LEYTON ORIENT
60 GREATEST MATCHES
OF THE TIJUANA TAXI ERA 1968–2012

LEYTON ORIENT
60 GREATEST MATCHES
OF THE TIJUANA TAXI ERA 1968–2012
MARTIN STRONG

DB PUBLISHING

This edition published in Great Britain in 2013 by DB Publishing, an imprint of JMD Media.

ISBN 9781780913131

Contents

Acknowledgements 7

Introduction
The Tijuana Taxi story   8

Game One
Birth of a legend   13

Game Two
Saved at the death   16

Game Three
The O's are going up   19

Game Four
Champions   22

Game Five
Laz the daz   26

Game Six
Not quite giant-killers   30

Game Seven
Giant-killers   34

Game Eight
Greatest day in the history
of the world?   38

Game Nine
Hatters hit by sparking O's   44

Game Ten
Heartache   47

Game Eleven
Orient's Double Rammy   52

Game Twelve
Last day happiness and a bit of turf   56

Game Thirteen
Canaries kop it   59

Game Fourteen
Bald eagle's blues   63

Game Fifteen
Kitchen sinks 'em   66

Game Sixteen
Boro buried   71

Game Seventeen
Kitchen saves the day   77

Game Eighteen
Day of the Jacko   80

Game Nineteen
Seagull special   83

Game Twenty
Hammered by Hurst   87

Game Twenty-one
Stan-tastic   91

Game Twenty-two
Return of a hero and the man
on crutches   94

Game Twenty-three
Night, night Knighton   97

Game Twenty-four
Kitchen Sinks 'em one last time   101

Game Twenty-five
Tiger Feat   104

Game Twenty-six
Cadette Force   107

Game Twenty-seven
Godfrey's golden game   112

Game Twenty-eight
King of the Castle   116

Game Twenty-nine
Eight-on Orient   121

Game Thirty
Kamara kops it in penalty drama   125

Game Thirty-one
Eight-on Orient (the follow up)   130

Game Thirty-two
Sooper-Cooper and a P.A. own-goal   134

Game Thirty-three
One wedding and a promotion   140

Game Thirty-four
Carters' cracker   146

Game Thirty-five
The Elleray Experience   150

Game Thirty-six
Cup Glory   154

Game Thirty-seven
Daggers dumped in nine-goal thriller   157

Game Thirty-eight
How's that?   160

Game Thirty-nine
Away The Lads! (Finally)   164

Game Forty
O's Seaside Special   167

Game Forty-one
Eight-on Orient (take three)   170

Game Forty-two
Taylor made for Wembley   172

Game Forty-three
A Corner Turned   175

Game Forty-four
Magpie's millionaires matched at the
Matchroom   178

Game Forty-five
Tigers tamed by Matt's magic   181

Game Forty-six
Pompey Chimed Out   185

Game Forty-seven
Lee licks Lincoln   190

Game Forty-eight
Messin' around by the river   193

Game Forty-nine
O's Steele promotion at the death   198

Game Fifty
Matt's perfect finish   206

Game Fifty-one
Table toppers toppled by the Trent   211

Game Fifty-two
Lion's mauled   215

Game Fifty-three
Bantam's battered   220

Game Fifty-four
Canaries kop it again   223

Game Fifty-five
Eight-on Orient (take four)   227

Game Fifty-six
Delia dumped out   231

Game Fifty-seven
Wednesday walloped   234

Game Fifty-eight
Swans silenced   237

Game Fifty-nine
The O's are better than Barcelona   242

Game Sixty
Over the Mooney in Derbyshire   250

Acknowledgements

Firstly thanks to my wonderful Mum and Dad, the latter apart from everything else, for taking me to Brisbane Road that first time on 1 April (appropriate ?) back in 1967 to see a cracking 0–0 against Swindon Town. I caught the bug that afternoon and haven't looked back since.

Much appreciation to my lovely wife of twenty-seven years, Sonia and to my two smashing daughters Barbara and Becky for putting up with those two and a half thousand Orient programmes, not to mention the hundred scrapbooks and memorabilia all round the house (I'll tidy them all up eventually dear, honest.)

Thanks to Rob for getting me all the programmes at the away games over the years, always arriving in mint condition.

Cheers to Dave Winter for the excellent photos that have have been used in the book, and to Dave Staplehurst for the valuable information provided regarding the early matches.

Thanks to the Randlesome Away Travel Service (aka RATS), that's Dave, Brenda and Suzanne for ferrying me all over the country to watch the mighty O's, and to all those friends I've made at Leyton Orient Football Club over the years – George and Lottie, Pete C., Bob, Gary, the Hiscocks, Sharon, Andy, Daniel and George up the road, etc, etc. And to the rowdy lot I sit near high up in the West Stand every home game.

To Dave Dodd, Simon on the door, Steve, Keren, Tim, Martyn and all the other heroes at the Supporters Club for making my home match days such a wonderful experience and apologies for my behaviour in the Clubhouse after games from time to time, when I've had a couple.

To all those responsible for producing the wonderful '*Leyton Orientear*' over the past twenty-six years and well done to anyone that's actually bothered to read my monthly column in it during that time.

Last but not least, thanks to all the players who have played for the O's over the past 46 years and given me enough memories to allow me to write this book. Some of you may not have been world-beaters but you've all I'm sure given your best when wearing an Orient shirt and it's been a pleasure watching you all perform.

Up the O's.
strongo.

The Tijuana Taxi story

On 10 August 1968 my Dad took his nine-year-old son to see the first home game of the new season against Rotherham United. We took up our usual positions sitting in the North Wing of the East Stand after we had bought the little white programme and I excitedly awaited the entry of our boys into the arena at around ten to three that afternoon.

As the mighty reds ran onto the pitch that day however there was a change to greet the new season – for the first time *Tijuana Taxi* sounded over the tannoy to welcome the O's onto the hallowed turf.

My Dad laughed aloud upon hearing Herb Alpert's catchy tune. 'What's this got to do with Orient or even football ?' he said to me ' I can't see them keeping it for long.'

Well forty-five years on and remarkably the O's still enter the field of battle at Brisbane Road accompanied by the same music that they first did back in 1968.

It was the idea of tannoy announcer Keith Simpson to play Herb's tune before every game. Orient had gone through, to say the least, a difficult period in the mid-sixties culminating in the infamous pass the buckets meeting of '66. Towards the end of the decade things had started to pick up a little and the playing of the catchy ditty along with other new ideas such as the introduction of the 'Golden Girls' at the ground to sell Goal-time tickets were aimed at modernizing the club and bringing them into 'the swinging sixties.'

The introduction of *Taxi* was greeted with a super game against Tommy Docherty's Rotherham, the 3–3 encounter rightly takes its place as the first of the sixty classics included within these pages. Little did we know on the day however that we had been there to witness the start of a Leyton Legend at Brizzy Road.

Said the programme for the following home game against Gillingham 'Listen out tonight for Orient's catchy new theme tune – Herb Alpert's swinging version of *Tijuana Taxi*. This record will introduce our team every time they take to the field and I hope it will become the signal for a really rousing cheer from the Orient supporters.'

With the wonderful new music, not surprisingly our clubs fortunes picked up dramatically in the late sixties culminating in the winning of the Third Division Championship in 1970. Throughout the seventies *Tijuana Taxi* was to introduce some classic matches at the old stadium many of them in the Cup, and all included here along with the heartache Villa game of '74.

The beginning of the eighties were not so kind to the Club or indeed our theme music.

At the start of the 82–83 season Keith Simpson was forced to relinquish his duties as Brisbane Road announcer in order to become the mandatory fourth official at home games.

He was replaced by a local DJ called Steve Day who inexplicably took away the Taxi and replaced it with '*Red River Rock*' by Johnny and the Hurricanes.

Along with letting Kitchen go to Fulham in '79 and the erection of fences in front of the North Terrace, at the time it seemed to me to be one of the worst decisions ever made at our home of good East London football.

Not surprisingly '*Red River Rock*' lasted no more than a year, the next season Simpson returned to the tannoy but for some reason still without our song.

Our fortunes without Herb Alpert declined and mid-decade we slipped into the bottom division. The calls for the reintroduction of *Taxi*, led by the *Orientear*, became louder as the team played poorer and poorer. Eventually to much jubilation it was reinstated with even those too young to remember it's first coming welcoming it's return.

With the tune back in it's rightful place the club's fortunes once more picked up culminating in the promotion season of '88-'89.

The tune remained in the early nineties, though in '92 there were strong rumours that it was going to be replaced – it was said that manager Peter Eustace wanted a more macho battle cry to lead the team out. In November of that year the story even made the '*Sunday Times*.'

Taxi survived that scare but when Barry Hearn took over the club in '95 he echoed the thoughts of Eustace and Alpert got the red card, to be replaced by Queen with '*We Will Rock You*'.

Sure we had a lot to be thankful for from Bazza in saving the club, but even he later admitted that it was not one of his smarter moves to remove Herb – the equivalent of a new owner taking over at Liverpool and banning *'You'll Never Walk Alone.'*

There was, of course another outcry from the Brisbane Road faithful and once again *Tijuana Taxi* came bouncing back. It goes without saying that our fortunes picked up upon it's return culminating in the first Wembley play-off appearance in 1999. Unfair it would have been to Scunthorpe that afternoon for *Taxi* to lead the teams onto the pitch, so it was played some twenty minutes before kick-off instead. It was still nice to know however, that our tune was there to play some small part of an historic afternoon for Leyton Orient Football Club.

The great man Herb Alpert is still going strong in the States, though nearing eighty he's still doing concerts across the country. Alas the composer is quite elusive and all efforts by myself to contact him with a view to him sending the club a message regarding the playing of his ditty have proved unfruitful.

Having spoken to his fans through the message board of his appreciation society they believe he knows of our club thanks to a reference of Leyton Orient on Alpert's Wikipedia page for many years, stating how his tune leads us out. That though seems about as far as it goes when it comes to getting it touch with him, which is a great shame.

It's certainly been there to witness many a Brisbane Road classic over the years, and I'm sure the tune has been there in spirit watching over all the unforgettable away games too.

The classics since '68 are all captured here, sixty corkers for all Brisbane Roaders to enjoy, starting from the Bloomfield age going right up to the present man-with-no-hair era. Hopefully they will bring back a memory or two to O's everywhere and lets just hope the ditty can accompany more good times in the years to come.

Hearing the tune come five to three every home game at Leyton Stadium remains for me as much a part of the Brisbane Road match-day experience as buying a programme or having a pint or six in the Supporter's Club before a game.

Introduction

And it still remains a standing joke between my Dad and myself that he got it so hopelessly wrong all those years ago when he said the tune wouldn't last long in leading the team out.

Enjoy the book, fellow O.

Game One

Birth of a legend

Orient 3 Rotherham United 3
League Division 3. 10 August 1968

The *Tijuana Taxi* era was welcomed in at Brisbane Road with an absolute cracker of a game against Rotherham on the opening day of the season in 1968.

After an abysmal 1967–68 campaign where we avoided relegation by just a point, there was more optimism around for the new season come August. Much of that was due to the fact that player/manager Jimmy Bloomfield had made a shrewd acquisition by signing Peter Brabrook from West Ham for around £8,000.

The experienced left-winger had played for England in the 1958 World Cup and appeared a fine signing. Bloomfield had what looked a good crop of youngsters who could supplement the likes of Brabrook and Bloomfield and as a result there was more hope around Leyton.

Rotherham had just been rather unluckily relegated from the Second Division and under Tommy Docherty were one of the favourites to go straight back up at the first time of asking.

A very respectable crowd of 7,979 gathered at East London's home of good football and none of them can have gone home disappointed at the fare they were shown on the afternoon.

Rotherham started the better team and were rewarded with a goal after just seven minutes. Steve Downes headed in a beautifully flighted corner kick from David Bentley over O's 'keeper Steve Bowtell – who was deputising for regular stopper Ray Goddard – to make it 1–0 to the visitors.

SEASON 1968-69

ORIENT

v

Rotherham United

Saturday, August 10th, 1968
Kick-Off 3 p.m.
FOOTBALL LEAGUE - DIVISION III

Official Programme 6d.

The goal certainly seemed to wake the home side up however, and for the rest of the half we played some wonderful football.

Roy Massey was obviously keen to do well against his former club and our midfielder was instrumental in creating the equaliser after twenty minutes. He prodded on a centre from Brabrook to Vic Halom who stabbed past Alan Hill to put us back on level terms.

With Malcolm Slater and Brabrook always threatening down the flanks, and Bloomfield and Dave Harper controlling midfield, the O's continued to look dangerous and the only surprise was that we had to wait until over an hour had been played to take the lead.

Massey was obstructed a yard outside the box resulting in an indirect free-kick. Bloomfield laid the ball off to full-back Mick Jones who rifled a fine shot past Hill into the back of the net. It must have been a sweet goal for Jones who had been let go by Docherty when he was manager at Chelsea.

Then twelve minutes later came the best goal of the game for the Orient. A breathtaking move involving Slater, Harper and Halom saw the ball ending up at the feet of Brabrook on the edge of the area and our former England man drilled home a fine left-footer to cap an excellent debut.

At 3–1 up entering the final quarter of an hour we looked to have the game in the bag, but unfortunately that was not the case. With just eight minutes left our full-back Bert Howe held Graham Leggatt's shirt just inside the area resulting in a penalty, which Leggatt himself converted. Then just two minutes later Bentley's corner kick for Rotherham was flicked on by James Storrie and Leggatt emerged from a ruck of players to stab the ball past Bowtell.

Both teams could have found a winner in the closing minutes, but the game finished a point a piece, though it was generally agreed that it had been a more than lucky one for the visitors.

Harper and Massey had both hit the woodwork and Hill had also made two excellent saves during the ninety-minutes. Some of our football had been magnificent.

Tommy Docherty, having his first taste of Third Division football admitted afterwards that his boys were fortunate: 'We were being torn apart until Graham Leggatt struck. Orient were an impressive side.'

'Orient Dazzle' headlined the *News of the World* the next day, while the *Sunday Mirror* chipped in with 'Cruel luck for Orient.'

It was a fabulous game with wonderful debuts on the day from Herb Alpert and Peter Brabrook.

Like most O's fans that afternoon I left the ground thinking that we had turned the corner and a fine season beckoned for us.

In typical Orient fashion however we ended the season just about avoiding relegation to the Fourth Division.

Orient: Bowtell, Jones, Howe, Harper, Mancini, Taylor, Slater, Massey, Bloomfield, Halom, Brabrook.
Goals: Halom (20s), Jones (62n), Brabrook (74n).

Rotherham United: Hill, Swift, Harrity, Quinn, Watson, Tiler, Leggatt, Storrie, Gilliver, Downes, Bentley.
Goals: Downes (7n), Leggatt (81s pen, 83s).

Star Man: Peter Brabrook (or Herb Alpert).
Attendance: 7,979.

After the given goal times in matches played at Brisbane Road, 'n' signifies the goal was scored at the Windsor Road - north end - of the ground, 's' denotes a score at the south end, now the 'Tommy Johnston Stand' end.

Game Two

Saved at the death

Orient 4 Shrewsbury Town 0
Football League Division 3. 28 April 1969

Looking back now, this match – our last game of the 1968–69 season – can be regarded as one of the most important in the clubs history. Losing it would have meant relegation to the Fourth Division for the first time in the clubs history and having already fallen from the First to the Third in the sixties, it may well have been difficult to stem the downward spiral in the bottom tier.

As it was victory that paved the way for a remarkable promotion just a year later, which in turn set the foundations for a whole decade in the Second Division, and some wonderful memories of seventies football at the Orient.

1968–69 had been a pretty painful campaign for the majority of it and we had suffered five straight defeats at the end of March and the beginning of April to land us right in the thick of a relegation battle. Our form had picked up a little as the climax to the season came however, and in the penultimate match at Bournemouth, we had picked up a priceless victory thanks to a single Barry Dyson goal.

That game was played on a Friday night and the win meant that we went into this Shrewsbury encounter on the following Tuesday knowing that a win would guarantee Third Division football at Brisbane Road for another year, at least.

The game turned out to be player/manager Jimmy Bloomfield's last for the club as a player, afterwards he hung up his boots to concentrate on managerial duties, a move that was to prove highly successful. Fittingly he turned in one of the best of his 47 appearances for the O's, controlling midfield and bringing back memories of his days playing at a higher level.

From the start Orient looked right up for it and threw everything at their opponents. Indeed it took the home side just five minutes to open the scoring. Malcolm Slater received the ball on the right wing and beat the full-back before delivering a cross into the centre. His ball was met by centre-forward

Mickey Bullock, who smashed home a wonderful volley from twenty yards out, into the back of the net.

An even better goal came for the O's thirteen minutes later, this time it was all the work of Barry Dyson. Our number ten collected the ball and lobbed it over a Shrewsbury defender's head. As the ball dropped Dyson hit a dipping volley which found its way into the corner of the goal. It was our man's tenth goal of the season, making him the leading scorer at Brisbane Road that year. It was doubtful if any of the others were as good as this one had been, or indeed as vital, as it gave us some valuable breathing space with a two goal cushion.

As it was such a crucial match – the Shrews were down the bottom as well – there was plenty of needle and it all got out of hand with half an hour played, when O's midfielder Terry Parmenter reacted badly to a poor challenge and got himself sent off for retaliating.

It was an indication of just how much the home side had dominated however, that going down to ten men had little impact on the game at all.

With the half-time score 2–0 it looked as if we would go on to win comfortably if we kept our heads, and that's exactly what we did. Five minutes after the restart Bloomfield floated a free-kick to the left of the penalty area where it was met by Mickey Bullock. Our forward nodded it into the centre where it was met by Terry Mancini, who headed past Town 'keeper John Phillips into the back of the net.

The scoring was wrapped up with just over an hour played, when a fine through ball from Slater, found its way to Dave Harper who cleverly steered it between defender and 'keeper and into the goal.

4–0 and the party could begin. There was a mini pitch invasion at the end, though nothing on the scale of when we won promotion to the First a few years earlier, of course.

We had saved ourselves from relegation with a clinical display that evening, which as it turned out was an indicator of how things were going to be the following season.

Ironically we defeated Shrewsbury at home again a year later, almost to the day, but this time the 1–0 win unbelievably secured the Third Division Championship for the O's.

There had certainly been signs that we had the makings of a good team, with Bloomfield starting to get together a good mix of experience and youth, but very few could have envisaged such a dramatic turnaround for the Club in only a year, after this match.

One who did however was Chairman Arthur Page. In his piece in the Shrewsbury programme he said: 'Both Jimmy Bloomfield, our manager, and myself agree that the skill to wage a promotion campaign next term is laced through our present side. That has been proved with some entertaining matches and good results against some of the most successful sides in our division.'

Our current Chairman, Bazza Hearn, often graces us with his ramblings in the programme these days, but I doubt if he'll ever match dear old Arthur for a better prophesy of a forthcoming Brisbane Road season.

Orient: Goddard, Jones, Rofe, Allen, Mancini, Bloomfield, Harper, Slater, Bullock, Dyson, Parmenter.
Goals: Bullock (5s), Dyson (18s), Mancini (50n), Harper(62n).

Shrewsbury: Phillips, Gregory, Fellows, Moore, Dolby, Clapham, Roberts, Wood, Harkin, Meredith, McLaughlin.

Star Man: Jimmy Bloomfield.
Attendance: 6,115.

Game Three

The O's are going up

Bradford City 0 Orient 1
League Division 3. 15 April 1970

The 1969–70 season was certainly a stunning one at the Orient. Whilst in terms of greatness the amazing promotion to the top division in 1961–62 will probably never be beaten at Brizzy Road, it's fair to say that the campaign that heralded in the seventies was also a monumental one, ranking not too far behind it.

The facts were that at the time, the club had been in decline since 1963 and were on an awful downward spiral that looked destined to finish with a place in the bottom division. Relegation had been narrowly avoided in 67–68 and 68–69 and financially the club were – just for a change – in turmoil.

Chairman Arthur Page had made a bold move in bringing young Jimmy Bloomfield to the club as player manager, though there were rumours that this was done with one eye on the finances, as in effect we were getting a player for free.

As it turned out however, this proved to be a masterstroke by the man at the helm with Bloomfield more than justifying the brave decision with a magnificent promotion in his second full season in charge.

Bloomfield had given up playing at the end of the 68–69 season to concentrate on management, and his policy of blending promising youngsters like Tommy Taylor, Dennis Rofe and Barrie Fairbrother with the experience of Terry Mancini, Peter Allen and Peter Brabrook reaped stunning rewards in 69–70.

By mid October with the O's handily placed in sixth place, just four points behind leaders Luton, Bloomfield signed experienced Mark Lazarus – who had started his career at Brisbane Road many years before - from Crystal Palace for £8,000.

It was the catalyst to spur the team on even more and a fine set of results took us up to third come Christmas. Boxing Day saw a massive game against leaders Luton, and in front of 17,619 we came out victorious at Brisbane Road, the game being settled by a single Peter Allen strike.

Then on 26 January we hit the top spot for the first time with a 3–0 home thumping of Bury as Luton went through a bad spell, and promotion started to looked a distinct possibility.

After a 4–1 home victory against Plymouth on Good Friday morning we sat second, two points behind leaders Brighton, but with four games in hand.

Then a 1–0 victory on Easter Monday at Doncaster took us back to the top where we remained for the rest of the season.

We travelled up to Yorkshire for this clash with Bradford City in April on a Wednesday night knowing that a victory would guarantee a remarkable promotion back to the Second Division.

It was a meaningless match for mid-table City and from the kick-off the O's, not surprisingly looked as if they wanted the victory more than their opponents. After just five minutes Mickey Bullock lashed in a vicious volley which rebounded from the crossbar, but this proved to be the best chance of the first half as both defences for the most part, remained on top. For the O's centre backs Terry Mancini and Tommy Taylor were having excellent games, while Ray Goddard in goal was equal to anything the Yorkshire men could throw at him.

The only real threat to the Orient goal in the first half came when Mancini hit a ball back to Goddard far harder than he meant to, and the O's 'keeper had to dive across his goal to make a splendid save.

The second period started much livelier than the first had ended and the visitors should really have taken the lead after 51 minutes. Peter Brabrook picked out Peter Allen with an astute pass, but our midfielder drove somewhat wildly from twelve yards out.

The O's received a blow with just over an hour played when ever consistent Dave Harper picked up an injury and had to be replaced by young Barrie Fairbrother, but this proved to be something of a blessing in disguise, as Fairbrother started to cause Bradford's defence some serious problems up front.

Barry Dyson cracked in a powerful 15 yarder which went close shortly after the substitution, and then after 75 minutes the games decisive moment came.

Mark Lazarus swept in a centre from the right which Mickey Bullock met with a fine diving header, the ball going just wide of Patrick Liney's fingertips to give us the lead.

It was Bullock's seventeenth league goal of the season, but was his first since 16 February. It was certainly a fine time to end his goal famine.

Bradford heads dropped somewhat after the goal and we could easily have added a second before the end. Peter Allen came closest to doubling the tally when his swerving thirty-yarder was tipped round the post by Liney for a corner, but the final score remained 1–0, so securing a superb promotion for the O's.

One imagines that the atmosphere on the way back to Leyton from Yorkshire that Wednesday evening must have been something special for players and supporters alike, something that very few would have anticipated some twelve months previously.

It now just remained for the boys to secure that Third Division Championship trophy to round off a truly historic campaign.

Bradford City: Liney, Atkins, Bayliss, McConnell, Hallett, Leighton, Hall, Ham, Corner (Bannister), O'Neil, Middleton.

Orient: Goddard, Jones, Rofe, Taylor, Mancini, Allen, Lazarus, Bullock, Harper (Fairbrother 62), Dyson, Brabrook.
Goal: Bullock (75).

Star Man: Mickey Bullock.
Attendance: 5,442.

Champions

Orient 1 Shrewsbury Town 0
League Division 3. 25 April 1970

The promotion clinching victory at Bradford on Wednesday was followed on Monday by a 3–2 home win against Southport, when the O's came from two down to triumph with goals from Lazarus and a couple from Bullock.

With Luton only drawing 0–0 at Mansfield on the same night, it was all set up for the club to secure a much deserved Third Division Championship. Just a point was needed to clinch it in their home game against Shrewsbury on the following Saturday.

I remember going to the game as excited as I had ever been going to watch a match at Brisbane Road. Since I'd been cheering on the team we had always been in the bottom reaches of the Third Division and avoiding relegation forever appeared the aim at the beginning of the season.

Here we were though, at the end of 1969–70 and we were on the brink of being crowned champions. I remember feeling a bit unhappy that I had not been able to be there when we had secured a place in Division Two with that

win at Bradford – an eleven-year-old was not allowed to travel up to Yorkshire on a Wednesday night – but here we were and I was about to be there at the game that saw my team win the title. It was a great feeling.

My word how the whole club had changed within the space of a few years. It had only been four years previously that Chairman Arthur Page had called a meeting at Brisbane Road one Sunday morning where buckets were passed around for money to save the Football Club.

Now he had called another meeting on the day after the Shrewsbury game, but this one was advertised as a celebration, where Page was to outline his plans for Orient's future.

It was not lost on a lot of people that we were ironically playing Shrewsbury for the Championship, when only a year previously almost to the day we had to beat the same opponents to keep our Third Division status at the other end of the table.

The encounter took place on a wet afternoon with a swirling wind blowing everywhere and as a result the O's did not put on one of their better performances of the campaign. Both sides gave it their all however, to produce a thrilling game given the difficult conditions.

Mark Lazarus provided the first threat to the Town goal when he cut inside Geoff Fellows and crossed to Barry Dyson, but our forward was narrowly beaten to the ball by Alf Wood and the danger was averted.

Mickey Bullock then volleyed over but Shrewsbury, even though they had nothing to play for, started to come into the game more and more and began to control midfield through the experienced Dave Roberts and Terry Harkin.

George Andrews chipped a shot against the bar for the visitors and then Mick Jones and Terry Mancini were forced to make desperate goalline clearances from Moore and Bridgewood.

Ray Goddard then had to make a couple of fine saves from Roberts and Harkin and the O's went in at half-time somewhat fortunate to still be 0–0.

When the second half started Orient had clearly been given a roasting by manager Bloomfield as they began a lot brighter.

They began to control the match and it came as no surprise when the breakthrough came for the champions-elect on 58 minutes.

There was a suspicion of handball as Bullock controlled a neat Tommy Taylor pass on the left. Our forward slipped past Tony Gregory and put in a telling cross beyond the reach of 'keeper Bob Tooze. Waiting at the far post was Lazarus who calmly guided the ball past Tooze with his head, into the back of the net to make it 1–0.

It was the fourth goal Lazarus had scored in six games highlighting what an astute signing Bloomfield had made back in October to acquire the experienced player from Crystal Palace. There followed what had become the wingers ritual celebration of doing a lap of honour before he returned to his outside-right position for the restart. The 13,268 of us in the crowd also celebrated ecstatically knowing that we were on the verge of witnessing a piece of Orient history.

Credit to Shrewsbury who never gave up, but the O's started to relax and play some of the good football that we had witnessed throughout a lot of the season. Bullock and then Barrie Fairbrother came close and then Lazarus could have easily been awarded a penalty when he was hacked from behind in the area, referee Hartley bizarrely only awarding Orient an indirect free-kick.

Wood had a last minute effort shave the post for the visitors, but the O's hung on to record a 1–0 victory and thus secure the Third Division Championship.

It had truly been a wonderful achievement by Jimmy Bloomfield and the team to turn the fortunes of the club around so dramatically, and 500 or so gathered at the ground on the day after the Shrewsbury win to hear chairman Page convey his thoughts:

'The last time I addressed you the situation was very different. If you remember we were passing the bucket round, asking you to help us save the Orient. Your attitude in that crisis convinced me that it was worth carrying on as chairman and now I'm jolly glad I did.'

Bloomfield said that his ultimate aim was to bring First Division football back to Brisbane Road and pointed out that more First Division managers had gone to Brisbane Road that season to watch our youngsters play than at any other time in our club's history. This, he said was a tribute to the youth policy at the club.

We still had one more game to finish the season after the win against the Shrews, a home match against Gillingham. The Gills were in the bottom four and had to win to avoid relegation to the bottom tier.

Remarkably – or maybe not remarkably – Gillingham won 2–1 inflicting only the second home defeat for the Champions at Brisbane Road all season. The Kent side thus secured safety and condemned Bournemouth to the Fourth Division. It was one of those results that I'm sure had it happened these days would have been looked into very closely by the authorities.

The O's were presented with the Third Division Championship trophy after that game and all 16,334 in the crowd that night went home happy, be they Orient or Gillingham fans.

I remember thinking at the time, how long would it be before I saw the club celebrate another championship triumph? Forty-three years later and I'm still waiting.

Orient: Goddard, Jones, Rofe, Taylor, Mancini, Allen, Lazarus, Bullock, Fairbrother, Dyson, Brabrook.
Goal: Lazarus (58s).

Shrewsbury Town: Tooze, Gregory, Fellows, Moore (Meredith 82), Wood, Mattais, Roberts, Bridgewood, Andrews, Hughes, Harkin.

Star Man: Mark Lazarus.
Attendance: 13,268.

Game Five

Laz the daz

Orient 3 Sheffield United 1
League Division 2. 15 August 1970

The O's started life in their new division with basically the same squad that had won us promotion the season before. The good news for fans was that Jimmy Bloomfield was still the boss, despite the fact that there had been rumours that Birmingham were interested in appointing him as their new manager.

The fixture list gave us a tough first game at home to Sheffield United. The Blades had a fine side and were one of the favourites to go up to the First Division at the end of the season. Indeed the team from Yorkshire were to have a fine campaign and finished as runners-up to Leicester at the end of it, thus going up to the top flight.

It was doubtful though that they had a harder game all season than their first one in 70–71. This encounter at Brisbane Road saw the O's, after a tentative start, play them off the park for much of the second half and ended up worthy 3–1 winners.

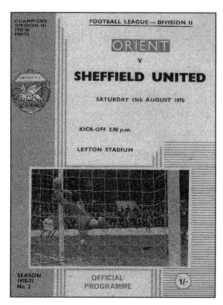

Two players in particular stood out for the Orient on the afternoon, veteran Mark Lazarus, who scored twice, and young full-back Dennis Rofe, the twenty-year-old playing the game as if he too had been around for years.

The O's started very much on the front foot, both Barry Dyson and Mickey Bullock coming close to opening the scoring before the visitors had even tested Ray Goddard in the Orient goal.

After sustaining the early pressure however, the Northerners began to show the resilience that had so very nearly earned them promotion the previous year.

After 23 minutes their full-back Ted Hemsley made a dash up field and let fly from thirty-five yards. Goddard was well beaten, but luckily for the home side the ball hit the post and rebounded to safety.

They started to get well on top and it came as no surprise when United took the lead on the stroke of half-time. Some poor Orient defending allowed Colin Addison to push home a cross from former Arsenal man John Barnwell for the opening goal.

One-nil down at the interval, most in the crowd would have feared the worst for our boys, especially seeing how the first forty-five had ended, but in fact after the break the O's came out a changed team.

We actually looked remarkably confident and Barry Dyson, Mick Jones and Dave Harper all had chances to put us back on level terms before Harper finally achieved the feat on 62 minutes.

A free-kick by Lazarus was punched clear by 'keeper Alan Hodgkinson, but only as far as Harper. From 25 yards our half-back sent a right-foot volley into the back of the net to make it 1–1.

It then took just six minutes for the Orient to take the lead. The architect of the goal was Rofe who made a characteristic burst up the left wing. Three defenders were caught out of position as the full-back crossed to the on rushing Lazarus who push the ball past Hodgkinson to give us a 2–1 advantage going into the last quarter of the game. A delighted Lazarus celebrated as only Lazarus did, shaking hands with the crowd behind the goal before taking off on his trademark lap of honour.

But the O's were not finished and just four minutes later Rofe again was instrumental in giving us another goal. He intercepted the ball on his chest and combined with Peter Brabrook before sending in another fine cross. Again the ball was met by Lazarus, this time with his head, and he nodded past the 'keeper to give us a two goal advantage. Cue repeat celebration from the goalscorer, before he made his way back to his own half for the re-start.

Our winger was not resting on his laurels however and went in search of a much deserved hat-trick. He let fly with a blistering left-footed drive which had so much power that Hodgkinson dislocated a finger as he saved it. The veteran Blades stopper had to be replaced by Alan Woodward in goal for the last five minutes and in the end United were probably happy to go home having not lost by more.

3–1 reflected a fine return to the Second Division for the Orient. Everyone knew that it was going to be hard at the higher level but this was a promising start. The local Guardian summed up the match perfectly with their headline: 'Laz the Daz switches O's on.'

The only disappointment about the afternoon for the Club was the attendance for the game. 10,584 was somewhat of a let down given our high gates for the last part of 69–70, though it could partially be explained by the Tottenham v. West Ham fixture being played at White Hart Lane at the same time as our match.

Explaining our second half revival Bloomfield said afterwards: 'I told the boys to tighten it up. They did just that, we got control of the midfield and scored some fine goals. It's a great start to the season and the players today have only underlined my faith that we can do really well in the Second Division.'

The season did in fact prove to be somewhat of a struggle for our boys but in the end we had to feel reasonably happy with our first campaign at the new level. We finished seven points clear of relegation which never seriously threatened us all season. The highlight league wise however, was this first game of the season encounter with the team from Sheffield, which had some of the Brisbane Road faithful leaving the ground talking about First Division football at the end of it.

One last strange quirk about our battles with the Blades that season – in the return fixture at Bramall Lane on 17 October the scoring was exactly the same as it had been at Brisbane Road, only in reverse.

The O's took the lead early on which they still held at half-time and United then scored three quick goals in the second period to triumph 3–1.

Orient: Goddard, Jones, Rofe, Taylor, Mancini, Harper, Lazarus, Bullock, Allen, Dyson, Brabrook.
Goals: Harper (62s), Lazarus (68s, 72s).

Sheffield United: Hodgkinson,(Barlow 85), Badger, Hemsley, Flynn, Colquhoun, Powell, Woodward, Barnwell, Addison, Currie.
Goal: Addison (45s).

Star Man: Mark Lazarus.
Attendance: 10,584.

Game Six

Not quite giant-killers

Nottingham Forest 1 Orient 1
FA Cup Fourth Round. 23 January 1971

Talk to many an old Orient codger about the seventies, and a lot of the happiest memories of the decade came through the FA Cup. There were the two runs in it in '72 and '78, as well as the classic encounter with Derby in '75.

Indeed our first FA Cup matches of the decade in 1971 set the tone nicely for what was to come in the following years. In the Third Round of the 70–71 season we had a magnificent result at Roker Park, where we got a totally unexpected win against Sunderland 3–0, the home side being well above us in the Second Division at the time.

We were rewarded with an away tie against First Division Nottingham Forest in the Fourth Round, and in the two and a half matches that we subsequently played against the midlanders we gave an admiral account of ourselves, and were unlucky to eventually lose.

There had been heavy overnight rain before the first match in Nottingham, but bearing that in mind the pitch was not too bad and the two teams put on a fine spectacle for the 25,349 present at the City Ground.

From the kick-off the O's were far from outclassed by their opponents from the higher division and Barrie Fairbrother was close to giving the visitors an early lead when he was narrowly beaten to a loose ball by Forest 'keeper Jim Barron.

Forest full-back John Winfield had a thirty-yard effort well saved by Ray Goddard, but this was matched soon after by his O's counterpart Mick Jones who saw a similar long ranger drift just wide of the post.

The pick of the midfield men on show in the first half was Forest's Tommy Jackson and it was he who came close to scoring when he met a Ronnie Rees free-kick that resulted in a fine Goddard save with half an hour played.

It was far from one-way traffic however, and Orient could easily have taken the lead when a Dennis Rofe inswinging corner was totally misjudged by Jim

Barron, who was fortunate to see the ball beat everyone else and drift away to safety.

Indeed it was the O's who eventually broke the deadlock with just two minutes to go before the break and a fine goal it was too. Mark Lazarus, who was having an excellent game slung over a wonderful cross from the touchline which was met by a superb diving header from Barry Dyson into the corner of the net. It was even met by applause from sections of the home crowd.

It looked as if we were certain to go into the break a goal to the good but it was not to be. Just a minute later the ball was put hopefully into the Orient box and as Terry Mancini and Peter Cormack went for it, referee Tom Reynolds controversially blew for a penalty. It was a decision hotly disputed by Mancini and the rest of the Orient defence, but the protests were to no avail and Ian Storey-Moore scored the subsequent penalty to level the game.

Credit had to be given to the O's, heads could easily have gone down after such a decision on the stroke of half-time, but our boys kept their composure and subsequently played a really good second forty-five minutes.

Goddard was called upon to make a decent save from a Storey-Moore header but at the other end Peter Allen nearly sneaked us into the lead when his first time shot surprised Barron, the 'keeper being relieved to see the ball also drift the wrong side of the near post.

Peter Cormack hit the post for the home side, though the referee had already blown for an Orient free-kick and then just before the end the O's had a great chance to secure a famous victory through the ever dangerous Lazarus.

Our man popped up in the Forest goalmouth and took the ball past Barron giving our number seven the chance to score with the goal at his mercy. Unfortunately however the angle was extremely acute and he was almost on the goal-line as he tried to tap it into the net. He consequently struck his effort against the post and the home side escaped with a goal-kick.

We had one last chance when a cross from Lazarus was fluffed by Barron, but in a crowded area the ball broke to a Forest defender who cleared.

So the game ended 1–1, certainly a moral victory for the underdogs from East London, but a result which could have been even better.

Indeed Matt Gillies, the Nottingham manager agreed afterwards that Orient were by far the better team on the day.

O's supremo Jimmy Bloomfield sportingly refused to talk about the controversial penalty just before the break and instead focused on how well his team, and in particular Mark Lazarus had played: 'Mark is going so well these days he inspires the side. My lads gave a marvellous team display, and in the last four games since I recalled him Mark has scored in the previous three and made today's goal for Dyson.'

So not for the last time in the decade Orient had put on a super show in the greatest-cup-competition-in-the-world against higher ranking opponents.

The draw at the City Ground meant a replay at Brisbane Road just two days later. The Monday night however turned out to be one of the most farcical ever seen at Leyton Stadium. There had been heavy rain throughout the afternoon and then a torrential downpour half an hour before kick-off time left a gigantic pool of water on the pitch.

Referee Tom Reynolds delayed kick-off by just over five minutes, but it was clear to everyone present when he finally allowed the game to start that it was a ridiculous decision to let the match go ahead at all.

After forty-five minutes Mr. Reynolds finally saw sense and abandoned the game with the score still 0–0. He defended his decision to start it in the first place by saying that there were eighteen and a half thousand in the ground – our biggest gate of the season – and he did not want to let the punters down.

Forest 'keeper Jim Barron however summed up the feelings of most afterwards when he said: 'It was ridiculous to let it go on in the first place. How can anyone stand, let alone play football in conditions like these ?'

Headlined the Daily Express the next day: 'Orient clash – it's a farce.'

The game was rearranged for a week later and Forest this time won 1–0. The pitch was still dreadful, but the O's though once more not outclassed, never raised their game as they had done in the first game.

We thus bowed out of the cup, the disappointing thing being that if we could somehow have overcome Forest we would have had a lucrative tie against Spurs in the Fifth Round. We would have to wait another twelve months before we entered that stage of the competition.

Nottingham Forest: Barron, Hindley, Winfield, Chapman, O'Kane, Jackson, Lyons, Fraser, Cormack, Rees (Collier 75), Storey-Moore.
Goal: Storey-Moore (44 pen.)

Orient: Goddard, Jones, Rofe, Bennett, Mancini, Allen, Lazarus, Brisley, Bullock, Dyson, Fairbrother.
Goal: Dyson (43).

Star Man: Mark Lazarus.
Attendance: 25,349.

Game Seven

Giant-killers

Leicester City 0 Orient 2
FA Cup Fourth Round. 5 February 1972

After the euphoria of the magnificent promotion in 1970, its fair to say that the new decade had began fairly quietly for the O's. We finished 17th in our first season back in Division II.

We needed something to really kick-start the seventies for us and that something came with the FA Cup run of 1972. The O's got drawn at home to Third Division Wrexham in the Third Round and won easily 3–0. The reward was an away tie against First Division Leicester City.

The tie was given extra spice by the fact that the Foxes manager was Jimmy Bloomfield who of course had been the architect of Orient's wonderful 69–70 season. His sterling work at Brisbane Road had caught the attention of clubs at the higher level and he had been rewarded with a job at Leicester at the start of the 71–72 campaign.

He was doing a decent job at the midlands club, coming into the game with the O's they were unbeaten in six and held a comfortable mid-table position.

The O's were struggling a little, placed fifth from bottom of Division II though there were some promising signs in the young team. Ian Bowyer and Phil Hoadley, both only 20, had been signed and looked decent acquisitions and the arrival of Tom Walley from Watford had given the side some much needed experience.

Orient had prepared for the game with a five day holiday soaking up the sun in Majorca, which at the time did not appear ideal preparation for a game played on a mud bath of a pitch at Filbert Street. On the day however, the O's were quite brilliant and thoroughly deserved to defeat their opponents from the higher league.

We had been handed a huge stroke of luck before the game, when Leicester found themselves without England goalkeeper Peter Shilton through injury, which meant that they had to give a debut to seventeen-year-old rookie Carl Jeyes.

As the game started we had to soak up some early pressure from the midlanders, but then started to come into the match with efforts from Mickey Bullock and Barry Dyson both going just wide.

Then, after twenty-seven minutes came possibly the crucial moment in the tie.

Leicester's Len Glover crossed from the right and the ball was met by John Farrington who headed goalwards. Goalkeeper Ray Goddard was beaten but Dyson was on the line appearing to handle before he cleared. To most present it appeared an obvious penalty but referee Colin Fallon waved play on.

Said the man in black (which is what they always wore in those days) afterwards: 'I had no problem whatsoever in waving play on. There is no doubt that the ball hit Dyson's hand, but it was purely accidental. The lad had no idea what happened and a penalty would not have been justified.'

His view was not shared by Bloomfield however: 'It was a clear penalty, but that's football.'

Even Orient manager George Petchey admitted afterwards: 'We were lucky to get away with that one.'

The decision was definitely a turning point. Just four minutes later the O's scored. A brilliant goal it was too. Peter Allen found himself surrounded by blue shirts on the edge of the City area. He laid the ball off to Ian Bowyer who shook off two defenders before unleashing a fierce twenty-yarder which sailed into the net giving the young 'keeper no chance.

Ironically one of his last acts as Orient manager had seen Bloomfield sign Bowyer from Manchester City. Speaking about the goal he said afterwards: 'It's just what I bought him for.'

Leicester were nearly gifted an equalizer just moments after when a back pass from Bullock was intercepted by Glover. He rounded Goddard and squared the ball for Alistair Brown. Thankfully for the O's however the home player missed badly, blazing wide with the goal at his mercy.

We went in 1–0 up at half-time and were good value for the lead. The second period started badly however, with Phil Hoadley colliding with Goddard resulting in what seemed a pretty bad injury to the Orient 'keeper. After receiving treatment our man continued bravely – there were no substitute goalkeepers in those days, of course – and remarkably managed to keep a clean sheet for the rest of the game. He was to miss the next two fixtures as a result of the collision.

Leicester started to press but Orient continued to pose a threat on the break and sure enough it was through one of these breakaways that a second was scored. Paul Harris blocked a Glover shot and cleared to Allen on the right. Our man advanced, then crossed into the area. Jeyes went for the ball with Bowyer, but somehow managed to let the ball slip past him and into the net.

Even allowing for his age it was a terrible mistake for the 'keeper to make and it virtually handed the game to the O's.

City vainly tried to test our injured custodian, but a limping Goddard was equal to anything the Filberts threw at him and we held on for a famous win.

The players celebrated wildly afterwards with champagne apparently flowing in the bath. Sportingly Bloomfield went to congratulate them, shaking every Orient player's hand.

He said: 'They deserved their win. Orient were the better side and I hope they do well in the next round.'

Said Peter Shilton of Carl Jeyes: 'You can't blame him at all for the defeat. He played well and had no chance with the first goal. The second was just an unfortunate incident which could have happened to anyone.'

It was certainly a magnificent result – bearing in mind the two clubs league positions, it was probably the best since I has started to support the O's in the sixties. I was not at the game – my Dad did not take me to away games, but he took me to Tottenham that afternoon who were at home to Rotherham in the cup. They recorded a routine 2–0 win, but I remember the highlight of the afternoon was when the man with the numbers for the half-time scoreboard put up 0–1 by the Leicester v. Orient letter.

It meant an agonizing wait until I found out the final score from Filbert Street, which I got from the Evening Standard around 6.30pm, but there was of course much joy when I found out. It was the first time I had known the O's to be giant killers. I knew that for a change we would get masses of coverage in the Sunday papers, I guessed it had to be the top story the next day.

As it turned out though, there was just one problem. The result of another match that afternoon: non-league Hereford United 2, Newcastle United, from the First Division, 1 – only the biggest cup upset in donkeys years, indeed one of the biggest ever.

The O's defeating a side in only the division above us was mere chicken feed by comparison. And our game, unlike the Hereford one was not on the television. As a result we got hardly a mention in the Sunday papers.

It was an anomaly, however, that was well and truly rectified by our result in the next round.

George Petchey and the Chelsea manager Dave Sexton were old buddies from their playing days and both lived on the south coast at the time. They appeared together on Radio Brighton on the Sunday after the Leicester game, and both joked that the two clubs would get drawn together in the Fifth Round the following day. It was a prophesy however that remarkably came true, so setting up another great day in the history of Orient Football Club.

Leicester City: Jayes, Whitworth, Nish, Cross, Manley, Brown, Weller, Farrington, Birchenall, Sammels, Glover.

Orient: Goddard, Hoadley, Rofe, Bennett, Harris, Allen, Fairbrother, Dyson, Bullock, Walley, Bowyer.
Goals: Bowyer (31), Allen (62).

Star Man: Ian Bowyer.
Attendance: 31,402.

Game Eight

Greatest day in the history of the world?

Orient 3 Chelsea 2
FA Cup Fifth Round. 26 February 1972

Quite simply, for me this encounter remains the greatest football game ever played. Many a match in the forty odd years since has tried to emulate it – the Oxford experience in 2006 came close – but the Chelsea classic is still top of the pile in my humble opinion.

The mere facts of that memorable afternoon speak for themselves. We were a below average Second Division team, while Chelsea were the holders of the European Cup Winners Cup. Due to play in the League Cup Final the following week, they were one of the top sides in Europe.

Their side consisted of famous names aplenty: Bonetti, Webb, Osgood, Hudson to name but four. They were two up after forty minutes and coasting it. Yet unbelievably we ended up winning.

In those days when we used to go to home games my Dad took me to sit in the North Wing of the East Stand. For this one however he was unable to get tickets for our normal place, so for the first time we stood in the enclosure towards the Coronation Gardens end of the ground.

It was four months before I became a teenager, so that it was quite a strain all afternoon to see the action at the north end of the ground. The Gods looked after me however in that four of the five goals were down our end including Fairbrother's unforgettable winner.

And with the Beeb's '*Match of the Day*' cameras present I was able to relive the action at both ends of the pitch later.

On a mud bath of a pitch Chelsea started well and it came as little surprise when they took the lead with just under half an hour played. A Peter Houseman corner was not cleared and found its way to the Chelsea winger once more. His cross from the right was met by ex-O David Webb with a looping header that sailed over Ray Goddard and into the net.

A second goal for the Blues followed ten minutes later. Again it came from a cross from the right, this time being met by Peter Osgood whose close range header doubled the lead.

Chelsea looked in complete control but I remember commenting to my Dad at the time that I had seen Peter Bonetti give away a 2–0 lead a couple of years before when playing for England against West Germany in the 1970 World Cup and I wondered if it would happen again.

Happen again it sure did. The game turned just on the stroke of half-time. One of the commentator's favourite sayings has always been that the best time to score a goal in any match is just before the break and if anyone needed any proof they only have to look at the video of this game to justify it.

With forty-five minutes gone and injury time looming a Mickey Bullock shot rebounded to Phil Hoadley for the O's. Thirty yards out our centre-half unleashed a fierce thirty-yarder which Peter Bonetti got his hand to but could not prevent from entering the net.

I was straining my neck at the other end of the ground but I must admit I could not see the goal. I knew by the reaction of the Chelsea fans gathered in the Coronation Gardens terrace in front of me and the roars from the rest of the crowd that we had scored however.

Seeing it later it was a wonderful goal, amazingly Hoadley's first for the club. I never forgave the BBC for incredibly only naming it third in their Goal of the Month competition at the time.

At half-time we were deservedly 2–1 down but the goal had certainly given us hope that a famous comeback win was on the cards and we were not disappointed.

The second half started and all of a sudden it seemed a different game altogether. Just four minutes after the restart Peter Allen picked the ball up on the right of midfield and played a long ball into the heart of the Chelsea penalty area. Peter Bonetti came to collect but David Webb beat him to it and diverted it past him. There at the far post with an empty net in front of him was Mickey Bullock and our striker duly obliged to hit the back of the onion bag, scoring the easiest goal of his career.

I went potty –the O's had equalized and it had all happened right in front of me. I had seen the goal.

Incredibly the goal really knocked the stuffing out of Chelsea. Allen and Barry Dyson began to take hold of the midfield and from being down and out at one stage we actually looked like we could go on and win it.

Sure enough with 89 minutes gone and a replay beckoning an O's winner came. Again it was a long through ball that caused chaos in the Blues defence, this time played by Tom Walley.

Peter Bonetti came to collect, but this time he collided with Orient forward Ian Bowyer. The ball broke to Barrie Fairbrother who side-footed into an empty net.

He wheeled away, arms aloft celebrating wildly. We've had Cooper's promotion winner in '89, Tehoue's Arsenal equalizer in 2011, but for me Barrie the beard's winning goal against Chelsea on 26 February 1972 remains my all time favourite moment at Brisbane Road.

The game of course was not over. Indeed following our third there was quite a big pitch invasion from the Chelsea hordes in an attempt to get the match abandoned. It was not to be the last time they were to create trouble at the ground in the seventies.

When play restarted, not unsurprisingly most of the action was down the end of the pitch where I was unable to see. Deep into injury time an almighty roar went up all around the ground. I knew that something dramatic had happened at the Windsor Road end, yet I knew from the reaction in front of me that it had not been a goal.

Seconds later I heard the final whistle as Barrie Fairbrother caught the ball from a Ray Goddard goal-kick. We had won. There was a wonderful moment as Fairbrother ran off clutching the match ball when PA man Keith Simpson played *Tijuana Taxi* over the tannoy. It was normally not played at the end of matches, but this was a glorious Orient moment and guess he thought it only right it should be shared with our magnificent theme tune.

Whilst we normally got back to Chingford around 5.15pm after home games, just in time for Dr Who, the late finish together with the massive crowd meant that I missed the Doctor that Saturday and even the start of *Dixon of Dock Green* afterwards, which was unheard of in those days.

Of course I cared not.

The result really did mean a lot to me. At school everyone else supported the likes of Spurs, Arsenal or West Ham. They had seen their teams win trophies and I had always been envious. I realised however that there was one thing that I could see my club do which they were unable to do. This phenomena called 'giant killing'. And here it was – for the first time I had seen the O's achieve it.

Despite the fact that I had missed some of the action being in the enclosure, it mattered little that evening. Most normal folk I guess would have considered standing in the new position lucky after the result we had witnessed, and returned there the following game. I decided however that the south enclosure was 'the Chelsea game' enclosure and actually vowed at the time that it would forever be so and that I would never stand there again. Its actually something that I've stuck to and I've never in the forty odd years since been in it either standing or as it is now, sitting.

I was on a different planet as you can imagine that evening, but the day still had a final lovely twist to it. '*Match of the Day*' was always on Saturday nights yet as it never started before 10 o'clock I had never been allowed to stay up to watch it.

With our game due to be one of the games featured that night, I begged my folks to let me stay up as a one off to watch it. As it turned out I was sent to bed normal time – 9.30pm – with the proviso that if we were the first game on the programme I would be able to go back downstairs and see it.

Of course I knew I was onto a winner as it was obviously the top game that day and would clearly be the first one on.

It was and I re-entered our living room with my Dad doing the *Telegraph* crossword. This was something he normally did at the match when we went to the Orient but with the big crowd he had been unable to do so that afternoon.

I just loved watching all the action for the second time. It was enhanced further by the wonderful commentary from Barry Davies. I was able to see for the first time Hoadley's glorious strike and I found out what the crowd had gone crazy about at the end of the game, deep into injury time. David Webb had been pushed up front and had contrived to miss an open goal at the Windsor Road end.

At the final whistle Davies summed up the afternoon perfectly: 'A tie that started off a private London affair has become one for the whole nation.' Magnificent stuff.

In years to come there was great debate amongst folk as to who was the Beeb's number one commentator Davies or John Motson. After his performance on 26 February 1972 for me there was only ever one winner.

Our victory was the major shock of the day, and this was reflected by the vast coverage in the papers the following day.

Said the *Sunday Mirror*: 'Little Orient, London's poor relations, gave high-stepping Chelsea a two goal start, then George Petchey's young East End pick-pockets pulled off the biggest smash and grab raid since the Great Train Robbery.'

The *Sunday Express* concentrated on our match-winner: 'Fairbrother, who scored the winning goal, defied an order from Petchey to shave off his beard. 'This beard is a lucky omen and it stays until we are out of the cup' said the irrepressible Barrie. Yet Orient do not need superstition – or lucky charms – if they take this brand of raw courage into their quarter-final.'

Petchey rightly praised his side for the great comeback: 'No praise can be too high for the players; to pick themselves up off the floor after being two goals down was a magnificent performance. I feel we have won many friends through our cup run, not only defeating such top class opposition but by the football we have produced in doing so.'

Chelsea manager Dave Sexton – himself once in charge at Brisbane Road – not surprisingly had less to say: 'That's the way it goes', was his take on it.

Indeed the defeat had a devastating effect on the club from Stamford Bridge. They played Stoke City a week later at Wembley in the League Cup Final. It was a game that they were expected to win easily, yet it was one that they ended up losing, with veteran George Eastham scoring the winner in a 2–1 victory for the Potters. I raised more than a little chuckle as I heard 30,000 Stoke fans taunting the Chelsea faithful with chants of 'Orient, Orient', before the start of the game.

It saw the start of a big demise for Chelsea in the mid-seventies. They got themselves into a lot of debt over a new stand that was built and they got relegated in to the same division as we were in. And of course their 'fans' continued to cause trouble wherever they went. It's fair to say that their problems all started that February afternoon in east London. Day of still the greatest football match ever played.

Orient: Goddard, Hoadley, Rofe, Bennett, Harris, Allen, Fairbrother, Dyson, Bullock, Walley, Bowyer (sub Brisley 90).
Goals: Hoadley (45n), Bullock (49s), Fairbrother (89s).

Chelsea: Bonetti, Mulligan, Harris, Hollins, Dempsey, Webb, Cooke, Kember, Osgood, Hudson, Houseman.
Goals: Webb (26s), Osgood (36s).

Star Man: Barrie Fairbrother.
Attendance: 30,329.

Game Nine

Hatters hit by sparking O's

Orient 2 Luton Town 0
Football League Division 2. 20 October 1973

After the excitement of the cup run in '72, the following season proved somewhat mundane at Leyton Stadium. The O's finished fifteenth and were knocked out of the FA Cup in the Third Round by Coventry.

There was certainly no hint of the drama that was to take place in the1973–74 campaign. Manager George Petchey had brought in Arthur Rowe from Tottenham to assist with the coaching however, and this proved to be an excellent move. Rowe had been instrumental in the 'push and run' style developed at Spurs and he introduced this with great effect at Brisbane Road.

Former Crystal Palace coach Petchey had pinched a couple of decent players from Malcolm Allison at his old club – Gerry Queen and Phil Hoadley – and things were starting to look up under his leadership.

By the time of this game in October we had gained twelve points from the first eleven games and were placed just two points behind Luton who were sitting second. Our exciting brand of football had seen us become the highest scorers away from home in the Division with ten, and we had been beaten twice only in the league thus far.

We had started to attract some very favourable headlines from the press and media and Brian Moore brought his '*Big Match*' cameras to east London for this fixture against the Bedfordshire club.

Another point of interest for the game was that it marked the debut of goalkeeper John Jackson, who had been another capture from Crystal Palace for a bargain £25,000. Jacko had been something of a legend at Selhurst Park, playing over 200 consecutive games but Allison unbelievably thought his best days were behind him and let him go. It was a controversial move at the time, not only at the Palace but also at the O's where Jackson replaced the popular Ray Goddard between the sticks.

At the time, Allison thought Jackson had a limited life expectancy in the game, though he was to be proved spectacularly wrong. Jacko went on to play 200 consecutive league games for the O's as well, and was instrumental in getting us to the FA Cup semi-final some four years later.

It was a move that mirrored a similar one regarding Pat Jennings around the same time. The Irishman had served Tottenham well but the club considered he was past his best and let him go to Arsenal for a ridiculous £40,000. It turned out to be one of the best pieces of transfer dealing Arsenal have ever done.

Luton were the division's leading scorers, so the game promised to be an entertaining one and it did not disappoint. Orient's passing game created many chances in the first half, but young Luton 'keeper Keith Barber had a fine forty-five minutes making crucial stops from a Mickey Bullock header and a Barry Fairbrother shot from the edge of the area.

Luton looked threatening when they attacked, but Jackson was having a fine debut. And when he was beaten following a poor Ricky Heppolette header, Derrick Downing was on the line to clear, thus preventing an own goal by Heppolette.

Just before the break a Mickey Bullock header hit the post, but the game remained goalless at the interval.

As the second half started the O's stepped up a gear and began to dominate. Derrick Downing was causing the Luton defence all kinds of problems with his runs down the left and it seemed only a matter of time before we scored. Gerry Queen once more hit the post and David Payne shot wildly over when in a good position, but then the breakthrough finally came.

There was a wonderful passing movement started by Terry Brisley in our own half, which was eventually finished off by the ever lively Brisley, who laid the ball back to Queen for the Scotsman to fire home from the edge of the area.

Peter Anderson had a header go just wide for the visitors, but we continued to look much the better team and it came as no surprise when we doubled our lead with seven minutes left.

Again it was a wonderful team goal with a fine one-two between Tom Walley and Queen resulting in a cross from the left by Walley being met by the head of Fairbrother to make it 2–0.

As the final whistle sounded the crowd gave the team a fine reception. It had been a wonderful performance and with a bit more luck and some better finishing the game could easily have ended four or five nil.

After this showing against a decent side we started to believe that, just for a change, the season was not going to be a battle to fight off relegation and that we could maybe even threaten the top three.

On the television the next day Brian Clough, analysing the game said it had been a credit to the Second Division, and he added that if we continued to play like that we were in with a chance of promotion come May.

Said Chris Harrigan in the *Sunday Mirror*: 'Orient brought high flying Luton down to earth with a bang and no one was more pleased than Orient's new import from Crystal Palace £25,000 'keeper John Jackson.'

Jacko indeed had had a fine debut for us and joked afterwards: 'I'd forgotten what being on a winning side was like.' - At the time Palace were bottom of the second without a win all season.

Looking back now we may have had bigger wins throughout the seventies, but considering the opposition (Luton ended up getting promoted) and the style in which we won that afternoon with some breathtaking football, this match is right up there ranking alongside some of the best performances of the decade.

Orient: Jackson, Payne, Downing, Walley, Hoadley, Brisley, Allen, Heppolette, Bullock, Fairbrother, Queen.
Goals: Queen (70n), Fairbrother (83n).

Luton Town: Barber, Shanks, Thomson, Anderson, Faulkner, Garner, Jim Ryan, John Ryan, Butlin, West, Aston.

Star Man: Terry Brisley.
Attendance: 11,135.

Game Ten

Heartache

Orient 1 Aston Villa 1
Football League Division 2. 3 May 1974

An integral part of being a Leyton Orient supporter is getting used to the many disappointments over the years.

In this respect, many a game stands out from decades past. From the two cup defeats to the Gooners in the seventies, the two play-off defeats at the turn of the century, right up to the recent capitulation to Southend in the JPT, there have been many a time when one wonders at the end of a match, why we put ourselves through it.

Yet for me even some forty years on, this game against Aston Villa remains the ultimate heartache game.

I do not think if I'm still watching Leyton Orient Football Club, or whatever they happen to be called then, in 2050 I will ever feel such pain after any encounter as I felt on that May night back in 1974.

This was the last game of the season and 1973–74 had been a remarkable one. After finishing 1972–73 in fifteenth position in the second division just three points off the relegation places there was not a great deal of optimism going into the new campaign. Most at Brizzy Road had expected at best a mid-table finish with a nice little cup run to possibly get us through the winter in good spirits.

Yet unbelievably we entered this final encounter only needing to win to secure a top three finish and with it promotion to the First Division. If we did not win, then it was to be Carlisle instead who went up.

It was the first season when there had been three up and down from the Second Division and at the start most thought that this would be bad news for the O's with there being more of a threat at the wrong end of the table, yet unbelievably it was the top that was concerning us.

We all take the number of promotion and relegation places for granted these days, yet on its introduction it was a highly controversial move to increase it from two to three, between the First and the Second. At the end of 1973–74 Manchester United occupied one of those places at the bottom of the First. Critics at the time said it was a disaster for the game in this country that they would have to go down and that they would never recover.

We were there on the other hand poised for the top league. I remember the day of this Villa game well even now nearly forty years on. I was nervous at school all day with only one thing on my mind.

At four o'clock I left for the game getting the number 69 bus from outside my front door in Chingford , arriving at the ground some twenty minutes later.

I reckon I had left for the game around the same time as the Villa coach had departed from the midlands.

I was first in the queue for the North Terrace and indeed the first punter to enter the stadium when the gates opened after five.

By about 6.15pm Leyton Stadium was absolutely packed. The crowd was 29,766 on the night and most of them appeared to be there about an hour and a half before kick-off. That of course is the difference between watching football then and now. In those days the game was not all ticket, our ground was three sides standing so you had to get there early for the big games to book your spot. It created the best atmosphere pre-match I've ever known at Brizzy Road that night, one that will alas never be repeated now at our theatre of flats, with the much smaller capacity.

There was singing a plenty with not a hint of a single away supporter – Villa had nothing to play for – and most were confident that we could do it on the night.

In fact we really should have secured a top three finish long before this last match after our great start to the season. We were comfortably second at Christmas. We had however only won one of of our home games from mid

January onwards and it was this that was ultimately to prove our undoing. After the magic in front of goal that we had seen in the first half of the season, the goals had dried up – we managed to score more than one in a match only once in the last eighteen games.

Still we knew that any kind of win this evening would do and surely Villa would let us get the two points we needed.

As the game started however, it became clear there was a good chance that things would not go to plan. The O's were fraught with tension and anxiety and the deafening noise before the game all but disappeared. We were not performing well at all. Earlier in the season we had been playing beautiful one touch football yet against the midlanders we were hoofing it high into the penalty area where the bombardment was being dealt with easily by giant centre-half Chris Nichol and goalkeeper Jim Cumbes.

There were only four chances created in a scrappy first half and three of those fell to the visitors. Indeed 'keeper Ray Goddard kept us in the game. He had turned over a Ray Graydon effort and produced a brilliant interception to cut out an Ian Hamiton centre. Brian Little also missed twice when in good positions. The O's only effort came from Gerry Queen, but he had been denied by Cumbes.

The only consolation at half-time was that poor as we had played, it was still 0–0 and we were hanging in there. Surely things had to improve in the second period.

Unfortunately however they did not and six minutes after the break came the killer blow. An otherwise impeccable Phil Hoadley chopped down the tricky Little in our penalty area.

Ray Graydon stepped up to take the resulting penalty and sent Ray Goddard the wrong way to put Villa 1–0 up. The stadium went silent.

We all began to realise that maybe this was not going to be Orient's night. The goal however, did seem to kick some life into our boys and indeed after sixty-six minutes Mickey Bullock brought the house down. Standing by the near post he collected a Bill Roffey throw and brilliantly hooked the ball over Cumbes and into the corner of the net for 1–1. Did the 29,766 go potty.

Game on. Still 24 minutes left, plenty of time to just get that one strike and the pot of gold that was the First Division.

We finally really came to life and started to put the away team under serious pressure. Alas though, those old shortcomings in front of goal came to the surface once more. Downing and Roffey fired wildly over and Barrie Fairbrother missed a golden chance that he would have taken easily before Christmas.

The time just ebbed away and it looked like it was just not going to happen. We entered injury time and then in its second minute Bullock had a superb point blank effort somehow kept out by Cumbes as if his life depended on it.

The final whistle sounded and it was heartache, pain and misery all round. The players sunk to their knees and it was said there were tears aplenty in the dressing room. Of all those present at Brisbane Road there was just one happy man – Carlisle goalkeeper Allen Ross who had made the trip down to watch the match and was apparently crying tears of joy as his side could contemplate First Division football for the first time in their history.

I was absolutely gutted. We had blown the chance of seeing top flight football, and deep down I think I knew that there was a very good chance we would not have the same opportunity ever again. The truth was that our division that year was very poor – Middleborough won it by fifteen points which was incredible considering there were only two points for a win in those days. The two other teams that went up – Luton and Carlisle not unexpectedly came straight back down, and of course Man United went straight back up in 1974–75. We also would surely have had just one season in the top tier, but even that would have been one season more than I have currently seen them play in it.

I just wanted to be alone after the game and walked all the way home arriving back in Chingford at around eleven, some seven hours after I had left for the match. I was greeted by my mother and told her that we had failed to win and would not be promoted. She asked what the score was and when I told her 1–1, she came out with one of the all time classic Orient quotes,: 'Oh well at least they didn't lose.' Not really what I wanted to hear at the time.

I'm a bit of a cricket man and watch the county game nowadays on Sky when they have it on. They often interview Jim Cumbes who is now chief executive at Lancashire Cricket Club. When ever he comes on my mind goes back, of course, to injury time at Brisbane Road on 3 May 1974 and I feel like putting something through the telly. Why did he have to make that save ?

Looking back now some four decades later, though there was pain that night we really should have looked at the positives for the club that evening. It had only been five years to the week before that, that Orient had played a crucial home game against Shrewsbury which if we had lost would have meant relegation to the Fourth Division at the time. To merely be talking about First Division football at the club had been some achievement in 1973–74.

Of course this was something that did not enter our heads that May evening. The really gutting thing as well was that we could all see that we needed to boost our team with a new striker to freshen things up around Christmas time in 1973. A new front man would surely have clinched us promotion. The board at the time however failed to invest. Yet the incredible thing was that in the close season in 1974 they bought Derek Possee for £60,000. No-one at Brizzy could understand why they did not make the move some six months earlier. But then that's Orient/Leyton Orient for you.

Orient: Goddard, Downing, Roffey, Allen, Hoadley, Walley, Fairbrother, Brisley, Bullock, Queen, Heppolette.
Goal: Bullock (66n).

Aston Villa: Cumbes, Robson, Aitkin, McMahon, Nicholl, Turnbull, Graydon, Brown, Morgan, Hamilton, Little.
Goal: Graydon (51pen, s)

Star Man: Mickey Bullock.
Attendance: 29,766.

Orient's Double Rammy

Orient 2 Derby County 2
FA Cup Third Round. 4 January 1975

4 January 1975 was a remarkable day in the history of the oldest cup competition in the world. In those wonderful days when every tie kicked off at 3 o'clock on a Saturday afternoon, five non-league teams entered the Third Round and come the draw for the Fourth Round on Monday lunchtime all five still had an interest in it.

Wimbledon, then of the Southern League won 1–0 at First Division Burnley. Altrincham and Wycombe held Everton and Middleborough who were both in the top flight, whilst in other ties Arsenal and Manchester United were held at home by teams from the lower divisions, York and Walsall respectively.

Not to be outdone by the other underdogs our boys produced one of their cup specials in a minor classic against Derby County. It was a match seen later in the evening by millions as the main game on *Match of the Day*.

We entered the day in 15th place in the Second Division, our season rap-

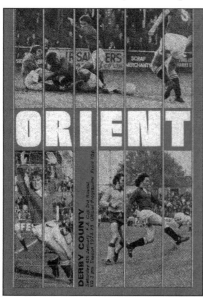

idly going nowhere after the near miss of 1973–74. Quite remarkably we had draw eight of our previous nine matches which included a goalless draw at Old Trafford against Manchester United, while Derby were then quite possibly the best team in the country and ended the season as league champions. Internationals aplenty rolled off the County team sheet – Nish, Rioch, Todd, Gemmill and Frannie Lee amongst them. Dave Mackay was their manager.

Yet unbelievably after just a quarter of an hour of this match at Brisbane

Road, we were two goals up and thoroughly deserved our lead, having played some wonderful football. A Phil Hoadley free-kick twelve minutes into the game had been punched clear by Colin Boulton to Derek Possee who drove the ball back fiercely past the 'keeper and into the corner to give us the lead.

Then just three minutes later Possee flicked on a cross to Gerry Queen who drove the ball home, so stunning the twelve thousand present at Leyton Stadium. A couple of goals to the good most teams in our position would have shut up shop and tried to preserve the lead, but we continued to go forward and hit both the bar and the post before having an appeal for a blatant penalty turned down. The referee must have been the only one present at Leyton that afternoon who did not believe a Derby defender had brought down Derek Possee inside the box.

Then however Derby got the break they badly needed just before the interval. Following a free-kick Archie Gemmill fed Colin Todd on the edge of the area and Todd shot. Now it was well known at the time that for all of his qualities as a defender, England international Todd never scored, and for him try his luck from distance, summed up just how desperate the Rams had become at the time.

To the disbelief of everyone however his poorly hit effort deflected off Derek Downing and past John Jackson into the net. The Leyton Stadium bovril still tasted good at half-time however, as we would all have gladly taken 2–1 at the turn around at the start of the day.

Not surprisingly our lads started to tire a little in the second half, but we hung on until the closing stages and the O's looked on course for a famous win. With just seven minutes to go however that man Todd struck again. He again hit a speculative shot from just outside the area but this time it hit his own teammate Rodger Davies and it deflected past a wrong footed John Jackson into the opposite corner of the net.

County thus escaped the afternoon with a draw. The O's fans, the Derby punters and the evening armchair fans must all have agreed they had got out of jail. Prior to the Orient game Colin Todd had not scored all season and indeed he never added to his tally of two after our encounter.

Said Dave Mackay of the O's after the game: 'The speed and skill of their quick counters completely put us off our stride. We just didn't expect it and it took some of the lads a long time to get going.' In fact it had taken them all of 83 minutes to get going – they had never really looked in it until it was 2–2.

In those days school beckoned for me and the replay the following Wednesday at the Baseball Ground was out of bounds. Instead I went to White Hart Lane where the home side, in another major cup shock went out of the cup losing 1–0 in a replay to Second Division Nottingham Forest. The visitors that night were playing their first game under a new manager, a chap named Brian Clough and I think that most present that evening felt that if he could carry on producing similar results to the one that night at Spurs he would have a bright future at the City Ground.

The O's meanwhile were at the same time being brilliant yet again, this time up in the Midlands. For this game, the replay action was shown late at night on ITV Barry Fairbrother had scored to make the score 1–1 at half-time and we were well and truly in the tie entering the second period. We replaced Peter Bennett with a young winger called Laurie Cunningham, making one of his first appearances in an Orient shirt. It's fair to say that for the rest of the game Laurie ran rings around Todd and Nish. One brilliant run saw him out pacing the home defence, but in the resulting one-on-one with Boulton he showed his inexperience as he just squeezed the ball wide of the post.

Unfortunately our brave resistance finally ended just five minutes from time when Bruce Rioch scored the winner to put us out of the cup. It had taken the League Champions designate exactly 175 minutes to finally get the better of us in the tie. Our lads had certainly done themselves proud over the two games.

Derby must have been glad as hell to get rid of us. Our admirable displays were put into perspective when County, with virtually the same side that played against us, shortly afterwards defeated the then top of the league Liverpool 2–0. Indeed just eight months later many of the players who had struggled at Brisbane Road against us were in the Derby side that defeated Real Madrid 4–1 in the European Cup.

The O's meanwhile ended the campaign in twelfth position. It's fair to say that it was not the most exciting season we had ever seen at Brisbane Road. Twelve of our forty-two league games ended in goalless draws. Our total of 28 goals was the lowest in the division.

However that third round afternoon in January was for sure top notch. Indeed despite the cup exploits of '72 and '78 and some of the displays in the 1973–74 near miss season, I'd put the first Derby game up there as possibly the performance of the decade for the Orient.

And now some thirty-seven years later I still hate Colin Todd.

Orient: Jackson, Fisher, Downing, Allen, Hoadley, Walley, Fairbrother, Bennett, Queen, Grealish, Possee.
Goals: Possee (12n), Queen (15n).

Derby County: Boulton, Webster, Nish, Rioch, Daniel, Todd, Newton, Gemmill, Davies, Bourne (Hinton), Lee.
Goals: Todd (43s, 83n).

Star Man: Derek Possee.
Attendance: 12,490.

Game Twelve

Last day happiness and a bit of turf

Orient 1 Hull City 1
Football League Division 2. 17 May 1977

After two mid-table finishes in 1974–75 and 1975–76 the following season saw a disappointing relegation struggle at Brisbane Road, despite the fact that the Final of the Anglo-Scottish Cup was reached.

A major problem for the club was the poor state of the pitch with many home games postponed because of it, meaning that by the last week in April we still had five matches at Leyton Stadium to play. We failed to win any of the first four and the one away fixture sandwiched in-between saw a 1-6 defeat at Fulham. Indeed due to the back-log of fixtures, the reserves had to play on three consecutive days: 18, 19 and 20 May and then again on 23 May to complete their Football Combination programme.

With all the other clubs around us having finished their season, we entered this last game against Hull on 17 May knowing that a defeat would relegate us to the Third Division. The irony was that a win or a draw for us would send Carlisle down. In other words three years after our failure to beat Aston Villa on the season's last day had given the Cumbrians First Division football, their destiny was again in our hands, only this time to go the other way out of the division.

In many ways this was a strange evening. Playing a game in the second half of May meant that there was little need for floodlights for most of the ninety minutes, and we were also told that after the game had finished we were allowed to go onto the playing area and basically dig up the turf (what there was of it) and take it home. It was, unsurprisingly to be relayed in the summer.

Hull were 14 and had nothing to play for, but we had failed to win in ten and had scored just six times in our previous twelve games.

Our gates had dipped below 5,000 but on this balmy evening 8,400 masochists were attracted to Brizzy to see if we could preserve our Second Division status.

Game Twelve

We started the game on the front foot but it looked like being the same old problem that we had been having all season, in that we were unable to finish off decent moves by finding the back of the net. However finally after 36 minutes Bill Roffey crossed from the left and Joe Mayo headed downwards for Allan Glover to thunder a drive into the net, to give us a half-time lead.

City came out for the second half in a more positive vein and the O's were forced into some desperate defending. Tensions began to rise as four Hull players as well as Roffey found their way into the referee's notebook.

Then with twenty minutes remaining John Jackson, who had been his usual reliable self all season committed a very rare error when in an off-guard moment he fumbled a hopeful shot by Paul Haigh, allowing the ball to slip from his grasp and into the net.

1–1 and at once Brisbane Road became a very nervous place and the clock seemed to suddenly slow down to a snails pace. Alan Whittle had a couple of chances to give us the lead once more, but the best chance in the closing minutes fell to City's Stuart Croft who thankfully sent his close range header wide of the target.

Just to prolong the agony even more, referee Burden added five minutes of injury time but he finally blew for the end of the match to start wild celebrations from the relieved crowd.

After years of being told to keep off the pitch it was strange to go onto it and even stranger to take some of it to keep.

I decided to take a patch of grass near the penalty spot on the north side of the ground just in front of where I stood, and I remember carefully carrying it onto the 69 bus to take home to Chingford.

When I got home home it was meticulously relayed in our garden. It was pure joy that evening to know that we still had Second Division football to look forward to the following season and also with the knowledge that I had a piece of my favorite place in the world in our back garden.

The evening highlighted the bizarreness at times of being a football supporter. Three years earlier we had drawn another match 1–1 this time against Aston Villa and we had all left Brisbane Road as if it was the end of the world. This despite the fact that we had ended the campaign in our highest league position for over ten years.

Yet on this night in 1977 despite ending up just a point away from relegation we were all ecstatic going away from Leyton. And God only knows what emotions they must have been feeling up in Carlise at the end of the evening.

1977–78 ended up being one of our most memorable ever with our appearance in the FA Cup Semi-Final, as well as all of Kitchen's goals, but one wonders what would have happened had Hull managed to sneak a winner that evening back in May '77.

Orient: Jackson, Grealish, Roffey, Bennett, Gray, Roeder, Chiedozie, Glover, Mayo, Allen, Whittle.
Goal: Glover (36n)

Hull City: Wealands, Daniel, DeVries, Haigh, Croft, Roberts, Nisbet, Lord, Sunley, McDonald, Galvin.
Goal: Haigh (70n).

Star Man: Allan Glover.
Attendance: 8,400.

Game Thirteen

Canaries kop it

Norwich City 0 Orient 1
FA Cup Third Round Replay. 16 January 1978

In the momentous history of Clapton Orient/Leyton Orient/Orient/Leyton Orient, few could argue that the 1961–62 promotion season stands out as our greatest ever achievement. For a club the size of the O's to reach the top flight, even in those days, was quite magnificent.

Not a million miles behind however, were the events of 1969–70 and 1977–78. In the former we had avoided relegation to the Fourth Division with a win in the last game of the season 1968–69, yet incredibly were crowned Third Division champions just a year later.

And in 1977–78 we unbelievably reached the last four of the FA Cup with a team so good we once more required a final day victory that season to avoid relegation, this time from the Second.

In fact it was not just that we got to the semi-final in 1978 but the way that we did it that made it such a great accomplishment that year. Other clubs from the second tier have made it as far as the Orient did, yet few have had such a difficult route as we had that year. Millwall for instance, back in 2004 got all the way to the final not having had to face a single team from the Premiership en-route.

Compare that to the mighty O's. Our path to that infamous afternoon at Stamford Bridge when Supermac 'scored' twice for the Gooners to finally knock us out, consisted of six matches against sides from the division above us. Three of those we won and three we drew. Two of those wins were away from home. Even the only game against a non top tier side was the one against Blackburn, who although a fellow Second Division club were way above us at the time, sitting in fifth place in the table.

It really was an outstanding achievement by the club. The journey began with this match up with Norwich in January. Orient were placed in fifteenth position in Division Two while the Canaries stood eighth in the First and were having a wonderful season. Just a month earlier they had beaten the League Champions Liverpool at Carrow Road, and could boast some fine players, amongst them '66 World Cup winner Martin Peters.

The draw gave us a Brisbane Road tie in early January. It had also paired West Ham at home however, with an attractive looking game (as much as any match involving the Shammers can be viewed as 'attractive') against Watford. With Tottenham also at home on the Saturday we got permission to move our fixture to the Friday night, 6 January.

It was probably a very good move, with 14,538 attracted to Brizzy for the evening match. The O's had had just one win from the previous six yet played superbly on the night. Peter Kitchen had given us a deserved 26th minute lead and although John Jackson made some good saves, we could easily have been two or three up with a touch of good fortune. Heartache came on the night however, when Roger Gibbens equalized in injury time to give the Canaries a rather fortuitous replay.

I remember getting to the King's Head in Chingford after the game feeling absolutely gutted. It was one of those where if you would have given us a draw at kick-off we would have taken it, but to miss out on a win so late on, it felt more like a defeat.

In fact I found the most painful part about the fixture came the next day at lunchtime. John Bond, the Norwich manager at the time obviously had a free day so he was invited to the Beeb to take part in their *Football Focus* programme. He had a great big smile on his face and was looking really smug knowing that his side had got out of jail. He had the nerve to say that Norwich deserved the draw and must have thought it would be a lot easier for them at home in the replay, where they were unbeaten all season.

At the time it was tempting to throw something at the telly, or even do something really bad to the yellow budgie we had at home.

The return match was due to be played the following Wednesday, 11 January. However heavy rain caused a postponement meaning the game was finally played on Monday 16 January. As one would expect Norwich as the home side, had more of the play in the second game but found Jacko in inspired form. The great man was playing his 153rd consecutive game for us and it was certainly one of his best. Four saves he made on the night were world class. It was not all one way traffic however, on the break we looked really threatening with young winger John Chiedozie causing more than a problem or two to the Canaries back four. Full-back Colin Sullivan cannot have had any harder afternoons against Division One wingers that season as he did against Chiedozie.

The young Nigerian, along with Big Joe Mayo, helped create a fine opportunity for Peter Kitchen after twenty-six minutes, Kitches side-footed volley bringing about an excellent save from veteran 'keeper Kevin Keelan. Whilst the home team generally had the better of the game our midfield did a fine job closing down Peters and Colin Suggett for City and as the game entered its closing stages it remained goalless.

Then with 87 minutes came the crucial moment. Following a Bobby Fisher throw-in to Joe Mayo the ball broke to Chiedozie. His low cross was met by Kitchen who fired past Keelan from close range, for his eighteenth goal of the season.

We held out for the remaining moments to record a famous victory. Being as the game was on a Monday night there was little other footy action that evening, so we got a lot of press the following day.

'Glory night for Orient and Kitchen' said the *Daily Express*.

'Jacko Orient's show stopper' reported the *Evening Standard*. Jacko indeed was man of the match – many were hinting at the time, that he should be called up to the England squad.

Manager Jimmy Bloomfield said: 'What pleased me most of all was that we won it deservedly over the two matches. The lads were heartbroken at being robbed in the last match. But none thought we would lose this time.'

Kitch said: 'I wanted to prove I was capable of playing in a higher grade – and this was a great way to do it.'

I looked for some quotes from John Bond about the replay in the papers, but they were notable for their absence. After a couple of quiet seasons for us in the FA Cup it was wonderful to once more have some success in it. Blackburn waited for us in the Fourth Round.

Norwich City: Keelan, Bond, Sullivan, Ryan, Forbes, Powell, Neighbour, Suggett, Gibbens, Reeves, Peters.

Orient: Jackson, Fisher, Roffey, Grealish, Hoadley, Roeder, Chiedozie, Gray, Mayo, Kitchen, Bennett.
Goal: Kitchen (87).

Star Man: John Jackson.
Attendance: 20,421.

Game Fourteen

Bald eagle's blues

Orient 3 Blackburn Rovers 1
FA Cup Fourth Round. 28 January 1978

When the topic of the '78 cup run comes up amongst veteran O's, it's fair to say that this game is often overlooked. Probably because it was the one game in our run to the semi-final that was not against Division One opposition, yet in many ways it was still a classic.

Indeed looking back the Blackburn game, more than any of the other encounters on the road to the last four, this was the one game where we were lucky not to lose.

Going into the game the Rovers were nine places above us in the Second Division, just four points away from a promotion place, with a game in hand on the clubs above them.

I remember being stood on the North Terrace as the northerners kicked towards us in the first half and watching somewhat one way traffic, with all the play being at our end. Our league form was still poor – we had been beaten the previous week at Oldham – and we had suffered a severe blow the day after the Norwich win when John Chiedozie had broken his leg playing for the youth team at Ipswich.

Half-time came at 0–0, but it's fair to say that Jacko had once more kept us in the tie with some wonderful saves in the first forty-five. One from point blank range, I still consider now one of the best I've ever seen at Brizzy.

We really did get pulled apart in the first period. Blackburn's two overlapping full-backs Kevin Hird and John Bailey gave us heaps of trouble and they had Gordon Taylor – now big wig in the PFA, of course – running the midfield.

We barely created a chance in the first half and the pattern continued after the break. After sixty-eight minutes Rovers finally got the break through they deserved when Stuart Metcalfe gave them the lead.

The O's looked out of it, yet thanks to a piece of Kitch magic we came back into the game with just twelve minutes remaining.

He just beat Rovers 'keeper John Butcher to a teasing through ball, clipping it wide to the right. Our goal gourmet chased it down and from an acute angle smashed it hard into the net. Just as this can be considered the forgotten match of the cup run, the opening goal from Kitchen on this day, could possibly be regarded as the forgotten goal. Everybody can recall his masterpieces against Chelsea and Middlesbrough, yet this effort really was in many ways just as good.

We had created very little all game, yet with just over ten minutes to go were right back in it at 1–1. And it was to get even better. Kitch put Joe Mayo through with 86 minutes on the clock and the big man shot. His effort was initially blocked on the line by John Waddington, but Kitchen was in the right place at the right time to poke the ball home.

2–1 up yet the O's still had not finished. Just before the end 17-year-old Kevin Godfrey, who had taken Chiedozie's place in the side put in a not very good cross which some how found it's way to Mayo, who slotted home. Young Godfrey with only a handful of matches under his belt had looked out of his depth all game but had somehow managed to help secure the win at the death.

It really was a bizarre encounter. We had not been in it for the majority of it yet had ended up winning 3–1. Because he had kept us in it for a long time, Jacko was once again our man of the match.

Rovers manager Jim Smith said afterwards ; 'I can't believe the result. They hardly had a kick and beat us.' Unlike John Bond in the previous round it was hard not to have some sympathy with the Blackburn boss.

In fact the O's came back to haunt Smith again some twenty-eight years later when we defeated his Oxford side in the famous 2006 game to knock the U's out of the league.

In his long and distinguished career as a football manager 'the Bald Eagle' will have had many a highlight but it's fair to say that this 3–1 reverse would not have been one of them.

Personally I loved the match. I've always said that the best games are the ones where you come from behind to win, preferably late on. And for me it always seems all that sweeter when, as in this instance, it has not really been deserved.

The draw for the next round took place, as always, on the Jimmy Young show on Radio 2 the following Monday at 12.30 pm. Chelsea were drawn away to Orient. Even to this day you look back and wonder why it was the O's and not Blackburn.

Orient: Jackson, Fisher, Roffey, Grealish, Hoadley, Roeder, Godfrey, Gray, Mayo, Kitchen, Bennett.
Goals: Kitchen (78n, 86n) Mayo (89n).

Blackburn: Butcher, Hird, Bailey, Metcalfe, Waddington, Fazackerley, Brotherston, Wood, Wagstaffe, Parkes, Taylor.
Goal: Metcalfe (68s)

Star Man: Peter Kitchen.
Attendance: 9,547.

Kitchen sinks 'em

Chelsea 1 Orient 2
FA Cup Fifth Round Replay. 27 February 1978

Needless to say there was great anticipation concerning our match up with the West Londoners in the Fifth Round of the Cup, six years since we had beaten them at the same stage of the same competition.

Unfortunately events on the day at Brisbane Road were marred by happenings off the pitch. Just after the start of the game a wall collapsed at the Coronation Gardens end of the ground resulting in some injuries.

I remember getting off the 69 bus in Leyton High Road at 1.30 that afternoon seeing around 50 or so armed with blue scarves running towards the ground with hammers and other tools singing 'Brisbane Road is falling down' and I feared the worst.

Sure enough with the first attack at the south end of the ground just after kick-off there was a big surge by the Chelsea supporters who were gathered there and the wall at the front collapsed. There were a few injuries, but it could have been a lot worse.

It was clear that a section of the away support had one thing on their mind, to smash up the Brisbane Road, yet amazingly afterwards the Chelsea chairman Brian Mears blamed the state of the ground for the casualties. His counterpart at Orient, Brian Winston was rightly furious with the comments and went on 'The Big Match' the next day to say so.

The FA set up a committee which decreed that Leyton Stadium was indeed unsafe and as a result the barriers behind the goal had to be dramatically strengthened. We were told that the same had to be done in the Westside but Winston and Co. decided that it would be cheaper to turn the terraces there into a seating area, so that from the start of the 1978–79 season there was no standing anymore in our biggest stand.

It's fair to say that the Chelsea hooligans with their actions that afternoon changed the complete complexion of Brisbane Road for good. And incidentally sitting on the FA's committee that initiated the changes was a certain Brian Mears.

The game ended 0–0 – Jacko made a couple of decent saves and Kitch had a goal disallowed – but generally it was a match to be forgotten.

Not so the replay some ten days later. Picking out the all time Orient classics, this one for sure makes the top five. Whilst two days before the encounter, we had earned a magnificent away draw at Tottenham in Division Two, we still had not won in the league all year.

It was not one of the great Chelsea teams but they had beaten Liverpool 4–2 in the Third Round and could still boost some fine players, notably a young Ray Wilkins in midfield.

On the night there was a good sprinkling of Orient fans amongst the 36,379 in the crowd and whilst most of those were in the seats there was a small pocket of us in the away end, behind the goal directly opposite the Shed End. Surrounded by police we actually felt much safer than we did in the Brisbane Road encounter.

From the start it was a much more open game than the first one had been, though chances were still few and far between to begin with. The O's best effort came from a Paddy Grealish thirty-yarder that flew narrowly over the bar.

Then after twenty-two minutes the long deadlock over the two games was finally broken in somewhat bizarre circumstances. A Chelsea ball to the edge of our area saw our full-back Bill Roffey under severe pressure from winger Clive Walker. Roffey panicked somewhat and attempted to lob the ball back to John Jackson. Unfortunately, however he got his angles all wrong and lobbed the ball exquisitely over Jacko and into the corner of the net.

The small group of us at the other end of the ground feared the worst for the rest of the game, yet quite remarkably the goal in many ways was the best thing that could have happened to us. It certainly woke us up and for the rest of the game we were absolutely magnificent.

Half-time came and we were still one down. It was a wet night but we still had hope and sure enough that was justified just four minutes after the re-start. Kevin Godfrey put Kitch through on the right. Our forward cut inside and beat Ron Harris, Mickey Droy and Ian Britton before slotting the ball past Bonetti. Although it could have been argued that all three defenders dived in like novices it was still magnificent play by the moustached wizard, a goal reminiscent of Jimmy Greaves in his prime.

Incredibly after the equalizer we started to control the game. Soon after Peter Allen produced a wonderful dipping shot which Bonetti just managed to turn over.

Then Kitchen turned provider with a teasing cross which found Mayo whose header clipped the post.

The only threat from Chelsea was coming from Walker, who struck a fine long ranger which called for a fine save from Jacko.

With eighteen minutes left came the moment that sent the small, wet group on the vast open away terrace into ecstasy. It all came from a Chelsea corner down our end. The ball broke to Glenn Roeder on the edge of our box. Our elegant defender took it forward into the middle of the park. From here he looked up and played a wonderful 40 yard cross fielder right to the feet of Joe Mayo on the left.

Big Joe took it down, advanced to the edge of the area then slipped a ball through to our goal poacher who was hovering menacingly. Kitch controlled the ball superbly and then proceeded to clip it over Bonetti and into the net for 2–1.

Kitch's first that night had been a super individual goal, but the second was a magnificent team effort from one end of the pitch to the other.

Needless to say when it went in we all went mad, at the same time being told by those directly opposite us in the Shed that we were going to get our heads kicked in.

We still had over a quarter of an hour to go however, and we knew that Chelsea would throw everything at us in the remainder of the game. That they certainly did, the Blues put big centre-half Mickey Droy up front but our defence stayed firm, led of course by the magnificent Jackson.

We hung on to record a famous victory. At the final whistle we celebrated wildly for some minutes, then hid our scarves away and tried to look glum as we headed for the station. There were four Chingfordians all travelling together that night and I remember once we got back to Walthamstow Central all hell broke out as we released all our pent-up happiness on the 69 bus back to Chingford. It had certainly been a wonderful evening.

The next day the papers were rightly raving about our win and especially the performance of our two goal hero. 'Viva Kitchen !' headlined the *Daily Mail*, reflecting on the fact that Kitch looked like a character from Viva Zapata (whatever that was): 'with his swarthy looks, dark moustache and hunched shoulders'.

They quoted our goal machine as saying afterwards on his first effort: 'That's got to be my best goal of the 22 I've scored this season. I was terrible in the first half. Ron Harris is hard to get past. I felt better in the second half. When I scored the opener it was the first time I'd been able to turn and take him on.'

Sadly Orient manager Jimmy Bloomfield missed the game having been in hospital after an operation. He was actually quite ill and went on to miss much of the rest of the season with his assistant Peter Angell taking control for a lot of the time.

Chelsea manager Ken Shellito said: 'I was very unhappy about our performance. We deserved what we got – nothing.'

And so the Orient FA Cup circus in 1978 rolled on to Middlesborough for the quarter-final. Would we be able to reach the semi-finals for the first time ever? With Kitch and Jacko in the team, most of us thought at the time that anything was possible.

Orient: Jackson, Fisher, Roffey, Grealish, Hoadley, Roeder, Godfrey, Gray, Mayo, Kitchen, Allen.
Goals: Kitchen (49, 72)

Chelsea: Bonetti, Locke, Harris, Britton, Droy, Wicks, Finnieston, Wilkins, Langley, Swain, Walker.
Goal: Roffey (22 og).

Star Man: Peter Kitchen.
Attendance: 36,379.

Game Sixteen

Boro buried

Orient 2 Middlesbrough 1
FA Cup Sixth Round Replay. 14 March 1978

The quarter-final draw had given us Middlesbrough away and led to one of those never to be forgotten days in the life of being an 'O'. The actual game at Ayresome Park turned out to be a quite forgettable one. It was a real backs to the wall effort by the team, but the defence were magnificent all afternoon, so much so that Jacko had very little to do in the way of saves. We got a 0–0 draw, another superb result against a side sitting comfortably mid-table in the First Division.

It was events other than the footy however that made it a day to remember for many of the 2,000 who had travelled up from east London.

Orient had chartered two trains to go up to the game from Stratford, something unheard of for the club in those days. When we arrived at Middlesbrough station we were greeted by the police who gave us an escort to the ground. There were a few yobs around but we sang all the way to the stadium because with plenty of police around we did not feel at all threatened.

We had not sold all of our allocation of standing tickets for the game and as a result we were moved from the away supporter's section in the ground, to the children's enclosure high up in the corner of Ayresome Park. On the day Middlesbrough had what was then a record attendance for them of 33,426 and before the game as well as during it we had constant abuse directed at us from everywhere. I was not too bothered at the time however, as I thought the boys in blue would be there for us after the game had finished to take us back to the station.

However with about ten minutes of the match remaining and the locals getting more and more agitated about their teams inability to break us down, the police who had been with us since two o'clock amazingly disappeared.

Just one remained in our enclosure and I questioned him as to whether we would be getting an escort back to the station from the police. No was the answer I was given, as they had to direct the traffic. I argued that we could have problems with their louts but he told me it was my fault for being a southerner.

Being in the kid's enclosure, just a low wall separated us from the Boro hard-core in front of us. When the final whistle sounded they poured over to join the Orient fans, and they weren't looking for our autographs. A few O's, I remember got a fair beating after the game. I got chased through some back street by three of their hoolies and sacrificed my scarf, but when I finally got back to the station seeing the state of some of our fans I realised I had got off lightly.

As an experience it devastated me at the time. I said on the train on the way home that I had had enough of football and that I would not be going to the replay because of the events of the afternoon.

I mellowed somewhat in the next three days and had my usual place on the North Terrace come Tuesday night, but looking back it was an awful experience, certainly the worst I've ever had at the 1,200 or so matches I've been to over the years with the O's.

It was certainly a bad day for away supporters in the FA Cup. On the same day Ipswich had won 6–1 at Millwall and I remember seeing on the news that many of their supporters had got a nasty beating from the home thugs that day at Cold Blow Lane.

Partly as a result of the goings on that took place on Saturday, I really wanted us to hammer the north-easterners in the replay.

As it was the O's put in a quite stunning display. The team's attitude was remarkable on the night. We had been happy in the first game to soak up a lot of pressure and did not even seem bothered to try and hit them on the break, yet in the second match we began the total opposite. We threw the kitchen (if you'll excuse the pun) sink at them from the kick-off and were unbelievably two up after just twelve minutes.

The first was another classic effort from Kitch. After six minutes he controlled a long ball from Kevin Godfrey with one touch on the edge of the area, then hooked it goalwards. It sailed into the net, via the post with boro 'keeper Jim Platt totally stranded.

Then just six minutes later things got even better for the O's. Big Joe Mayo tried his luck from the edge of the box. It was not the greatest shot he will ever have had, but with an awkward bounce, Platt somehow managed to let the ball slip past him and into the goal. 2–0.

Middlesbrough were totally stunned – as indeed were all of us on the terraces. There was a feeling of unreality around the place as people started to realise that for the first time in our history we could be going to see our team play in an FA Cup semi-final.

Middlesbrough as one would expect started to come more into the game and David Mills headed just over, but it was not all one way traffic and the ever-threatening Kitch went close once more with an overhead effort.

Bill Roffey in particular was impressing for the O's, our full-back putting in some highly impressive crosses for Kitch and Big Joe.

Things started to get a little heated just before the break, first Alan Ramage was booked for the visitors, then Phil Hoadley and Boro's Billy Ashcroft both had their names taken after a scuffle.

Half-time came and we were still two goals up, though we knew it was going to be a mighty long last forty-five.

The second-half started and still remarkably the O's pressed forward. They were now kicking towards us on the North Terrace, and within minutes of the restart Kitch was put through and had a glorious chance to put the tie to bed. Unchallenged in front of goal he sliced wide, however. I remember some wag near me shouting down: 'Kitchen you're rubbish' at him.

Ashcroft then should have scored for the visitors but his header was weak, and it started to look as if it could well be our night.

We started to tire a little and had to do more and more defending, but time was running out. Then with just five minutes left there was a scramble in the Orient box and David Armstrong poked the ball home for 2–1.

A long five minutes followed, but it was a successful five minutes as we held out for a quite magnificent victory. We had done it, and were through to our first ever FA Cup semi-final. After the events of Saturday I felt justice had been done. Of course it turned into a long night afterwards, but a thoroughly enjoyable one, of course. Just to put the cherry on the cake we found out that West Spam had lost 1–0 at QPR that night, sending them into the bottom three in the First.

There had really only been one downside to the victory and that had been the semi-final draw the day before. The winners of our clash had been drawn against Arsenal in the semi-final. The other two teams left in it were West Brom-wich Albion and Ipswich. Great as it was to be playing anyone in the last four, I felt that we would have had a much better chance of reaching Wembley if we had been playing the Baggies or the Town.

They were average First Division teams at the time, much on a par with the three that we had already defeated. Arsenal on the other hand were, I felt a class above the other survivors.

I always thought that they would have a touch too much for us at Stamford Bridge and indeed they did beating us 3–0.

Looking back some thirty-five years later, if you could take the ninety min-utes of the game away, the semi-final was actually a glorious day. A mass of red and white heading from east to west London, the great atmosphere before the game, the 'Kitchen fries Rice' banner, the pleasure of watching your side play in an FA Cup semi-final.

What a pity the referee had to blow the whistle to start the match that after-noon. Truth was for pretty much the whole of the ninety minutes we were awful. Rumour was that Kevin Godfrey froze in the dressing room just before kick-off and had to be replaced by Derek Clarke in the starting eleven at the last minute.

We got an early corner which Pat Jennings plucked out of the air, away from the oncoming Big Joe, but that was as good as it got for us all afternoon.

It still took two deflected efforts from Malcolm MacDonald to defeat us, however. I remember feeling sick as he walked back to the centre circle after both efforts, arms aloft as was his usual celebration, hating him almost as much as I hated Middlesbrough fans at the time.

Graham Rix got a third after the break, which really killed the tie.

It was all turning into a massive anti-climax. Many an 'O' started to leave at 3–0. The Gooners down the other end to us in the Shed started to sing anti Spurs and Chelsea songs – e.g. 'this is worse than White Hart Lane', directed at the ground. I remember getting really agitated as a big cheer went up in front of me from a group of O's 'fans'. It transpired that the Hammers had just taken a 2–1 lead at Leeds in a crucial relegation match. I did not like having Claret and Blues amongst us.

Quite remarkably however, the best part of the day was still to come. It seems incredible now, but back then there were three massive games in the capital that afternoon, all kicking off at the same time. There were the two FA Cup Semis, and also Spurs v. Bolton, a crucial promotion clash in the Second Division which actually attracted a bigger gate than either of the cup games at Stamford Bridge or Highbury. These days the police (or Sky, of course) would never allow it, but back then we all just accepted it.

We dejectedly started to drive home after the match, but as you can imagine the traffic all over London was a complete nightmare. A decision was made by our driver Mike to therefore to stop off at a pub on the Embankment around sixish to let the mayhem subside for a short while.

I can just about remember staggering out of the pub about five hours and eight pints later shouting abuse about John Bond, Middlesbrough fans and Super Mac. The pub had been full of footy fans, there were scarves of West Brom, Ipswich, Spurs and the O's present with everyone waiting for the traffic to get better, yet there was not a hint of trouble.

It was an evening to restore one's faith in the great game, despite our result that afternoon.

I said at the time that I was not going to watch the Arsenal v. Ipswich FA Cup Final that year, but in the end I relented and saw it, and jolly glad I did too. With Arsenal losing 1–0 and playing even worse than we had done at Stamford Bridge, it remains one of my all time favorite club games I've ever seen, where the O's have not been involved.

And there was Malcolm MacDonald who, just as he had done for Newcastle in the Cup Final some four years before, had another stinker. It became a standing joke at the end of the seventies – what is always taken to the Cup Final and never used? The standard reply was the ribbons of the losing team, but an alternative answer became Malcolm MacDonald.

And even now when there's a goal scored at Brisbane Road that has taken a wicked deflection you can always rely on some veteran wag around you to shout: 'Malcolm MacDonald's claiming it.'

Yes memories of that wonderful Cup Run back in 1978 are still there in many an old O to this very day.

It really was a magnificent achievement reaching the last four – what would we give now to have another evening to celebrate an FA Cup semi-final appearance, as we did on 14 March 1978.

Orient: Jackson, Fisher, Roffey, Grealish, Hoadley, Roeder, Godfrey, Gray, Mayo, Kitchen, Payne.
Goals: Kitchen (6s), Mayo (12s).

Middlesbrough: Platt, Craggs, Bailey, Mahoney, Boam, Ramage, Mills, McAndrew, Ashcroft, Cummins, Armstrong.
Goal: Armstrong (85s).

Star Man: Peter Kitchen.
Attendance: 18,051.

Game Seventeen

Kitchen saves the day

Cardiff City 0 Orient 1
Football League Division 2. 9 May 1978

1977–78 to this day remains my all time favourite Orient season. This may seem a weird thing to say bearing in mind that we were in a relegation scrap for all of it and only secured our Second Division status with this win in our last match, but for me it still brings back so many happy memories.

There was the amazing run through to the semis of the FA Cup of course, but almost as important for me was the fact that for the first time in my Orient supporting career we had actually found a decent goalscorer in Peter Kitchen.

Remarkably out of the last fifty seasons 1977–78 remains the only season when one of our players has managed to score twenty or more league goals in a campaign. It really is quite an unbelievable statistic, something that no other club who have been in the league during this time can come anywhere near to matching.

Saddo that I am, I remember looking back at those days now, how I used to get up on a Sunday morning back in '78 and search for that place in the Sunday papers where they gave the leading goalscorers in each of the divisions. I just stared in awe at seeing an Orient player up there at the top.

Kitch even treated us to two hat-tricks during the campaign – no Orient player had previously managed one since 1971 – and he ended the season having notched 29 out of our 57 goals in the four competitions we entered that year.

It could well be argued however, that despite his seven in the FA Cup, his winner in this game at Cardiff was possibly more important than any of the other 28 as it kept us up at the end of the season.

The truth was that we had struggled badly in the league all year despite all of the cup exploits, and so entered this final match needing a win to avoid relegation to the Third.

The teams around us had finished their programme and Cardiff were safe which helped us considerably, but going to Ninian Park that day we had only won once all season away from Brisbane Road in the league and had generally been truly awful on the road, the cup excluded.

Indeed our victories at Norwich and Chelsea meant that going to Wales for this encounter, we had won more games away in the FA Cup than we had in Division II in 1977–78.

Cardiff on the other hand were unbeaten in eleven home matches.

Over a thousand supporters made their way from east London swelling the crowd to 8,270 though there can not have been too much optimism amongst them on the journey down that evening. I was unable to get time off work and indeed had no idea of anything that had happened in Wales till I heard the final score on the radio at 10.00pm that evening.

As it was our boys, by all accounts, put in a really fine performance totally out of character to what had gone on before on their travels and thoroughly deserved their narrow win and with it survival.

A corner count of sixteen to three in Orient's favour reflected how we took the game to the Welshmen, and just how well we played throughout the game.

The big moment came in the thirty-seventh minute. Paddy Grealish took a long throw near the corner flag which was nodded on by Joe Mayo into the path of Derek Clarke.

Clarke's shot took a deflection to send the ball spinning into the air where Phil Hoadley connected. The ball dropped to Kitchen who toe-poked home past Ron Healey from just a few yards to give us the lead.

It was far from being a pretty goal, but then that could have been said for a lot of Kitch's efforts that season, and we certainly cared not.

The rest of the game was an obvious nervous affair for us, but the good thing about those days of course was that we had another great man – John Jackson – in goal, so we always had a chance of a clean sheet if we took the lead.

There was needless to say great relief at the final whistle as we secured the 1–0 win.

Amazingly the division was so tight that the two points lifted us six places to fourteenth in the division at the end of it, one of seven clubs that ended on thirty-eight points that year.

The team that were relegated instead of us were Blackpool. Remarkably they learned of their fate in the States, where they had gone on an end of season jolly obviously believing that they were safe. They must have been truly gutted on hearing their dreadful news so far away.

It could be said that it took the Lancashire club twenty-three years to get their revenge on Orient, when they defeated us in the play-off Final of 2001.

Another remarkable statistic from the season was the fact that though Peter Kitchen's 29 goals in all competitions made him the divisions leading scorer in all games, the most league goals were scored in 1977–78 by relegated Blackpool's Bob Hatton with 21.

It's certainly somewhat unusual for a division's leading scorer to play the whole season in a side that drops down at the end of it. Indeed Hatton had actually scored a hat-trick for the seasiders in Orient's first home game of the season, when the Pool won 4–1 at Brisbane Road, back in August.

Orient: Jackson, Fisher, Roffey, Grealish, Hoadley, Roeder, Clarke, Gray, Mayo, Kitchen, Bennett.
Goal: Kitchen (37).

Cardiff City: Healey, Dwyer, Pethard, Campbell, Pontin, Larmour, Grapes, Bishop, Evans, Went, Buchanan.

Star Man: Peter Kitchen.
Attendance: 8,270.

Game Eighteen

Day of the Jacko

Ipswich Town 0 Orient 0
FA Cup Fourth Round. 27 January 1979

Being an O's supporter these days it seems hard to remember those lovely days when we used to get a bye through to the Third Round of the FA Cup. Yes there was a time when we did not need to worry about the old tinpot until January. Trips to Alfreton or Droylesden before the turn of the year were just not on the agenda.

In the seventies, as a Second Division club we'd be straight in there with your Man U's and Liverpools first week in Jan.

Back in '79 we'd scraped past Bury 3–2 at home in the Third Round to set us up against the then holders of the trophy, Ipswich in the Fourth. It was a tie that could easily have been the final the previous season had we beaten the gooners in that Stamford Bridge semi-final.

The Suffolk club had just been drawn against Barcelona in the quarter-final

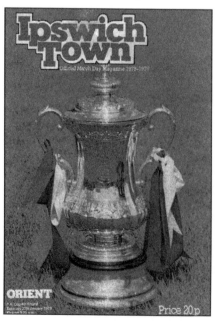

of the Cup Winners Cup and were one of the better sides in the First Division at the time. The team was awash with internationals: Mills, Beattie, Wark and Mariner and they had Bobby Robson as manager. Coming into the game they were unbeaten in five games, which included a 5–1 walloping of Chelsea.

The Orient for their part were also in the middle of a good run and were undefeated in seven, which had included wins against West Ham and Millwall, as well as a draw at top of the table Crystal Palace.

Our boys were very handily placed at seventh in the Second Division and were playing some entertaining stuff with Ian Moores, Joe Mayo, Peter Kitchen and John Chiedozie all featuring together in the forward line.

With the cup exploits of the previous season still fresh in many supporters' minds we took two thousand up to Portman Road for the Ipswich encounter. They gave us half the covered end behind the goal – all standing of course which created a wonderful atmosphere – similar to that at Middleborough the previous season, but without the animosity that we had encountered in the north-east in '78.

Conditions up in East Anglia that day were well dodgy. Our match had been in some doubt on the morning of the game and bearing this in mind it was a thoughougly entertaining ninety minutes, even though there were no goals.

Ipswich left winger Clive Woods, who had been man of the match in the Cup Final some eight months earlier, was the Town danger man for a lot of the afternoon giving Bobby Fisher a torrid time for a lot of the game. But despite the fact that Fisher was often beaten out wide, John Jackson in the O's goal had one of his classiest days catching cross after cross from the England international.

Jacko made one outstanding stop from a Kevin Beattie drive after twenty-five minutes but it was in the second half that he really came into his own. Our 'keeper made a series of wonderful saves, culminating in two classics both from Whymark in the last five minutes.

We constantly brought all eleven back for corners with the likes of Mayo and even Kitch doing some sterling work propping up the defence. I remember the last ten minutes seemed to last an eternity as we struggled to hang on, but hang on we did as we held on for a draw and a moral victory. Orient chances had been very few but it mattered little as we had achieved a fine result.

After the game Paul Went – who was supporting a fine black eye which he had got during the game – said on the television that Jacko's performance had been the best goalkeeping display he had seen in his sixteen years as a pro.

The game was highlighted on '*The Big Match*' the following day with Jackson rightly getting the accolades from the ITV team. Ipswich 'keeper Paul Cooper sportingly waited to applaud his opposite number off the field at the games conclusion.

Of the game the *Sunday Telegraph* said: 'Orient's defensive wall wet down everything that Ipswich could ignite in the icy air.'

Added the *Sunday Mirror*: 'In the second half Orient's penalty area resembled a traffic jam on rail strike days – yet it was the Ipswich stars who went off the rails.'

In those days there was no need a wait ten days for a replay. We hosted the Blues just three days later for the rematch in front of 19,000 punters at Brizzy.

Regrettably we lost the second game 2–0, with Paul Mariner scoring them both. I can remember going away from the ground that night feeling very disappointed. Having reached the last four in the competition the previous season, yet only reaching Round Four this time round, at the time appeared an almighty anti-climax.

Nowadays of course a visit to the Fourth Round is far from a failure, some might say highlighting the difference between the Club then and now. Little did we know back in 1979 that in the years to come being an Orient fan would mean having to endure defeats to the likes of Hendon, Enfield and Margate in the greatest cup competition in the world. Nothing can ever take away those magical moments of Orient in the FA Cup in the seventies, however. Happy days indeed.

Ipswich Town: Cooper, Burley, Talbot, Mills, Osman, Beattie, Wark, Woods, Muhren, Mariner, Whymark.

Orient: Jackson, Fisher, Roffey, Grealish, Gray, Went, Chiedozie, Moores, Mayo, Kitchen, Coates.

Star Man: John Jackson.
Attendance: 23,337

Game Nineteen

Seagull special

Orient 3 Brighton Hove Albion 3
Football League Division 2. 7 April 1979

This golden game from the seventies was indeed a classic against our friends from the south coast. After the league traumas of 1977–78, the following campaign despite a wretched start was turning out a lot better for the O's as it approached its climax.

Thanks mainly to our home form – going into this match we had won eleven out of the seventeen played at Brisbane Road – we entered April in a highly respectable seventh place with no fears of a drop to the third at the end of the season.

Nowadays, of course in the same position we could have pushed for a play-off place but back then with just the top three going up automatically and just two points for a win, being nine off third with just seven games left meant that the season was effectively over for us.

There were few grumbles at the time about this however at Brizzy. It was indeed quite nice to watch some end of term football without the pressures of a relegation fight just for a change.

For Brighton though the situation was different. Going into our match they stood top of the league a point clear of rivals Crystal Palace and were looking good for First Division football come August for the first time in their history.

The game always promised a lot so much so that Brian Moore brought his 'Big Match' cameras down to Leyton for one of the last times. And Moore and co. cannot have been disappointed with the fare they were offered by the two teams that afternoon. The resulting six goal thriller was described by Ralph Coates the next day on the programme as the most enjoyable game he'd ever played in.

Full credit had to go to Alan Mullery's Brighton who came looking for the win at a time when so many teams went away packing their defences, knowing that 0–0 was a more than acceptable outcome to a match on the road.

83

The Seagulls brought a large following, packing the North Terrace and making up a large proportion of the 11,567 present that afternoon.

The punters present witnessed ninety minutes packed with incident from the second minute when Orient's Alan Whittle (who we had nicknamed the Ayatollah as he'd just finished a spell playing in Iran) brought down Gerry Ryan for an obvious penalty that the referee did not give, to the last minute when the O's forced two corners and could easily have sneaked it. A draw was probably a fair result in the end, though it has to be noted that Brighton were without two of their better players on the day, captain Brian Horton and Teddy Maybank who were both suspended. They also included a certain Mark Lawrenson in their side that afternoon.

The scoring was started by Big Joe Mayo in the eighth minute when he pounced onto a loose ball following a corner to slot past Eric Steele.

Eleven minutes later the visitors were level however after a bad error from Paul Went in the Orient defence. He sliced an attempted clearance and the ball finally fell to Peter Sayer who fired home from the edge of the area.

It was the afternoon that Brighton's Martin Chivers chose to score the last of his 220 league goals and probably the only one he had ever scored whilst sporting a beard. The former England man had been signed by his former international colleague Mullery a couple of weeks previously from Norwich for £15,000. In the 27th minute Big Chiv sent Peter Sayer away on the right and followed up the resulting cross with a powerful header from six yards, so reminiscent of his heyday at White Hart Lane.

It proved to be his one and only goal for the south coast club in the second of the four games he played for them before he became a full-time publican. In fact by the size of his belly and his lack of speed that day, it's fair to say it looked as if the pints had already began to take their toll on the big man.

Having been treated to a goal from the Spurs League Cup Final hero of 1971, just three minutes later we were treated to one from the Spurs League Cup Final hero of 1973, Ralph Coates. And what a goal it was too.

Ralph himself said of his twenty-five yard drive on the half-hour which levelled the scores that it was the best goal of his career. Alan Mullery commented afterwards 'Blimey, I played with him for eight years at Spurs and I never saw one like that.'

Going in 2–2 at half-time, most agreed it had been the best forty-five minutes we had seen at Brisbane Road that season.

One imagined the players could not keep the pace of the game going into the second half yet straight from the kick-off Brighton stormed through and could have scored again after just six seconds, a drive producing a fine save from John Jackson. In fact they had to wait just nine more minutes before they took the lead once more this time a low shot from Paul Clark (who was later to become assistant manager at Brisbane Road) evaded Jacko to send the Seagulls behind the goal into raptures.

The way the game had panned out though an O's equalizer was always on the cards and sure enough it came with fifty-eight on the clock courtesy of another Spurs old boy, Ian Moores (hero of no League Cup Finals) who nodded home from close range after some not very good defending.

3–3 with still half an hour left, the surprise was that no more goals were scored in the remainder of the match. This was down mostly to the competence of the two 'keepers Jackson and Steele, with both teams continuing to create chances. For Jackson it was his 204th consecutive league game for the O's.

At the end of the game the players rightly earned a standing ovation from all present at Brisbane Road. The good news for Brighton was that Palace lost so that the Seagulls remained top of the league at the end of the day.

When questioned about his strategy for the game afterwards Alan Mullery said: 'At this stage of the season many teams in our position would go defensive, but we like to attack. We play the same home or away and that will not change. It was a bit disappointing to score three times in an away match and only draw, but it was a super game for the fans.'

Orient manager Jimmy Bloomfield was also lavish with his praise and tipped Brighton for promotion: 'They are the best team I have seen this season.' He said. 'They competed for every ball, never gave up and had more individual skill than other teams.'

At the end of the season Brighton got their promotion, though in the end they had to settle for the runners-up position thanks partly to Palace winning at Brisbane Road on the last day of the season.

As for the O's we finished in a highly respectable eleventh place. To end up in the top half, having just avoided relegation the season before and having been fourth from bottom after eight games was a fine achievement for Jimmy and the boys.

As is the way with the Orient it wasn't all a bed of roses. We followed up the Brighton thriller with a 2–0 home defeat to West Ham in the next home game and then we all had to endure one of the worst home games of the Seventies – a goalless draw with Oldham on the 21 April. It was a match where we had little to play for and it showed. In ninety minutes absolutely nothing happened.

Thankfully the TV gantry was empty for the Oldham game. We had certainly livened up the nation's Sunday afternoon some three weeks previously though with this seagull special.

Orient: Jackson, Hughton, Roffey, Grealish, Gray, Went, Chiedozie, Moores, Mayo, Whittle, Coates.
Goals: Mayo (7n), Coates (30n), Moores (58s).

Brighton and Hove Albion: Steele, Cattlin, Williams, Sayer, Rollings, Lawrenson, Ryan, Poskett, Chivers, Clark, O'Sullivan.
Goals: Sayer (18s), Chivers (32s), Clark (54n).

Star Man: Ralph Coates.
Attendance: 11,567.

Game Twenty

Hammered by Hurst

Orient 3 Chelsea 7
Football League Division 2. 10 November 1979

It really does seem almost impossible to believe nowadays, but there was a period during the seventies and early eighties when Orient and Chelsea had quite a rivalry between them.

Apart from the epic cup contests between the two teams in '72 and '78, we also had some fierce battles in the Second Division, and hard as it may seem to recall these days we often got the better of them. In 1975–76 we did the double over them with Laurie Cunningham scoring and staring in both matches – the 3–1 win at Brizzy Road on Boxing Day was particularly memorable.

Then there was a game at Stamford Bridge in December 1980 when Big Joe Mayo scored the only goal as we dented their chances of a promotion push that season. Indeed you got the feeling that for a long period we were not their favourite club.

It was not always a bed of roses against them for us however, as this bizarre

encounter at the end of the seventies showed.

Looking back it really was one of the strangest results you could ever wish to see at a football game. Going into the encounter Orient were on a good run of form. We had got nine out of the previous ten points on offer, and the previous Saturday had had an excellent 2–1 victory at Burnley.

Chelsea on the other hand had not had a particularly good start to the season. They were only placed eleventh having appointed Geoff Hurst as their new manager just a month before and until bringing his side to Leyton had not seen his side win under his leadership.

Chelsea's two main forwards Gary Johnson and Tommy Langley were both injured so Hurst was forced to play Clive Walker, who had been substitute for most of the season, and Lee Frost who had made just one first team appearance, as a makeshift strike force.

There had been a lot of talk in the media prior to the game that the Blues were about to sign the European Footballer of the Year Kevin Keegan from Hamburg and it was certainly the talk of the Chelsea contingent that made up a large proportion of the 13,005 present at our east London theatre of dreams.

Before the match Chelsea trainer Norman Medhurst (maybe knowing that his main men up front were not playing) promised a fiver for any of his players who scored a hat-trick. Hurst supported that sponsorship by offering to double the amount, and apparently assistant manager Bobby Gould chipped in that he would double it again.

One wonders if the current Chelsea manager would these days offer Fernando Torres or Demba Ba a tenner if he hit the back of the net three times. How times change.

As the game started there was no sign of the pandemonium that there would be for much of the afternoon, a lot of it in the Orient penalty area. Indeed after ten minutes the O's could quite easily have been a couple of goals to the good after efforts from Ralph Coates and Joe Mayo.

But everything changed with thirteen on the clock when Frost put Clive Walker in the clear on the right and Walker crossed for Ian Britton to head low past Mervyn Day. From this moment onwards, Walker became almost unplayable for the Orient defence.

After twenty-eight minutes he went on another fine run down the right and slipped the ball to Frost who fired home. Then just seven minutes later a Walker shot was intercepted by Mick Fillery who drove past Day into the roof of the net.

Standing with fellow O's on the Coronation Garden terrace we all stood there at half-time feeling stunned, knowing we had to endure a further forty-five minutes of possible mayhem, this time with the Blues kicking towards the end where we were standing.

It may have been an idea for Orient manager Jimmy Bloomfield to accept damage limitation in the second half but the boss had other ideas and substituted defender Henry Hughton, putting on striker Ian Moores at the break. We thus played with four up front for the rest of the game.

In fact it looked initially as if it could have been a stroke of genius tactically as we scored within a minute of the re-start – Joe Mayo headed down Bill Roffey's cross for Billy Jennings to score from six yards. The comeback lasted all of five minutes however, as Frost again broke free to fire through Mervyn Day's legs and into the net with 51 minutes.

Walker then made it 5–1 after 65 minutes shooting home after snapping up a perfect pass from Fillery. And it took him just three more minutes to score his second as the O's defence parted allowing the striker the freedom of Leyton to make it six.

Billy Jennings then scored his second of the game stabbing home from close range but the five goal advantage the visitors had was restored when Nigel Gray brought down Walker and Frost bagged his hat-trick with a penalty, with eighty-one on the clock.

Then, as if to sum up what a weird afternoon it had all been Orient full-back Bobby Fisher, who hardly ever scored let fly from thirty yards for the best of all ten goals to make the final score 3–7. It was Fisher's first of the season and he did not manage to hit the target again till April. And by this time many an O had left and were heading home.

Looking back the game could have ended up 8–8, it was just one of those days when both defences decided not to turn up. It turned out to be Paul Went's last game in an Orient shirt and it was probably his worst, although in fairness to him he did get injured in the second period but had to stay on, as we'd used our sub.

The victory was Chelsea's 1,000[th] in the league in their 75-year history. It was the first time they had scored seven away from home in the Football League. Negotiations were started with Keegan, but a deal to bring him to the Bridge was never completed.

Methurst, Gould and Hurst all handed over the money to hat-trick hero Frost, although anyone at the game would have known that Clive Walker was the real man of the match.

Said Jimmy Bloomfield afterwards: 'I tried to buy Walker when he was in the reserves last year. I was worried when I saw he was playing today and I was right.'

The next day the *News of the World* gave the Chelsea forward a marking of ten, which was almost unheard of.

The game had certainly been a weird one, the kind of which comes around only once in a blue (or red in our case) moon. Just four days before however on the same ground the O's youth team had defeated Portsmouth 10–1 in the FA Youth Cup, meaning that freakishly within two matches the back of the net had been hit an amazing twenty-one times at Brisbane Road.

And one last footnote – in our next match we went to Cardiff and in true Orient fashion kept a clean sheet in a Ninian Park goalless draw.

As for Chelsea they failed to go up at the end of the season. Despite hitting us for seven they remarkably missed out on the top three on goal difference to Birmingham. I thought that was funny.

Great player as Hurst was, the truth was that he never really hit the heights as a manager.

I bet he looks back now however, when wondering about his greatest achievement in football and thinks to that afternoon in Leyton when he managed a team that scored seven. That surely stands above scoring a hat-trick in a World Cup Final for him.

Orient: Day, Fisher, Roffey, Went, Gray, Taylor, Chiedozie, Hughton (Moores 46), Mayo, Jennings, Coates.
Goals: Jennings (46n, 78n), Fisher (85n).

Chelsea: Borota, Locke, Wilkins, Bumstead (Hales 75), Pates, Chivers, Britton, Fillery, Frost, Walker, Harris.
Goals: Britton (13n), Frost (28n, 51s, 81pen s), Fillery (35n), Walker (65s, 68s).

Star Man: Billy Jennings.
Attendance: 13,005.

Game Twenty-one

Stan-tastic

Orient 4 Preston North End 0
Football League Division 2. 4 October 1980

It's probably not unfair to say that as far as the eighties were concerned, the Orient peaked a mere ten months into the decade with this performance against Preston.

It was a win that took us up to sixth in the Second Division after nine matches, and had many of us (don't laugh) actually thinking we could end up getting promoted into the First Division.

Yep, it seems impossible to believe now but back then, at the start of the 1980–81 campaign, Orient really were one of the top thirty teams in the country.

During the close season manager Jimmy Bloomfield had pulled off what looking back now, must go down as one of the best Orient transfer coups ever, when he signed Stan Bowles from Nottingham Forest.

Stanley was still more than a half-decent player, but he had gone missing

prior to Forest's European Cup Final against Hamburg, and as a result had been put on the transfer list by the club. It was thought that Bowles would go back to Queens Park Rangers, but at the time the West Londoners were on tour and Jimmy nipped in quick to secure the England international's transfer to Brisbane Road.

Stan had been keen to move back to London and had a few days earlier turned down the chance to go to Sheffield Wednesday. In fact he revealed some years later that he actually rejected the Yorkshire team because he thought that they were in the Third Division, when they were actually in the Division above.

Our new man started the season in superb form. He lacked pace but was content to hang around in midfield spraying passes around the pitch, a lot of them to our ultra-nippy winger John Chiedozie.

Doing the donkey work in the middle of the park were Steve Parsons and John Margerrison and the three of them made for a wonderful combination.

In defence we had Mervyn Day in goal with the three stalwarts of the '78 cup campaign Bill Roffey, Bobby Fisher and Nigel Gray being joined by Tommy Taylor.

Up front our main man was Ian Moores who scored for the fourth time in five matches in this defeat of North End.

It was a fine side as the early season results had proved.

We started the Preston annihilation looking sharp from the kick-off, and it took us just ten minutes to take the lead. Ian Moores hit a curling 15-yard left footer past Roy Tunks to set us up for the afternoon.

Our build up play continued to impress with most of the moves going through Stanley, and it took an inspired Tunks to keep the Northerners in the match. In a one sided first half, the Preston custodian made fine saves twice from Joe Mayo headers and also from Moores.

It came as no surprise however, that we finally doubled our lead a couple of minutes before the interval. This time Tunks failed to hold on to a Chiedozie drive and Parsons nipped in for the second.

Then after 52 minutes Stan got the ball midfield, looked up and sprayed a wonderful pass through to John Chiedozie who ran on to fire in the third.

Bowles then took centre stage himself as he breezed beyond three defenders and calmly placed the ball past the 'keeper for the fourth twelve minutes before the end.

We could have had more – Big Joe cruised past the Preston defence and was unlucky to see his effort come back off the post – but in the end no O could have left Brizzy Road disappointed having witnessed a magnificent display from our boys.

Said Preston manager Nobby Stiles afterwards,: 'Orient were simply magnificent. We were lucky to get away with 4–0.'

'Fantastic.' Said Jimmy Bloomfield. 'That's my type of football.'

Indeed great to watch it certainly was.

It really did look like we were going places that season. Six weeks after the Preston game we signed Peter Taylor from Tottenham for £150,000 in what was intended to be a final push for promotion to the First.

But in many ways the 1980–81 season sums up just what it's like being a supporter of the Orient.

Despite the big new signing we totally went to pieces in the second half of the season,ending up sixth from bottom just two points away from getting relegated.

In the return match with Preston in March we lost 3–0 and Stanley got himself sent off.

True, we lost Steve Parsons when he broke his leg at Grimsby in February, but despite this there was no real reason for the total capitulation of form from the team.

Over thirty years on, the Preston match in October though remains one of the most compete performances I've ever seen from an O's XI in a league match and for me will always be up there with the all time classics.

Orient: Day, Fisher, Taylor, Gray, Roffey, Bowles, Margerrison, Parsons, Chiedozie, Mayo, Moores.
Goals: Moores (10s), Parsons (43s), Chiedozie (52n), Bowles (78n).

Preston North End: Tunks, Taylor, Baxter, O'Rierdan, McAteer, Sayer, Doyle, Coleman, Elliott, McGee, Houston (Blackley).

Star Man: Stan Bowles.
Attendance: 4,295.

Game Twenty-two

Return of a hero and the man on crutches

Leyton Orient 2 Preston North End 1
Football League Division 3. 17 December 1982

The second memorable ninety minutes of the eighties again features an encounter with Preston, but how things had changed in the two and a bit years between the first and second games.

Bloomfield had gone, Went had come for 21 days and gone, and Knighton had come down from the north east to take charge, bringing Frank Clark with him.

On the face of it, the club only appeared to be heading in one direction at the time though, and that was not up.

After relegation to the Third Division at the end of the 1981–82 season Knighton had made some notable player changes at Brisbane Road however, and as a result there was an air of optimism at the Club around August time in 1982.

After an opening day win at Chesterfield, the general feeling at the time was that we would more than hold our own in the new lower division.

However come the middle of December that feel good factor had totally evaporated. The season up till then had been nothing short of a disaster.

Incredibly there had been three 5–1 home defeats in the space of just five matches and the O's were third from bottom of the Third and heading for the Fourth for the first time in their history.

Something had to be done to stop the rot and that something turned out to be the re-signing of seventies Orient legend Peter Kitchen.

The great man had had spells at Fulham and Cardiff and had moved on to play for Happy Valley in Hong Kong.

Knighton signed him in the week leading up to the Preston game and indeed it had a moral boosting effect on the Club, especially as the week before had seen us crash out of the FA Cup, thanks to an 84th minute goal conceded at Newport County.

Said the manager of the signing: 'I'm absolutely thrilled. Kitch has a proven goal scoring record and could prove a very valuable asset. His general fitness is very good and he's raring to go. Just his presence will be good for the side.'

Indeed such had been the excitement level generated by the signing that for this game all of 1,668 attended Brisbane Road on the Friday before Christmas. At the time it was the lowest attendance for any match in the Third Division that year and a record low for the O's in the league.

The Salvation Army played carols on the pitch before the game and a few of them stayed behind to watch the match. Whether they were included in the official attendance figure I know not, but either way the number of punters present was not a high one.

Important though it turned out to be, the match itself was hardly a classic. Orient took the lead in the seventh minute with a penalty from David Peach, awarded for handball given against Preston defender Simon Westwell as he tried to clear an Andy Sussex corner-kick.

Preston were just two places above us going into the game and were not very good. But then neither were we and after 29 minutes they equalized.

Central defender Coleman collected the ball from Westwell on the wing and his floating shot bounced off Colin Foster and into the corner of the net.

We went in 1–1 at half-time, but as the second half started we began to take control. Peach had a good chance turned round the post for a corner but for all our possession we were getting continually frustrated by Preston's offside trap.

Then around midway through the period came an extraordinary incident still talked about among Orient veterans to this very day.

Without any warning, from the East-side enclosure a middle-aged man on crutches 'invaded' the pitch. A few of the other 1,667 cheered as without any-one approaching him he made it to the centre-circle.

There he threw his crutches to the ground and waited. After a little while two of the policemen on duty that night, who thought they would not have to do anything for their overtime that evening, woke up and entered the playing arena to escort him off, to more cheers from the rest of us.

It was reported that the man – an O's supporter named Ken – had done it to protest about a refereeing decision, though I would imagine the performance of the team could well have been a contributory factor as well. Interestingly he was not banned from the ground and continued to watch the team in games afterwards – these days a long or even life-ban would surely follow such an act but times some thirty-odd years ago were vastly different.

The incident certainly lifted the one and a half thousand or so, and it could be argued the 11 home players as well, as we secured the all important win just five minutes from the end.

Kitch collected a through pass from Kevin Godfrey and the returning maestro rounded 'keeper Litchfield and blasted into the empty net from just inside the area.

It was a typical Peter Kitchen goal – at the time it seemed like the clock had been turned back some four years. There had been very few magic moments since he had left and boy how good did it feel when he scored that night. For the first time since the beginning of October we ended the game out of the bottom four and had renewed hope for the second half of the campaign, with Kitchen back.

Indeed it cannot be overemphasized the impact Kitch had at the time, on turning the season. His return sparked a revival that saw a run where we won six out of seven and remarkably took us to the top half of the table.

Unfortunately however in the last of those matches – a 2–1 home win over Portsmouth - the legend broke his toe, and straight away the upturn ended.

He was out of action for a month and a half during which we slipped to fifth from bottom and into yet another relegation dog-fight.

Orient: Day, Roffey, Peach, Foster, Cunningham, Cornwell, Osgood, Godfrey, Houchen, Sussex, Kitchen. Sub not used: Smith.
Goals: Peach (Pen 7s), Kitchen (85n).

Preston North End: Litchfield, Westwell, McAteer, O'Riordan, Coleman, Gowling, Walsh, Sayer, Elliot, Naughton, Houston.
Goal: Coleman (29n).

Star Man: Peter Kitchen and a bloke named Ken.
Attendance: 1,668.

Game Twenty-three

Night, night Knighton

Orient 4 Sheffield United 1
Division 3. 14 May 1983

The O's had slumped back into relegation trouble as the end of season approached in 1982–83. In typical Orient fashion we had plummeted from eleventh in mid January to fourth from bottom with just one game to go in May. Entering the final afternoon the bottom of the Third Division read as thus:

	Pld.	Pts.	G.Diff.
Exeter	45	53	-23
Millwall	45	52	-14
Wrexham	45	51	-19
Orient	45	51	-27
Reading	45	50	-16
Doncaster Rov.	45	38	-38
Chesterfield	45	37	-24

Basically avoiding relegation was out of our hands. Wins for Wrexham, Millwall and Exeter would mean that even an O's victory at home to Sheffield United would not be enough to keep us up. The two good bits of news for Orient that afternoon however, were that the Sheffield team were mid-table and had nothing to play for, and Reading – who would be desperate for a win – were at home to Wrexham. This was an ideal fixture for us. If we won and Wrexham didn't we were safe.

The *Waltham Forest Guardian* called it the most important game in the Club's 102-year history and it was hard to argue against that.

Whilst these days folk would have one eye on the game and one eye on their mobiles relaying scores from the other relevant matches, it was different back then of course.

I was standing on the South terrace armed with my little tranny which would hopefully keep me abreast of events elsewhere.

As it was the O's produced one of their best performances of the season which in the end just proved enough for safety.

From the kick-off we attacked with a vigour and determination that had rarely been seen at Brisbane Road all season.

We peppered the United goal for half an hour and whilst the score remained goalless it seemed only a matter of time before we would go ahead.

Sure enough the break through came courtesy of Keith Houchen after 32 minutes.

His first shot was blocked on the edge of the area but it rebounded to his other boot and the subsequent effort sailed past Sheffield custodian Keith Waugh and into the net.

And we only had to wait another five minutes for the second. It came about as a result of a well worked free-kick – something totally out of character for the O's that season.

Barry Silkman floated the ball to Nigel Gray who nodded down into the goalmouth, where Kitch sneaked in, stooping to head home the second.

And at around the same time it filtered through that Kerry Dixon had given Reading the lead against Wrexham which was more good news for us.

In typical Orient fashion however, just as it looked really rosy we conceded just before half-time as Stewart Houston headed home from a corner.

Still 2–1 up at half-time and out of the relegation zone, it was nervy yes, but looking more than hopeful for a successful outcome to the afternoon.

Whether news of the Reading v. Wrexham match had made its way to the home dressing room at Brizzy we know not, but the O's started the second period as if they really meant business.

Within just two minutes a delightful through ball from Barry Silkman put Kevin Godfrey in the clear and our man slotted home to give us some much needed breathing space.

Indeed our second half showing impressed greatly and though good chances were squandered by Cornwell, Silkman and Kitch,with no more goal news coming from Reading it was looking promising for the day to have a successful outcome.

Then with 89 minutes on the clock Bill Roffey raced forward and banged in a fourth. Our mighty full-back – the player of the year – celebrated with a somersault and we knew we had done our part in the great escape with a fine performance.

It was now just a question of keeping fingers crossed that it was enough for safety.

Just as the final whistle sounded it was confirmed that Reading had indeed held on to defeat Wrexham 1–0, and we could look forward to another season in the Third.

The results meant that we had leapfrogged the welsh side to end up fifth from bottom.

In fact an 85th minute equalizer for Exeter at Newport meant that despite their win, Reading were also relegated, amazingly with 53 points. (Some twenty-eight years later in 2011–12 the O's escaped the drop with a grand total of just 47).

The wonderful news travelled around Leyton Stadium quickly after the conclusion of our match and we all celebrated wildly. There was the inevitable pitch invasion and we all congregated around the player's tunnel singing 'Whatever will be will be, we're still in Division Three.'

Similar scenes had not been seen at Brisbane Road since we defeated Middlesbrough in the cup quarter-final back in '78.

There then followed a pretty strange episode. Ken Knighton appeared in the Director's box pointing his arms skyward, then punching the air in triumph. For some reason we all started chanting his name, proclaiming him a hero.

Yep, the man who had been the boss as we got relegated from the Second Division and followed it up by taking us to within a point of doing the same thing in the Third a year later was being hailed a saviour.

He took to the mike and told us that the next season was going to be much better and we all cheered again. If ever you needed proof that football fans are a weird species you just had to be at Brisbane Road that afternoon.

I suppose it was an occasion when we all just got wrapped up with that particular game and conveniently put to the back of the mind the last 45 games of hell he had put us through.

Not surprisingly the euphoria died down and a week later Knighton was sacked.

It was though quite ironic that his last game in charge had seen one of the best displays by the Orient in all his seventeen months as manager of the club.

Orient: Day, Roffey, Peach, Cunningham, Gray, Silkman, Godfrey, Cornwell, Houchen, Kitchen, McNeil. Sub: (not used) Sussex.
Goals: Houchen (32n), Kitchen (37n), Godfrey (47s), Roffey (89s).

Sheffield United: Waugh, Henderson, Charles, Richardson, West, Houston, Towner (sub: Brazil 45), Trusson, Edwards, Morris, Cooper.
Goal: Houston (38s).

Star Man: Barry Silkman.
Attendance: 4,468.

Game Twenty-four

Kitchen Sinks 'em one last time

Orient 5 Millwall 3
Football League Division 3. 21 April 1984

In typical Orient style, when Ken Knighton was sacked after the 82–83 campaign, his right hand man Frank Clark was promoted up to become manager.

It did not take rocket science to see that it was a move done out of financial need rather than for football reasons.

Both Clark and Knighton still had two years of their contracts to run after relegation had been narrowly avoided and with the need to pay off Knighton, promoting his fellow north-easterner was the cheap option for the powers that be at the Club.

Yet remarkably Clark got off to a wonderful start as the new man in charge. After five games of the new season the O's amazingly found themselves at the top of the Division Three table.

A 1–0 win at Rotherham had made it four wins out of five and we found ourselves looking down on the other twenty-three clubs in the Third tier.

We knew it could not last of course and it didn't, but just for a change we entered the final part of the season in 1984 without any concerns about relegation.

After thirty-nine games we had amassed 54 points and were placed twelve. Going into this game, Millwall were also on 54 so it was the definitive 'mid-table six-pointer'.

With no pressure on either team the two sides produced a classic encounter with the O's three times coming from behind to snatch the three points.

Peter Kitchen became the first O to score four goals in a league match since 1958, as he notched his third hat-trick for us, the first since his return to Brisbane Road at the end of 1982.

On a lovely afternoon weather wise things started badly for the home side when Keith Osgood headed into his own goal following a cross from Kevin Bremner.

Soon afterwards however John Cornwell who was captaining Orient for the first time equalized following a pass from Kitch.

Dean Neal then had the ball in the net for the visitors but the referee belatedly blew for handball. It was a short-lived reprieve however as Millwall pulled ahead once more after thirty-seven, again with more than a little help from Osgood. Our man got involved in a terrible mix-up with 'keeper Richard Key allowing Steve Powell the simplest of jobs in putting the ball into an empty net.

It was then that the Peter Kitchen show kicked off. A minute later there was good work from Mark McNeil down the right, his shot was parried to an unmarked Kitch who tapped in his first.

Half-time came at 2–2 and we'd seen a fine first forty-five, but the second period proved even better.

In fact it was the Lions who were the better team initially from the restart and it took a superb save from O's 'keeper Richard Key to keep out Neal.

The visiting forward got his goal however, when some poor home defending saw him run around a statuesque home defence to make the score 3–2 with nearly an hour played.

Then Kitch ran riot. First he collected a pass from midfield and advanced towards the area before slotting home past Paul Sansome for what was the best of his four successful efforts.

He missed the chance of his hat-trick when he headed McNeil's cross wide, but with seventeen minutes left a close range header gave him his third following good work from Osgood.

Finally with just five minutes remaining an Andy Sussex pass gave him a fourth and completed a 5–3 win.

The two games with our London neighbours that season, had therefore yielded 15 goals following our 4–3 defeat at the Den on Boxing Day.

We gained some nice revenge this afternoon for that yule-tide loss, when at one stage we had been 2–0 up. It was just a shame there were not more at Brisbane Road to witness the 5–3 - 3,874 was a disappointing crowd – though remembering the antics of certain Millwall loonies at our place over the years many an O would have been more than happy that few had bothered to venture across the river that day.

The O's finished the season in 11th place, a fine achievement following the traumas of 82–83. Possibly a little surprisingly Kitch left on a free transfer at the end of the season, though it's probably fair to say that apart from this Millwall encounter his form had dipped somewhat towards the run-in.

Nevertheless he left the club a true Orient legend having scored a total of 60 goals in his 127 appearances for the club. No Orient supporter of course will ever forget his seven cup goals in '78 which propelled us to an FA Cup semi-final and amazingly he remains the last player to score twenty league goals in a season for us.

Whilst his first telling contribution in an Orient shirt had been in a 5–3 victory over Oldham in 1977 when he scored twice, it's fair to say his last was also in a 5–3, this time against the Lions.

Orient: Key, Hales, Wilkins, Corbett, Osgood, Cornwell, Silkman, Brooks, Sussex, Kitchen, McNeil. Sub: Banfield (not used.)
Goals: Cornwell (31n), Kitchen (38n, 60s, 73s, 85s)

Millwall: Sansome, Stevens, Stride (Neal J.), Lovell, Nutton, Cusack, McLeary, Bremmner, Neal D., Otulakowski, Robinson.
Goals: Osgood (16 o.g.s), Lovell (37s), Neal.D. (58n).

Star Man: Peter Kitchen.
Attendance: 3,874.

Tiger Feat

Orient 4 Hull City 5
Football League Division 3. 10 November 1984

It may seem a little silly to inaugurate into your clubs great games a match where the team concedes five at home and loses, but this encounter from 1984, was so extraordinary it simply could not be left out.

In a nutshell we were 4–1 up with 24 minutes to go and we lost 5–4.

I still remember now feeling distraught when the ref blew for full-time, just standing on the North Terrace stunned, thinking 'how on earth did that happen?'

Going into the match the O's found themselves third from bottom of the league. After the mid-table finish of the previous year normal service had been resumed in 1984–85 and another relegation struggle beckoned for our club.

We had only won one game out of the last seven going into this Hull encounter and had got hammered 3–0 by Walsall in our previous home match.

Nevertheless we started the game against the Tigers brightly and took the lead after 16 minutes when Barry Silkman's corner was headed on by Pat Corbett, for Kevin Godfrey to nod home from close range.

Things got even better just three minutes later when good work from Kevin Hales and Silkman set up new signing Chris Jones, who drilled home from twenty yards.

Then a Hales cross set up John Cornwell to make it 3–0 with less than half an hour gone.

For sure it was out of character from what we had seen previously that season, but with Silkman running the show in midfield and the defence operating a well drilled off-side trap you could not see City getting back into the game.

They got their first just before half-time when Billy Askew scored direct from a corner when 'keeper Rhys Wilmot really should have done better, but queuing for the half-time burger at the kiosk on the corner of the North Terrace the three points looked pretty well assured.

Incidentally call me a sad case but it's strange how certain obscure things from your Orient supporting past stick in your mind.

Back then the terrace for away supporters had just been moved from behind the goal on the north side of the ground to behind the goal on the south side of the ground.

Us home fans had therefore been forced to move to the other end of Leyton Stadium where the refreshments were sold in the corner, unlike at the Coronation Gardens end where the kiosk was in the centre in a really handy place. This annoyed me at the time and I was not happy either that the stall on the North Terrace would also serve patrons of the West Side, which could mean a lengthy wait to get your grub.

So even though we were locked in a deep relegation battle in 1984–85, the refreshment scandal was just as big a deal for me at the time.

For the second half of this Hull encounter our boys were kicking towards the end where we were standing and after the first half, we were confident we would see a lot of action right in front of us in the final forty-five.

And sure enough with 11 minutes played after the break Mark McNeil set up Silkman and our man fired home a wonderful thirty-yarder to restore our three goal advantage.

With under a quarter of the match remaining we were 4–1 up but then, unbelievably, it's fair to say that not only did the wheels come off but so too the roof, the bonnet, the engine and the sat-nav, if they'd have had those gadgets in those days.

Steve Massey got a second for Hull after 66 minutes, there was then a mad goalmouth scramble after 70 with Andy Flounders claiming their third, though we then nearly made it 5–3 when Jones saw his header come back against the bar.

The visitors got the equalizer however when a handball allowed Stan McEwan to score from the penalty spot and the winner came courtesy of Flounders again, just two minutes from the end.

Being an Orient supporter you thought you should have got used to disappointments over the years but this one really was something different, even by O's standards.

Just how we blew it so spectacularly we will never know, but we sure did somehow.

Hull's player-manger Brian Horton said afterwards he knew his team had goals in them and he was always confident his team could turn things around, but at 3–0 and 4–1 can't really believe he honestly thought that way.

By strange coincidence the match-day programme for the game had pointed out that exactly five years to the day previously we had lost at home 7–3 to Chelsea in what was another of those daft games that seem to come along once every ten years or so, but this one for me outdid even that match in terms of bizarreness.

It was certainly a very satisfying victory for the Tigers. In beating them 3–1 at Brizzy Road some seven months earlier we had virtually ended their promotion hopes, so it was sweet revenge indeed for them.

And just to really rub it in when we played them at Bothferry Park the following April they once more scored five against us, this time with just one in return.

Unsurprisingly we were relegated to the Fourth Division for the first time in our history come May. We had, it's fair to say, been rubbish in the league all season (apart from the first 65 minutes at home to Hull)

A relegation/refreshment-fiasco double meant 1984–85 was pretty much a disastrous one for me.

Orient: Wilmot, Hales, Stride, Corbett, Banfield, Cunningham, Silkman, McNeil, Jones, Cornwell, Godfrey. Sub: Brooks (not used).
Goals: Godfrey (16s), Jones (19s), Cornwell (26s), Silkman (56n).

Hull City: Norman, McNeil, Swann, Horton, Skipper, McEwan, Flounders, McClaren, Whitehurst, Askew, Massey.
Goals: Askew (45n), Massey (66s), Flounders (70s, 88s), McEwan (76 pen.s).

Star Man: Barry Silkman.
Attendance: 2,365.

Game Twenty-six

Cadette Force

Orient 2 West Bromwich Albion 1
F.A.Cup Third Round. 5 January 1985

As any O will tell you, the FA Cup is just magical. So many favorite Orient moments in my time as a supporter, have come from the greatest Cup competition in the world, and I'm sure it's a phenomena that will continue for as long as I follow the side.

On so many occasions over the years we've been really struggling in the league yet we will play a game in the FA Cup and look a totally different team.

Among the many examples include Portsmouth in '02, West Ham in '87 and this one – West Brom in '85.

1984–85 league wise was a shocking season, yet from out of the blue at the beginning of January we pulled off a completely unexpected victory against a side then in the top six of the First Division.

The O's had got to the Third Round thanks to an easy draw in the first two rounds. We had beaten non-league Buckingham Town and Fourth Division Torquay to take us into the draw with the big boys.

We were the first ball out of the hat and the Baggies were the second.

The game was a nice break from the tribulations of the Third Division at the time, though not even the staunchest of Orient fans can have expected to win.

I Remember before leaving for Brisbane Road that day watching *Football Focus* on the Beeb at lunch-time and hearing Desmond Lynham tipping the Baggies to go all the way and win the trophy.

Leaving to get the 69 bus from Chingford to Leyton, I just hoped the O's players had seen the programme which would have given them plenty of incentive, I figured, to go and defeat the top flight club.

At the time the one bright spark for the Orient that season had been the form of youngster Richard Cadette, who had scored three times in the last two home games before the Albion match. He really did look one for the future, as indeed he was to show this afternoon.

West Brom were managed at the time by Johnny Giles and had a few internationals in their line-up, including ex-O Tony Grealish, who had been one of the stars of our '78 cup run.

The game started quietly but came to life after 16 minutes when Orient's Kevin Hales and Albion's England full-back Derek Statham clashed in midfield with a collision that resulted in the Baggies man being stretchered off. Hales was booked and had the foul occurred these days he would more than likely have been red carded, though our Kevin was certainly not a dirty player and it could have been argued that he was competing for a bouncing 50–50 ball.

The O's appeared to be holding their own until just before half-time when West Brom took the lead. Steve Hunt met Jimmy Nichol's centre with a close-range shot that Rhys Wilmot managed to block, but the ball fell for Nicky Cross who fired home.

It was a lead that the visitors just about deserved and the way things had gone for the O's throughout the season I think most of us thought the Albion would go on to win easily.

That was certainly not the case however. Remarkably Orient came out looking a different side in the second half.

Barry Silkman started running the show in midfield and after 56 minutes his speculative long-range effort slipped through the grasp of Tony Godden and into the net. It was one the 'keeper should have saved, but it was a goal we nevertheless thoughoughly deserved as a result of our play after the re-start.

Indeed the O's could have taken the lead just minutes later when Tommy Cunningham volleyed over from a few yards.

Soon after Leo Donnellan embarked on a run that ended with a shot that flashed just wide as our boys continued to impress.

Richard Cadette then entered the penalty area and was nudged off the ball by Jimmy Nichol, giving Silkman the chance to put us 2–1 up from the spot.

His penalty was well struck high to the 'keeper's right but Godden made up for his earlier error with a brilliant save, certainly to this day one of the best I've seen at a spot kick from a 'keeper at Brizzy Road.

The miss could easily have deflated our boys and been a big turning point, but we kept going and with just eight minutes remaining pinched a deserved winner. Cadette latched onto a Chris Jones overhead kick to fire past Godden from just inside the area.

For just a split second like many O's present I wondered if the goal had been disallowed as there was no trade-mark run to the crowd from Cadette as had been customary with his goals before then.

Explained our man afterwards, 'I suppose I was a bit tired and I just wanted to get on with the game.'

When the crowd finally got their act together and realized what had happened, there was a mini pitch invasion from some of the 6,000 or so O's present. It was a wonderful moment, so out of character with the way the 84–85 season had gone up till then.

And we hung on for the remaining minutes to secure a famous win. It was a freezing cold day standing on the North Terrace, but it suddenly got a whole lot warmer jumping up and down like a looney when the final whistle sounded.

Barry Silkman was the man of the match but it was nineteen-year-old Richard Cadette who stole the headlines.

His was the kind of story the newspapers loved. In the previous season he had been playing in the Isthmian League for Wembley, but had given up his job in double glazing to join the O's on a trial basis. Before that he had been with Luton on the Government's £25 a week Youth Opportunity Scheme.

Cadette had come into the side following a bad defeat to Bournemouth just before Christmas and had scored four in four following the Albion winner.

'I just hit the ball instinctively and I was delighted when it went in. You dream about things like this happening, but when they do you can't believe it for a while. Last season I was a non-league player now this – it's tremendous.' he said.

Cadette had a fine game, but then so too did most of the O's that afternoon. It's fair to say that Leo Donnellan in midfield and Neil Banfield in defence were not two of the greatest ever to don an Orient shirt, yet both excelled that day.

Donnellan and Silkman were up against England international Steve Hunt and Paddy Grealish in the centre of the park and both came out of it with flying colours.

Banfield was employed as a sweeper on the day and he too did a sterling job.

Frank Clark, O's boss, was understandably jubilant afterwards.

'It was the best result in my two years at the club.' he said. 'I am delighted for all the players and the loyal fans that turn up every week. This is all a new experience for me. I've always been on the receiving end of giant-killing feats. It hasn't quite sunk in yet.'

Poor old Frankie. In all his time when he was manager of a club whenever a cup game came along he was always reminded that he was a part of the Newcastle team that got beaten by non-league Hereford back in '72.

He had attracted the headlines just a week before this West Brom clash when Brian Clough had announced that Clark should be the man to follow in his footsteps as Nottingham Forest manager, something indeed that did eventually happen.

In typical Orient fashion we came back down to earth with a big bump by losing our next game 2–0 in the league at Gillingham after the West Brom heroics, but at least by then we had been rewarded for our cup exploits with a plumb home tie against First Division Southampton in the Fourth Round.

It was a much needed game at the time as there had been rumours that the O's were – just for a change – in big financial trouble. Chairman Neville Ovenden was said to have been close to putting the club up for sale just a few weeks earlier.

Indeed a crowd of 17,662 for the visit of the Saints ended up producing record gate receipts.

Remarkably just four days before the Southampton FA Cup clash just 804 had attended at Brisbane Road as we drew 0–0 with Aldershot in the Freight Rover Trophy.

And to complete a not very good night for Orient against the Shots, Richard Cadette suffered a bad knee injury ruling him out of the Fourth Round clash.

We lost 2–0 against a very good Southampton side who scored through Joe Jordan and Kevin Moran, but we put up a fine display in a game covered by the Beeb on 'Match of the Day'.

Looking back now it's hard to know where the displays against Southampton, and particularly West Bromwich came from that season.

We ended the campaign third from bottom and were relegated to the Fourth Division for the first time in our history. We had been dire in the league all season.

But then that's the Orient and the FA Cup.

We may not have sampled Wembley in a final of the magnificent competition, but at least it may be argued Wembley came to us for a day back in '85 in the shape of Richard Cadette.

Orient: Wilmot, Hales, Castle, Cunningham, Foster, Silkman, Godfrey, Cadette, Jones, Donnellan, Banfield. Sub: Sussex (not used). Goals: Silkman (56n), Cadette (82n).

West Bromwich Albion: Godden, Nicholl, Statham (Robson 16), Hunt, Bennett, Forsyth, Grealish, Thompson, Mackenzie, N. Cross, Whithead. Goal: N.Cross (45n).

Star Man: Richard Cadette.
Attendance: 7,061.

Godfrey's golden game

Orient 2 Tottenham Hotspur 0
League Cup Second Round First Leg. 23 September 1985

For me this was the game of the decade. It truly was one of those glory, glory nights at Brizzy Road. By and large memorable evenings in the League Cup have been few and far between for the O's over the years.

We like the FA Cup lots and lots but it's fair to say that the love affair does not extend to the countries second knock-out competition, where our record must surely be one of the worst in the League.

This game for me still stands head and shoulders above any other performance for us in it.

Going into the match Spurs had never lost to a Fourth Division team in any competition. Just two days before they had destroyed Sheffield Wednesday 5–1 for their fourth consecutive victory, in which time they had scored 15 goals.

At the same time the O's had blown a 1–0 half time lead to lose at home to Colchester.

Whilst the Tottenham team had cost around three million our XI was mustered together for under £100,000.

Those were the days when everybody took the League Cup really seriously. No one dared to put out an below strength side – they knew they would have a big fine to deal with – and unlike today when there are play-offs finals, FA Cup semi-finals, etc etc at the time it was one of only two chances for any team to play at Wembley, if you got to the final.

As for the small clubs financially the second cup tournament could be more rewarding than the FA Cup in that the two teams split the receipts 50–50 each game, whereas they would only get a third of the takings each in the FA Cup.

The meeting with our north London rivals unusually took place on a Monday night to avoid a clash with West Ham who were at home the following night, and also so that it did not coincide with the start of Yom Kippur.

The match saw the return to Leyton of John Chiedozie for Tottenham, while Chris Jones and Pat Corbett faced their former clubs for the O's.

A crowd of 13,828 was over five times the size of the gate just two days earlier.

Initially the visitors started really brightly with wingers Chiedozie and Chris Waddle looking lively down the flanks. In the centre of defence however John Sitton and Colin Foster were in fine form for our boys, dealing admirably with all their crosses.

When the back pairing were breached Orient 'keeper Peter Wells was in magnificent form. He made a wonderful save after 18 minutes stretching to turn away a dipping shot from Ozzie Ardiles and was equal to anything the Spurs front line could throw at him.

As the game progressed the Orient came more and more into the match and as the second half started still goalless their confidence grew.

Ardiles almost found a way through after 55 minutes but Wells again was the hero saving bravely at the Argentinean's feet. The turning point though came just after the hour.

Ardiles, Hughton and Hoddle combined in a fine move, which resulted in Sitton clearing off the line with Wells for once beaten.

Just seconds later, our 'keeper launched an 80 yard punt which Paul Shinners was allowed to flick on thanks to some lackadaisical Tottenham defending, and Kevin Godfrey latched on to the ball to fire home past Ray Clemence via a post.

The O's present naturally went wild but there was more to come. Just twelve minutes later Colin Foster crossed from the right and an unmarked Kevin Godfrey hooked in at the far post.

It was unbelievable. Indeed just minutes later our Kevin, his confidence now ultra-high was close to a hat-trick, his shot from the right just clearing the crossbar.

After our second in fact, Spurs heads actually went down as a cheeky chant of 'easy, easy' went up around Brizzy.

We saw out the game and the inevitable mini-pitch invasion followed the final whistle.

It had certainly been a stunning display on the night from the Fourth Division boys in red. Whilst every player was a hero it was generally acknowledged that Peter Wells had been man of the match for keeping us in the game for the first hour.

For his two goals however, it was Kevin Godfrey who captured all the headlines the following day.

'Godfrey double trouble' was the *Guardian's* headline. 'Tottenham are stunned by Godfrey' said the *Daily Telegraph* and 'Godfrey Gold' was the *Daily Mail's* take.

The fact that our Kevin captured all the glory made the night all the more special for me. Here was your definitive 'bread and butter' footballer. Our longest serving player who had been with us since he was 16, someone who was never going to hit the football heights but he was having his moment of fame and it was thoughoughly deserved.

In character with the shy guy he ducked out of any interviews after the match and just drove home to South London. It was nice that he had done it in front of watching England manager Bobby Robson. He was there to watch his Spurs internationals, but after Godfrey's performance on the night I awaited with baited breath his next squad announcement to see if our Kev had impressed enough to have been chosen in it.

Not surprisingly on the night, Frank Clark unlike our two goal hero, was more than happy to say a few words afterwards.

He called it 'The best win I have ever achieved as a manager. There was no waving of a magic wand at half-time – I just said "you have done half the job, don't let us collapse as we did on Saturday." We got the breaks at vital times and also defended well.'

Fair play too to Tottenham manager Peter Shreeve who was very magnanimous in defeat. 'The night belonged to the Eastenders of Orient,' he said. 'They played extremely well and we were dumped on the night. It's not my job to make their fans happy, but it was nice to see the pleasure on their faces, because it's a super club.' Wonderful stuff.

There was still the second leg to come however and we all knew we couldn't really expect a repeat performance at White Hart Lane. As it was, due to riots in Tottenham the follow up match was not played until five weeks later.

Spurs beat us 4–0 on the night, though that was a score which certainly flattered the hosts.

We had held out for exactly 44 minutes and seven seconds, before Graham Roberts scored the decisive first goal, during which time we could easily have been awarded a penalty when Gary Stevens brought down Chris Jones in the box.

It wasn't given by Keith Hackett however and we went on to concede three in the second period. We were though far from disgraced.

Even if we had lost by seven or eight at White Hart Lane however, nothing would have taken away the glory of the first Spurs encounter.

For me personally it had been a special evening. Born and raised in Chingford, Tottenham had always been the club of most of my local mates and I had had it drummed into me since they won the Cup in '67 how superior their team was to mine. I had seen a few gallant performances against our near neighbours over the years – notably the two 1–1 league draws in the 1977–78 season – but this was the first time I had seen them defeated by us.

It was a result that had been totally unexpected, even more so bearing in mind it was achieved in a competition where we were traditionally rubbish.

Orient: Wells, Hales, Dickenson, Sussex, Sitton, Corbett, Foster, Brooks, Shinners, Godfrey, Jones.
Goals: Godfrey (64s, 78s).

Tottenham Hotspur: Clemence, Thomas, Hughton, Roberts, Miller, Allen, Ardiles, Falco, Chiedozie, Hoddle, Waddle.

Star Man: Peter Wells.
Attendance: 13,828.

Game Twenty-eight

King of the Castle

Orient 1 West Ham 1
FA Cup Third Round. 10 January 1987

If the previous match, the Spurs game, was for me match of the decade, this one for sure pushed it all the way for that prestigious accolade.

At the start of 1987 the O's were in a bad, bad way. Our first season in the basement division 1985–86 had not been too bad. We had finished fifth, just one place away from a promotion place. (Unfortunately this was the season before the play-offs were introduced.)

But the first half of the next campaign was proving to be nothing short of a disaster. With the league form hopeless, not for the first time in our history the saving grace was once again proving to be the FA Cup.

We had been a bit fortunate in the first round, just scraping past Woodford Town thanks to a late, late goal from Colin Foster, but we had had a wonderful result in the second winning 1–0 at Bournemouth.

At the time the south-coasters were pushing for promotion a division above us and we had been 7–1 outsiders with the bookmakers before the game. A Lee Harvey goal however had given us the victory and consigned the home team to their second defeat in four days at Dean Court. (the home supporters gave their manager a real roasting following our win – chap by the name of Harry Redknapp.)

It was well known that (just for a change) our club were in dire straights financially and were desperate for a money spinning tie in the Third Round.

Well when the balls were pulled out of the hat on the Monday after the Second Round it was pure heaven for the Orient.

The draw produced two mouth-watering derbies – Manchester United verses Manchester City but more importantly Orient verses West Ham.

The headlines of course were predictable. The Evening Standard announced 'Battle for Eastenders'. The papers picked up on the fact that the previous two times we had faced West Ham in the Cup in 1964 and 1980 the Hammers had gone on to win it.

The man most pleased must have been Frank Clark. With Chairman Tony Wood spending most of his time in Ruanda, Clark had recently been made up to the post of Managing Director at the club, which meant that he was closely involved with the money situation at Brisbane Road, as well as looking after the playing side.

'The team are delighted. We will get a good crowd – I hope for 20,000 plus – and it should prove to be a nice windfall for us.'

As the tie approached though, our form on the park was shocking. In two Freight Rover games in December we had lost 3–0 at Swindon and then had got trounced 5–1 at home to Brentford in front of just 749 die-hard nutters.

Then just a week before we entertained the Hammers, we hit an all tome low in the league losing 3–1 at home to Halifax.

Just 2,207 had been present at Brisbane Road that afternoon to see us end the day fourth from bottom of the entire Football League – the lowest position in our entire history.

Unsurprisingly for those that had bothered to attend, the battle-cry of the day had been 'Clark Out.'

It's fair to say that December had not been too kind to our Frankie injury wise. Paul Shinners, Ian Juryeff, Andy Sussex and John Sitton had all been out with knocks, and with Henry Hughton cup-tied for the West Ham clash expectations before the match were to put it mildly not too great.

Said Mr Clark before the encounter with the team who were 79 places above us in the League: 'It's about confidence more than anything else. I'm just hoping that a big occasion like this will lift a little of the pressure. No one expects us to win. If we were playing at the top of our form it would be difficult enough, but at this moment in time the task facing us is enormous. I've seen West Ham recently and I wish I hadn't.'

I remember before leaving Loughton, where I was now living, to get to Leyton on the Saturday of the game, watching Ian St John and Jimmy Greaves – aka *the Saint and Greavsie* – on their lunchtime preview show on ITV.

And there they were interviewing our own celebrity fan Julian Lloyd-Webber. Asking him to play a tune on his cello in keeping with our chances in the game, he played the funeral march.

I actually thought it quite amusing. Indeed anyone who had watched us play over the previous month or so would have thought that Lloyd-Webber was spot on.

What an unexpected afternoon it turned out to be, though. For ninety minutes we totally belied our league position with a quite brilliant performance.

It all started very low key with barely a chance in the opening half hour, but all O's would have settled for that the way our season had gone up till then.

Then came the opening goal from the Hammers. A Mark Ward free-kick was met at the near post by centre-half Paul Hilton and we were one down.

Surely one suspected, that would open the flood-gates. Incredibly though it didn't. Even more incredibly for the remainder of the game Orient were by far and away the better team.

Before half-time West Ham 'keeper Phil Parkes was called upon to make two blinding saves from Chris Jones and Shaun Brooks to keep the score at 1–0.

A fine through ball from Brooks then put Kevin Godfrey in with a chance and our striker narrowly shaved the post with his effort.

And there was more of the same in the second half. Shaun Brooks began to run the show in midfield despite being up against Paul Ince and Alan Devonshire.

Peter Wells was largely redundant in the O's goal.

With just fifteen minutes left we continued to press, but Parkes continued to be outstanding in the Hammers goal and it looked as if it was going to be a gallant failure for the boys in red.

A two substitutes rule had just been introduced by the FA in the FA Cup and our Frankie sent on Alan Comfort and Lee Harvey for Hales and Godfrey in a do or die move.

And it certainly turned out to be 'do' rather than 'die'

With just two minutes left Parkes held a twenty-yarder from Jones and gallant as we had performed, I think that after that most of us thought our chance had gone.

How wrong we were though. With the game entering injury-time Alan Comfort robbed George Parris near the touch-line, right in front of where I was sitting in the East Stand. He crossed into the area and the ball struck Hilton's hand.

Straight away referee Neil Midgley blew and pointed to the spot. Now from where I was I had a perfect view and I have to say that the decision was – well let's say – a tiny bit generous to the O's.

Of course we all cared not. Generous or not we had been outstanding after going behind and thoughoughly deserved a slice of luck.

Remember thinking at the time – who the hell's going to take it? To my astonishment youngster Steve Castle stepped up to take responsibility from twelve-yards. He was shooting in front of the thousands of Hammers gathered behind the Coronation Gardens goal and he had never before taken a penalty.

There was no need to worry at all though. Parkes dived to his left while our Steve blasted high just to the 'keeper's right. 1–1. Magnificent. We all went bananas, while Castle gave a little punch to those in claret and blue behind the goal.

Just seconds later Midgley – what a man – blew for time. We all went even more bananas.

Said our goal scoring hero after the game: 'No, I didn't volunteer to take the penalty. You could say I was volunteered for the job by my mates. They all just left me to it. Although I'd never taken one before, it didn't bother me. I just shut everything out of my mind and knocked it home.'

Said our Frankie: 'I knew Steve would score. He's that sort of lad. He has a bit of character about him and a bit of bottle. I'll let the lads go out for a few pints tonight.'

It certainly was an unbelievable result. It had generally been accepted at the time that the Halifax match a week before had seen one of the worst ever Orient showings to take us to our worst ever league position, and now virtually the same players had almost beaten one of the best teams in the country.

But then that's the Orient and the FA Cup for you.

After a few days reflecting Clark said: 'My initial reaction was that we're still in the competition and have gained a draw. But having had time to think about the game I'm a little disappointed that we didn't actually win it. We had many more chances than they did.' He was spot on. While the papers were generally divided between Castle, Brooks and Phil Parkes as to who was man of the match, I'd have given it to the big Shammers 'keeper, who had a blinder.

In the *Daily Express* on Monday, Castle said: 'A lot of things were said on television that upset the lads – we could have done without the funeral march. We didn't need much motivating for the match, but what we heard made us all the more determined and gave us that extra edge.'

The replay was delayed by the weather and not played until three weeks after the first game. We ended up losing 4–1, but with just 10 minutes to go it had been 1–1 and once more the O's had been magnificent.

We had equalized after 57 minutes through a wonderful Shaun Brooks free-kick when Kevin Dickenson had just been denied when his chipped effort past Parkes was ruled out because referee Roger Milford had already blown up.

Three very late goals unfortunately sent us out, but no way had it been a 4–1 match.

The two games against our neighbours were certainly the catalyst to kick start our season.

Amazingly after the way things had looked at the start of '87, we just missed out on the play-offs by a single point, following the infamous last game of the season at Burnley.

Thoughts of that 1986–87 league campaign however have by and large been well and truly dumped to the back of the memory some twenty-five years on.

No way can the same be said about that West Ham encounter, though. Castle went on to have a fine career at the O's but for me nothing he ever did in an Orient shirt topped his penalty on 10 January 1987.

Orient: Wells, Hales (Comfort 80), Foster, Cunningham, John, Dickenson, Cornwell, Castle, Brooks, Jones, Godfrey (Harvey 75).
Goal: Castle (pen. 90s).

West Ham: Parkes, Parris, Hilton, Martin, Walford, Ward, Ince, Pike, Devonshire, McAvennie, Cottee.
Goal: Hilton (31s).

Star Man: Steve Castle.
Attendance: 19,225.

Game Twenty-nine

Eight-on Orient

Leyton Orient 8 Rochdale 0
Football League Division 4. 20 October 1987

One of the most satisfying experiences when watching the same team play week in, week out is when every once in a while your boys will totally surprise you and give you a nice afternoon or an evening that you just haven't expected to see.

This Rochdale game was one of those such occasions.

Ok so we only beat Rochdale at home on the night and back then we always beat Rochdale at home, but for Leyton Orient to score eight? Leyton Orient simply did not score eight in any game, full stop.

Since I had been going I had never seen them score more than five and quite honestly never expected to see them score so much as even six. And yet this night we did it and in reality could comfortably have even notched up double figures.

The club had had one major change in the middle of 1987 when Orient Football Club were suddenly no more, only to be replaced by Leyton Orient Football Club.

Yes after twenty-one years we brought back the name of the place where we played, after a campaign led by the 'Orientear' fanzine which was finally backed by Chairman Tony Wood.

When the new season began the O's made a not-too-bad start and were handily placed come mid-October.

Three days before this Rochdale encounter however we had been easily beaten 2–0 at home to a Cambridge United side who were below us in the league a result which had taken us down to fifth place.

Said our Frankie after the Cam U. result: 'Even if you play Liverpool at home you'd expect to make more chances than we did today. It's hard to find anyone who played well.'

That game had attracted our biggest gate of the season, but after the performance that day and with the Tuesday evening being an awful one weather wise it was no real surprise that the terraces were sparsely filled for the mid-week encounter with the Dale – indeed we followed up our best number punter wise with our worst – just 2,995 were in attendance on that wet night.

There were a few Orient regulars I know who just did not bother turning up. My how they must have regretted their decision when they saw the final score.

We started the game playing some half-decent football yet with quarter of an hour gone, it was still scoreless.

We had come close a few times and I remember turning to the lads on the North Terrace at the time, and stating that it was just going to be one of those nights – we were never going to score that evening. An hour later, that was certainly one for the Martin Strong book of Orient quotes.

Alan Comfort's corner after eighteen minutes found its way to centre-half Mark Smalley who smashed the loose ball home and that finally opened the flood-gates.

Goal two arrived after 32 minutes when a terrible back pass from John Bramhall was latched onto by Alan Hull and as Dale 'keeper Keith Welch came out the ball broke to Paul Shinners who converted.

The third was a Kevin Hales penalty driven in after Comfort had been tripped in the box by Ronnie Coyle.

Then just a minute before the interval the O's completed a marvellous opening half when Hales blasted home from 15 yards with the help of a deflection off Bramhall.

One of the nice things about going to Brisbane Road in those days was that you were able to move from the North Terrace to the covered West-side during the game – if I remember right it was a quid to do so – and at half-time the not unexpected decision was made by me to make the said move, so as: a. I would not get soaked in the second half and probably more importantly: b. I could go and sit towards the Coronation Gardens end of the stand where we were kicking towards in the second period.

Bearing in mind our 'keeper Peter Wells had touched the ball five times in the first forty-five, all of them through pass backs, and he had not even had to take a goal-kick let alone save a shot it was not one of the most difficult decisions I have ever had to make in my Brisbane Road career.

On the hour Kevin Dickenson burst through from just inside the Rochdale half. On reaching the edge of the box he played a fine one two with Shinners before tucking home low into the corner. 5–0.

The sixth was the best of the night, Steve Castle layed off to Comfort and our tricky winger swerved one way then the other before curling a brilliant 18 yarder just two minutes after the fifth.

He then scored again ten minutes later with a left footer and the eighth came after seventy-five when Shinners rose to head home a Comfort cross. 8–0.

There were still fifteen minutes left when the last went in but 8–0 it finished. Shinners should have completed his hat-trick when he missed a clear chance just before the end and bearing in mind Steve Castle had hit the bar and Hales had another disallowed we could easily have hit ten. Indeed remarkably all eight goals had been crammed into the middle hour of the game

It could be argued that the match became more even in the second half – Rochdale got far enough up the pitch to force Wells into taking a goal-kick after 55 minutes and after our eighth had gone in they actually forced a corner prompting a massive cheer from the not-very-many Dale fans who had managed the long journey south.

For O's fans present, it was a wonderful evening. We had equalled the clubs best ever victory against Crystal Palace some thirty-two years earlier, and in so doing had moved up to second in the division. Our total of 34 goals was nine more than anyone else in the division had managed at the time. Even away from home we were the only side at the time still unbeaten.

In the local *Waltham Forest Guardian* reporter Richard Lewis called it 'one of the most sensational evenings of soccer I can recall seeing.' After the game the bookies even made us favorites to take the Fourth Division title.

Frankie was needless to say a changed man from the previous Saturday: 'Yes it was a magnificent result. The players were a credit to the club and their profession.'

The mood amongst the Brizzy faithful of course was well bullish afterwards. The talk was that we would go up automatically – anything less would be a disappointment.

But maybe they were just forgetting that we are after all Leyton Orient. Four days after the Rochdale massacre we went to seventh from bottom Swansea and lost 3–0.

And at the end of the season we didn't even make the play-offs.

Still at least we could look back on an evening back in October with some amount of pride, even if we did go home a little wet.

Leyton Orient: Wells, Howard, Dickenson, Smalley, Day, Hales, Castle (Sussex 87), Godfrey (Harvey 74), Shinners, Hull, Comfort.
Goals: Smalley (18n), Hales (36 pen n, 45n), Shinners (33n, 75s), Dickenson (60s), Comfort (62s, 72s).

Rochdale: Welsh, Lomax, Hampton, Mycock, Bramhall, Smart, Parker, Simmonds, Parlane, Coyle, Gavin.

Star Man: Alan Comfort.
Attendance: 2,995.

Game Thirty

Kamara kops it in penalty drama

Stoke City 1 Leyton Orient 2
Littlewoods Cup Second Round Second Leg. Aggregate 3–3.
11 October 1988
(Orient won 6–5 on penalties)

The eighties quite remarkably actually gave us three memorable games in the second most important cup competition in the land. Not content with the excitement of defeating Spurs in '85, just two years later against all odds we defeated a team two divisions above us over two games in the same competition. And to round off the decade we went up to Goodison Park and put on a fine showing against Everton just before the nineties arrived.

This defeat of Stoke was also memorable in that it finally saw us win our first penalty shoot-out after ten years of trying.

After the disappointment of just missing out on the play-offs in 1987–88, the next campaign had started pretty abysmally for our boys.

We had defeated Aldershot over two matches in the Littlewoods Cup First

Round to set up the Stoke encounter, but going into the first leg we had only just got our first win in the league and were fourth from bottom in the basement division.

In the first leg at Brisbane Road, the O's had started the game well and took the lead with a cracking Ian Juryeff twenty-five yarder after thirty-seven minutes. After the break however it had all changed – Simon Stainrod headed past Peter Wells after 48 and then a mistake from our custodian allowed a chap named Chris Kamara to hit the winner for the Potters.

We had only narrowly lost to a side in the second tier but after the game our Frankie still got very upset: 'If we're going to play like that in the return leg we may as well not bother going. Peter (Wells) should have done better with the second goal, but he can't be blamed for losing us the game. It was a dreadful team effort.'

So two weeks later we ventured up to the Potteries, with expectations not massive. This despite the fact that we had thumped York 4–0 at Brizzy the week before and a goalless draw at Scarborough on the Saturday had lifted us to the dizzy heights of sixth from bottom in the league.

As it quite unexpectedly turned out the game at the Victoria Ground was a classic.

The hero for us was Kevin Hales who hit the winning penalty. It must have been all the more pleasant for our man who had been going through a rough period at the club. Ten days before Hales had given up the captaincy because he thought it was affecting his own game and he felt he wasn't getting any response from his teammates.

We had started the game well, more than matching our opponents but the home team were quite relaxed knowing a 0–0 would more than be enough to take them into the next round.

After forty minutes however the complexion of the tie changed when the O's were awarded the first penalty of the night.

Ian Juryeff had collected a ricochet and rounded City 'keeper, Scott Barrett who brought our man down. Hales stepped up to send us one up and tie the aggregate score.

The small group of us travelling fans camped in the enclosure at the side of the ground naturally celebrated wildly.

The score still meant however that we were still behind in the tie thanks to the away goals rule, but to still be in with a shout with just forty-five minutes left was more than many of us would have hoped for travelling up north that night.

Both teams created more chances in the second period but things looked grim for the O's when Keith Day climbed all over Simon Stainrod to concede the second penalty of the match.

Incredibly though Stoke winger Peter Beagrie blazed well over the bar and it remained 2–2 overall.

As the game entered the last five minutes it looked like it was going to be a heroic failure from the boys from east London and this feeling was further enhanced when referee Tom Fitzharris very harshly awarded Stoke another penalty with just four minutes left.

Kevin Dickenson this time was adjudged to have pushed Stainrod though from where I was it appeared a poor decision (not that I was biased)

This time Stainrod himself took responsibility and made no mistake to make it 1–1 on the night and 3–2 to City on aggregate. That surely was it as far as Orient's chances of winning the tie went.

Well no it wasn't. With just a minute left on the clock Alan Comfort brilliantly saved the day. He went on a mazy run into the penalty area then slotted home magnificently. 95% of the crowd went silent, the 5% of us in the side enclosure naturally enough did not.

The ref blew shortly afterwards and there was a feeling of stunned disbelief amongst us O's. We were still in it with thirty more minutes to play.

I can't actually remember much happening during extra-time. Both teams had given everything in the first ninety, and the O's in particular did not want to undo all their good work by giving away a silly goal.

So it ended 3–3 on aggregate and it was all down to spot kicks. After losing 2–1 at home and at 3–2 down entering the last knockings of the second match we would of course have taken penalties throughout most of the tie. The only small problem now, however was that Orient had always had a phobia about spot-kick lotteries. Up till then we had never been successful in any that we had taken part in.

It was decided that the penalties were to be taken at the end nearer to where us O's were congregated, though it was in front of the hoards of Stokies behind the goal.

I was none to confident but the small pocket of away support three times went crazy as Peter Beagrie, with his second unsuccessful attempt from 12 yards that night, Cliff Carr and Simon Stainrod all almost unbelievably missed for Stoke.

Meanwhile Paul Ward and Ian Juryeff had scored for us. Wardy's effort was particularly memorable for the lovely little wave he gave to the Stoke end after he had calmly side footed into the net.

After Stainrod had blasted his effort against the bar it was all down to Hales with our fifth effort to score to put us through. Our number one penalty taker had no problem sending Scott Barrett the wrong way to send us into delirium.

We had ended the evening with a tremendous giant-killing act and in so doing had also won our first ever penalty shoot-out. Scott Barrett, unsuccessful custodian for Stoke that night, interestingly became Orient hero from a spot-kick lottery some eleven years later against Rotherham in the play-off semi-final.

Needless to say our Frankie's reaction was totally different to the one he had had after the first leg ; 'It was a great evening for ourselves and football in general. The game was played in a marvellous spirit and the fans applauded both teams off the pitch. I would have been upset if we had gone out.'

Speaking about the winning conversion he said: 'Kevin showed great composure and courage. It's quite an ordeal to have to take a penalty in such a high pressure, but he kept his nerve. I can only remember Kevin missing one penalty in the last three years.'

I actually recall going into one at the time, when Hales did not take the first penalty for us. I've always thought the best penalty taker should always take the initial one in any shoot-out. Well I was proved wrong here.

Indeed I remember going into one again some eleven years later at the Rotherham shoot-out for the same reason, when our regular taker Matty Lockwood did not take the first. Once again I was proved wrong when he hit the winning fourth one for the O's.

The evening at the Victoria Ground finished very late. I got back home at some ridiculous hour, but of course it mattered not.

We got drawn away to Ipswich in the next round, not really the kind of tie Frankie and co. were looking for, and we reverted back to our standard League Cup form, losing 2–0.

Nothing though could detract from that glorious evening in the Potteries, and it remains to this day number two in the list of all time League Cup classics I've witnessed, just behind the Spurs epic.

Stoke City: Barrett, Gidman (Carr), Beeston, Kamara, Hemming, Henry, Hackett (Ware), Ford, Shaw, Stainrod, Beagrie.
Goal: Stainrod (85pen).

Leyton Orient: Wells, Howard, Dickenson, Hales, Day, Sitton, Baker (Harvey), Ward, Hull, Juryeff, Comfort.
Goals: Hales (40 pen), Comfort (89).

3–3 on aggregate, Leyton Orient won 6–5 on penalties.

Star Man: Kevin Hales.
Attendance: 5,756.

Game Thirty-one

Eight-on Orient (the follow up)

Leyton Orient 8 Colchester United 0
Football League Division 4. 15 October 1988

The O's faithful who witnessed the glory of the match at Stoke back in '88 quite remarkably had to wait a mere four days to see another of the decade's best games, this time though it was played at the Mecca that is Brisbane Road.

Yes this was the second of the three match '8–0 trilogy' from the eighties and nineties, this the one sandwiched between the Rochdale and Doncaster experiences.

Regrettably I was not there to see our first 8–0 game back in 1955 – when we defeated Crystal Palace – so I can't give judgement as to which was the best of the four, but for various reasons in many ways this Colchester match was for me, the most enjoyable of the trio that I saw.

For starters, unlike the Dale and Rovers matches here we were smashing local rivals. And in both the Rochdale and Doncaster encounters, we scored

our eighth well before the end of the game.

You were left then with a feeling that in both cases we could have gone on to reach double figures but that we had virtually 'declared'. Strange as it may seem you actually left those two games with a small sense of disappointment.

Against Colchester however, we hit the target for the last time just before the end to round off a fine effort from the team for the entire ninety minutes, with absolutely no let up at the end.

The performance against our Essex rivals was also the least expected of the big victories. Before the match we had only scored seven in nine league games. We were sixth from bottom of the league with United two points better off than us.

We also went into the match without Paul Shinners - generally regarded as our number one striker at the time – who had just had an appendix operation. Our two encounters the previous season had both ended goalless.

So at the end of the afternoon the 3,421 at Brizzy had witnessed a rout and it had certainly been one that came out of the blue (or red as I prefer to say).

Before our scoring began though that afternoon, we could easily have fallen behind. After just eight minutes United's Richard Wilkins found himself clean through with just Peter Wells to beat, but he struck tamely straight at our 'keeper. That was as good as it got for the visitors though.

We then completely took charge and by twenty minutes incredibly were three up.

The first two both came from Alan Comfort corners. Paul Ward flicked the first one on to Alan Hull who fired home from six yards.

The second saw centre-half John Sitton rise to meet the kick with a bullet like header past Mark Walton in the Colchester goal.

Midfielder Steve Baker then turned on the edge of the area with nineteen played to fire home the third via a post.

Colchester's afternoon was probably best summed up by our fourth. Alan Comfort blasted in a stinging shot which Walton punched in the air and he turned in horror as the ball looped over him and into the net.

There was no let up in the second period. The fifth and sixth both featured fine interplay between Hull and Ian Juryeff with Hull slotting home from 12 yards for the fifth while the same player headed home for the sixth.

Then with just six minutes to play Colchester's Colin Hunter handballed on the line allowing Kevin Hales to convert from the spot, his third penalty success for us in five days.

Finally Keith Day met another corner with a fine header to complete the rout with 89 minutes on the clock.

Day's effort hitting the back of the net signalled my two lasting memories of the afternoon. Firstly our centre-half's wildly over the top celebrations at his goal as if it had been a crucial last gasp winner. This came about as he had been released by our opponents and it clearly meant a hell of a lot to him to score against them.

Then as the game entered injury time I remember standing on the North Terrace and some wag to my left tried to start up a 'Clark Out' chant. This had been the anthem of the season thus far but this time it was greeted with much laughter by the O's faithful.

Hull's hat-trick was his first for the club – indeed he had scored but one in the league all season before that afternoon. He had turned his back on a banking career in the City to play professionally for our club.

In fact although our diminutive front man scored three, a prime candidate for man of the match would have been his strike partner Ian Juryeff who despite being magnificent all match, failed to get on the score sheet even once.

Said our Frankie afterwards: 'Ian will surely get his reward over the next couple of games for a performance like that.'

Clark, of course was very upbeat generally post match: 'One club was going to get a whacking from us. That's the way we've been playing and I could really sense it. We were just so sharp today and our finishing was absolutely clinical.'

It had for sure been a wonderful display. We won the Barclays Performance of the Week award, which carried a cash reward of £300 for a local community project. Cameraon Athan Youth Club in Walthamstow bagged the money.

For Colchester they had suffered their heaviest ever defeat in the league. The 0–8 reverse beat their previous worst capitulation of 0–7, again against us in 1952 and also against Reading four years earlier.

To nobody's great surprise their manager Roger Brown resigned three days later.

For us it really did kick start the season that had started so badly and indeed it remarkably ended up with the O's achieving promotion via the play-offs.

Before the game we were 66–1 to win the division and indeed you would have probably given similar odds on Frankie still being the man in charge come May, before the Colchester game.

Leyton Orient: Wells, Howard, Dickenson, Hales, Day, Sitton, Baker, Ward, Hull, Juryeff, Comfort. Subs not used: Harvey, Nugent.
Goals: Hull (9s, 52n, 73n), Sitton (11s), Baker (19s), Comfort (41s), Hales (Pen 84n), Day (89n).

Colchester United: Walton, Headman, Cartwright, Barnett (Radford), Hicks, Hill, Hunter, White, Tempest, Swindlehurst, Wilkins. Sub not used: Daniels.

Star Man: Alan Hull.
Attendance: 3,421.

Sooper-Cooper and a P.A. own-goal

Leyton Orient 4 Scunthorpe 1
Football League Division 4. 13 May 1989

Certain players become your favourites from the moment they don the magnificent Orient shirt. The likes of Kitch, Big Joe and more recently for me Gary Alexander and Matty Lockwood are names that fit into that category.

There are others though that have had to work for their adulation at Brizzy Road. Terry Howard, John Sitton and currently Scott Cuthbert are examples.

Then though there was the strange, indeed unique, case of Mark Cooper. A player it's fair to say pretty much hated for various reasons at the start of his Brizzy Road days who wonderfully turned it round to become if not quite a Leyton legend certainly someone you look back on with many a happy memory remembering him in an Orient shirt.

Coops came to the club in February 1989. He had been signed for £10,000 from Gillingham and he had already had an interesting career, to say the least, by the time he arrived. At only 21 he had already played for Cambridge, Totten-

ham Hotspur, Shrewsbury and the Gills who had paid a club record £102,500 for him from the Spurs.

At around the same time as Cooper's arrival at the club, Frankie made another signing – Kevin Campbell made his way across north London, on loan from Arsenal.

The O's record improved considerably in the next few months with the two new players but without being overly unkind to Cooper it's pretty fair to say that it was down a whole lot more to the Highbury man than the former Gill.

Whilst Campbell scored nine times in his fifteen appearances before he went back to his parent club, in the same period Cooper managed just one.

Campbell had been quite brilliant, while at the same time Cooper had been quite dreadful.

When King Kev left at the beginning of April it was clear that if the O's were to get up a division, Coops was going to have to up his game and take over the Campbell mantle as lead striker.

So what did Cooper do in the very next game ? Contrive to get himself sent off for a ridiculous off the ball incident with Wrexham skipper Joey Jones.

At the time despite the 1–0 victory in North Wales this looked to be a disaster for the O's.

Having already lost the services of King Kev, we would now be without the banned Cooper for three games. It was the club's first sending-off of the season and it therefore seriously damaged our quest to win the £25,000 Barclays were giving in their Blue Riband Award for fair-play and goals that season. Our Frankie was clearly furious with Coops and added a club fine to the three game ban.

You would have thought at the time that Cooper could not do any more to further dent his standing with the Brisbane Road management and punters, yet in the last game before his suspension he managed it.

Just to put the icing on the cake he contrived possibly the worst miss ever seen at Brisbane Road in the match against Torquay. In shooting wide with an empty net a few yards in front of him it looked as if he could well end up an all-time infamous Orient figure of hate.

Coops served his three game ban and came back into the side in the penultimate match of the season away at Lincoln.

Our man actually had a pretty decent game on his return at Sincil Bank, though he still managed to miss a golden chance with a header in the first half. Since his arrival some three months earlier our new forward had still only hit the back of the onion bag on just one occasion.

And then remarkably, came this last game of the season against Scunthorpe.

Unbelievably, completely out of the blue Super Cooper, hit one of the best hat-tricks I've ever seen from an O and he left the field to a standing ovation. It was a stunning turnaround.

Although we were already assured of a top seven spot before the victory, it certainly gave us much needed momentum before the play-offs. And ironically in scoring three times Cooper's goals meant we secured the £25,000 Barclays Blue Riband Award, which his earlier sending off had put in jeopardy.

Going into the game, Scunthorpe were sitting in an automatic promotion place and knew that a win or possibly even a draw would see them in the Third Division the next season. The third spot was between themselves and Crewe. Not unexpectedly the Iron brought a big following down to Brisbane Road, helping make it the biggest crowd of the season at Leyton Stadium.

The fun for the home fans though started after twenty minutes. Cooper received a short ball some twenty-five yards out and in one moment he turned and thundered in an unstoppable shot high and wide of 'keeper Musselwhite.

It was for sure a magnificent goal our fifty-eighth at home in the league in 1988–89, many more than anyone else had managed in the division. Arguably it was possibly the best of the lot, and it had been scored from a man who up till then had been totally derided by the Orient faithful. Someone who hadn't managed to score even one of the previous fifty-seven successful home efforts.

It was a deserved lead for Orient who had began very brightly with John Sitton coming close with a header and Terry Howard shooting just wide even before the opening goal.

It took just nine more minutes for the O's and indeed Coops to double their tally for the afternoon. A Keith Day free-kick wasn't cleared by three static United defenders and the ball found its way to Cooper some eight yards out, who coolly drilled past Musselwhite.

At this point Scunny finally woke up and Paul Heald had to make a superb tip over from Tony Daws' shot just before the break

At the interval the O's though thoroughly deserved the two goal lead after a fine first forty-five.

Not surprisingly the biggest cheer of the afternoon from the Coronation Gardens end of the ground where the Iron were gathered, came when announcer Keith Simpson relayed the news that Crewe were a goal down at already promoted Tranmere. That meant that if results stayed the same even if they lost to us, Scunthorpe would still achieve automatic promotion that afternoon.

The news may well have been relayed to the Scunny dressing room as they came out looking well fired up for the second half, and within four minutes had scored.

Kevin Taylor played a one–two with Daws and upon receiving the return pass slipped the ball passed Heald.

It gave the visitors hope, yet the O's responded magnificently and within sixty seconds were again two goals to the good. Steve Baker crossed from the right, Cooper – who was having one of those afternoons – flicked on to Steve Castle who smashed home our third.

In fairness to Scunthorpe they didn't throw the towel in and forced two good saves from Heald, but the last word of the afternoon fittingly went to Super Cooper.

With just three minutes left a Day free-kick saw Musselwhite rushing out to punch clear, but his effort only found it's way to Coops who looked up and with the 'keeper out of his goal lobbed superbly from distance into an empty net.

Indeed Cooper was just a fraction away from adding a fourth when with just a minute left he had a header which came back off the Scunny post.

It mattered little though. In just ninety minutes the man had quadrupled his goals tally for the season and had left the Brizzy punters stunned.

The game ended 4–1 and Cooper left the field of play to an amazing reception, clutching the match-ball.

In a fairly surreal moment however, there then came a strange incident, still talked about by many a veteran O to this very day.

Man on the P.A., Simpson bizarrely announced to the travelling Scunthorpe supporters that they had achieved automatic promotion when they hadn't. Crewe had equalized with fifteen minutes to go at Tranmere though no-one had obviously informed our announcer of this information.

There was mass celebration at the Coronation Gardens end of the ground but it was all wrong. There were no mobiles of course in those days so they just accepted initially that the news was true. I must admit though I was armed on the North Terrace with my trusted tranny and I was quietly chuckling to myself knowing that they had been given false information. The information was then corrected, but the damage had already been done.

Keith Simpson was a wonderful man. Orient through and through he had been doing the announcing at the home games since the sixties and had played a part in having the beloved *Tijuana Taxi* lead the team out from 1968 onwards.

Yet ask many a Brisbane Road oldie their lasting memory of him and it will be the Scunny promotion cock-up from '89.

Going back to the match, it had for sure been a remarkable ninety minutes. Before the game nobody could quite understand our Frankie's thinking in leaving out Ian Juryeff who had scored fourteen times that season and playing Mark Cooper in his place.

By the end of the match though the big man had totally justified his manager's decision.

Said Clark: 'Mark Cooper was superb and maybe his hat-trick will bring the fans onto his side.'

In a final twist to the afternoon Frank barred the hat-trick hero from talking to the press 'until he scores his next hat-trick', he stated.

Ironically Coops did manage to score three of the four Orient goals in the four play-off games and so in the end was a major player in our promotion year. The terrace jeering certainly became a thing of the past.

I've seen better players wearing an Orient shirt over the years, but when it comes to ones that have gone from zero to hero Coops for sure is the number one. A quite remarkable transformation.

As for Scunthorpe it must have been one hell of a long journey home for them and their army of fans that evening. They were in the play-offs but lost to Wrexham in the semis.

It's fair to say it probably took them ten years to get revenge for our P.A. gaff when they beat us 1-0 in the play-off final at Wembley in 1999. Would love though, to have heard some of the comments made about us and in particular Simpson on their way back to Humberside that evening back in '89.

Leyton Orient: Heald, Howard, Dickenson, Hales, Sitton, Day, Baker, Castle, Harvey (Juryeff 80), Cooper, Comfort (Carter 88).
Goals: Cooper (19s, 29s, 86n), Castle (52n).

Scunthorpe United: Musselwhite, Smalley, Longden, Taylor, Nicol, Cork, Hodkinson, Cowling, Daws, Flounders, Hamilton.
Goal: Taylor (51s).

Star Man: Mark Cooper.
Attendance: 6,366.

Game Thirty-three

One wedding and a promotion

Leyton Orient 2 Wrexham 1
Fourth Division Play-off Final, Second Leg. 3 June 1989

After the Scunthorpe victory the O's were paired with Scarborough for the play-off semi-final. It was our first attempt at the end of season jamboree, a new experience for the O's team and fans alike. The games with the Boro were very nervy affairs.

In the first game at Brisbane Road it was once again our new found hero Mark Cooper who was the star. He calmed the nerves after just six minutes when Kevin Hales delivered a perfect cross for our big man to loop a header past the Scarborough 'keeper Ian Ironside.

The visitors had a 'goal' disallowed for offside just before the interval, but much of the match was a pretty dull affair, though it finally livened up with just eight minutes left on the clock.

Scarborough centre-half Craig Short dithered badly on the ball and was robbed by Lee Harvey. Our man looked clean through but he was blatantly pulled down by the Boro defender. There followed the inevitable 'handbags at six paces' moment between the two sets of players and when tempers had cooled Short was booked – these days he would have been sent off.

From the resulting free-kick Coops stooped low to brilliantly head home and give us a two goal advantage for the return in Yorkshire.

Despite Frank Clark's claim before the match that we were not going there to shut up shop that's pretty much what we were forced to do for long periods in the game and when Martin Russell scored with seventy played those of us that had made the trip feared the worse.

Scarborough were kicking towards the goal behind which we were standing and to this day I still say those last twenty minutes were probably the longest I've ever known at any O's match.

They just seemed to go on and on as we endured wave upon wave of Scarborough attacks. Balls were kicked off the line, Healdy made save after save as we hardly got out of our own penalty area for the last quarter of an hour. But the defence failed to crack – John Sitton in particular was magnificent – as we held on to reach the final.

Alas it was just before the finals were moved to Wembley, but in finishing the season above our opponents Wrexham, we at least guaranteed that we could play the second leg at home, such were the rules in those days.

The first leg was another nervous affair with chances few and far between. Mark Cooper hit the bar with a header in the first half but it finished in a goalless game, so setting up a grand finale to the season at Brisbane Road on 3 June.

It was to be our sixty-first and final game of a marathon season. We had certainly never played a competitive game in June before and the unexpected lateness to the end of the campaign caught out many. Long serving physio Bill Songhurst had already planned a trip to the far east to celebrate his silver wedding anniversary and so missed the match, though it was player Alan Comfort who attracted all the talk before the encounter.

Our man had already booked his wedding to take place on the same day at 5.30 in the afternoon at Bangor in Northern Ireland. One sensed leading up to the match that there was more than a little annoyance on our Frankie's behalf that the winger had not changed his plans to tie the knot on the biggest day for the club in years.

The lucky thing was that England were due to play Poland at Wembley in a World Cup qualifier in the afternoon meaning that there was a 12 o'clock kick off at Brizzy that Sunday. This at least gave the Comforts a little more time.

Seeing a nice little story with some good publicity the *Daily Express* offered a helicopter to airlift Comfort from near to the ground on to Heathrow, allowing him to get up to Belfast in time for the service.

Needless to say there was great anticipation around Leyton Stadium in the days preceding the season's finale. After years of pain we were finally within touching distance of our first promotion for nineteen years and the first through the play-offs.

It had all the makings of being one of the great Brisbane Road days and it did not disappoint.

13,355 gathered in East London and actually witnessed a surprisingly decent game considering what was a stake, and there was a more than decent result at the end of it.

Whilst our three previous play-off matches had been tight affairs with not a lot of attacking flair this was quite a surprisingly open ninety minutes.

Wrexham started brightly clearly looking for an away goal which would have been crucial. It took a brave save from Paul Heald to deny Ollie Kearns and they looked a more potent attacking threat than they had done at the Racecourse Ground in the first match.

The O's though were dangerous when they went forward and Kevin Hales, Alan Comfort, Cooper and Lee Harvey all had efforts not too far away.

A goal looked as if it could come for either side at any time and finally the breakthrough came in first-half injury time.

And what a breakthrough it was. A cross from the left found its way to Lee Harvey on the edge of the area and our man hit a screamer into the top corner past 'keeper Mike Salmon. I was standing right behind the effort on the North Terrace and I don't think I can remember seeing a strike being hit so hard.

Harvey had worn the number nine shirt in the later stages of the season but this corker was his first goal in twelve games. For many an O I know, this remains the best ever Brisbane Road goal, partly because of the greatness of the shot and partly because of its importance at the time. It was for sure one of the most magnificent Orient moments ever seen at the Herb Albert Stadium.

Despite ending up by miles the division's top scorers we had not hit the target in the previous two play-off matches, resulting in much nervousness among home punters before the strike.

At half time though we were all suddenly a lot more relaxed.

We were 1–0 up at home, 1–0 up on aggregate, Welsh heads were surely bound to drop following the goal just before the interval and we would go on to win easily.

Well that was what the thinking was at the time, but we are of course Leyton Orient. Within two minutes of the restart Wrexham had equalized.

The Robins had introduced Steve Buxton as substitute at half-time and his knock back was met by an unmarked Jon Bowden who nodded in from all of two yards. As soft goals to give away go, this was up with the best of them.

Although the goal was not quite in the same class as Lee's one, those that had set off at the crack of dawn and were gathered on the visitor's South Terrace cared little.

It was 1-1 and they had their precious away goal.

The rules stated that only after extra-time would the away goals rule come into play, meaning that we still had plenty of time to get a winner, but there were certainly many nervous folk around at the time. And extra time, of course would have created more problems for the Comforts and their wedding, time wise.

After their equalizer it has to be said the Welsh team's tactics were a tiny bit baffling. They had shown throughout the first half that they were more than capable of scoring, yet they decided to sit back and defend the advantage they had.

We had scored over one hundred goals in all competitions that season so it was a risky strategy to take and one that proved ultimately unsuccessful.

The O's pressed forward but with just under ten minutes remaining of normal time the score remained the same. Then Lee Harvey found himself with space on the right and he crossed into the area. It was met by Super Cooper who had broken clear of Joey Jones to volley past Salmon and into the net.

It was pretty poor defending and the goal was not half as good as Harvey's effort but down the other end of the ground to where it was scored, we naturally cared little about that on the North Terrace.

Of course we knew that even at 2-1 the job was far from done. They had to come at us now which they certainly did for the rest of the match.

Like the game at Scarborough there were some desperate moments down our end in the final minutes. One Welsh effort from point blank range I remember hit Healdy full on in the face. A great save though it was, he seemed to know little about it.

We hung on though for a famous win. At the conclusion there were some never to be forgotten scenes at our theatre of dreams. For many an Orient fan it was the first promotion they had experienced. In some ways it may have been nice to clinch it at Wembley – the play-offs were moved there the following year – but it was lovely to do it at our lovely little place of worship in East London, where we had witnessed so many years of agony.

There was a pitch invasion, which I don't think would have been allowed at Wembley and hundreds gathered in front of the director's box in the East Stand.

The players and our Frankie came out to be greeted by the obvious great reception. Words were said over the mike by our leader and we even forgave Ooh Terry Howard when he started singing.

It was of course quite ironical that Clark had got cheered so heartily by the Brizzy faithful, given that throughout a lot of the season he had got barracked by many on the terraces.

Going into March we had been fourteenth and had looked a million miles away from being a promotion side.

We had got knocked out of the FA Cup by non-league Enfield and another season in the basement division looked assured well into it.

The previous time an Orient manager had been given such a great ovation from the Director's Box had been Ken Knighton when relegation was avoided in '83. Ten days after that Knighton was sacked, a fate that was never likely to be repeated this time round with Frank.

Clark's take afterwards was: 'It's a great day for the club. It's a great day for the chairman and I'm delighted for the players and the fans. Oh, yes, I'm a bit pleased myself.'

Another pleased party on the day was the *Sunday Express*. Comfort was whisked away for his wedding and he just got there in time. The paper got their story – they just happened to have a photographer by the helicopter before take off and at the church after the wedding – and of course it was made all the sweeter for them with our victory.

Leyton Orient: Heald, Howard, Dickenson (Ward), Hales, Day, Sitton, Baker, Castle, Harvey, Cooper, Comfort. Sub not used: Hull.
Goals: Harvey (44n), Cooper (82s).

Wrexham: Salmon, Salathiel, Wright, Hunter, Beaumont, Jones, Thackeray (Buxton), Flynn (Cooper).
Goal: Bowden (47n).

Star Man: Alan Comfort.
Attendance: 13,355.

Game Thirty-four

Carters' cracker

Everton 2 Leyton Orient 2
Littlewoods Cup Second Round. Second Leg. 3 October 1989
(Everton won 4–2 on aggregate)

Frankie and the boys had started brightly in their new division in 1989–90, picking up a creditable nine points from their first five games and they also hammered Gillingham 7–1 on aggregate in the Littlewoods Cup.

The draw for the O's in their generally-most-unfavorite-cup competition gave them a plumb Second Round tie against First Division giants Everton, with the first leg to be played at Brisbane Road.

An excited Clark anticipated a crowd of around twelve or thirteen thousand for the match – with chairman Tony Wood spending much of the time out of the country, Frank looked after much of the finances – and he must have been a touch disappointed that only 8,214 came through the turnstiles on the night of the first game. Indeed much of what Clark said to the press at the time seemed to concentrate as much on money matters as events on the park for the Orient.

The O's had beaten Wigan at home 1–0 in the game before the Everton first leg, yet Frankie appeared more concerned that the club were forced at the time to fork out three grand to remove all brushwood from behind the South Terrace and the West Stand at the ground.

Somebody had also taken the decision to make the Everton match all ticket which must have hit prospects of a good attendance figure hard.

In the game itself the O's peaked in the first four minutes with their best two chances. First Terry Howard hit a fierce goal bound drive which was blocked, then Danny Carter had a decent chance which he hit wide.

The Toffee men gradually took control after this and despite a not-too-bad effort from the boys in red they ran out fairly comfortable 2–0 winners.

So Orient headed for the return at Goodison with expectations of winning the tie pretty low but there were hopes at least that we would put on a good showing up on Merseyside.

As it was the hundred or so of us who ventured up north two weeks later witnessed one of the better performances of the coming-to-a-close 80's decade, with the highlight of the night being arguably the best goal of the decade scored by an O.

We were aided on the evening, it has to be said, by the Merseysider's skipper Kevin Ratcliffe hobbling off after only four minutes with a groin strain, to be replaced by Stefan Rehn.

This meant a complete rearrangement of the Everton defence which was a big bonus for us. Though chances were few and far between we were more than matching our opponents as half-time approached and indeed it did not come as a major surprise when we took the lead a minute before the break.

And what a goal it was too. Winger Danny Carter intercepted a pass from Rehn, sidestepped Ian Snodin, and curled a twenty-five yarder past Neville Southall.

Those of us in the away enclosure at the opposite end to where the goal was scored went a little doolally, though I even heard some applause from the home supporters such had been the magnificence of the strike.

Said Southall after the match: 'The only time I saw it was when I picked the ball out of the back of the net.' Praise indeed from arguably the best goalkeeper in the league at the time.

The goal had the effect of waking up the home side immediately and they almost equalized straight away with a long range strike from Rehn, but we hung on and went in at half-time a goal to the good on the night.

I Remember spending the whole of the interval staring gob smacked at the scoreboard at the other end to where we were standing: 'Everton 0 Leyton Orient 1.'

One imagined that there must have been strong words in the home dressing room at half time. Whatever manager Colin Harvey said there was a totally different Everton in the second half.

As the O's began to tire the Toffeemen midfield led by Norman Whiteside, began to take control. Paul Heald continued to stand firm in the Orient goal however, pulling off fine saves from Kevin Sheedy, Graeme Sharp and Mike Newell.

With the score still at 1–0 on the night, 1–2 on aggregate, I remember out of the blue we created one decent chance with Mark Cooper heading narrowly over right in front of the away support.

Blimey I don't know what I'd have done if that had gone in.

The game and tie unfortunately though turned after seventy-one minutes. At this point Harvey had clearly had enough of the way his team were playing and he brought on Tony Cottee in place of Sharp.

The substitution effectively turned the match. Within a minute of coming on, with only his second touch of the ball Cottee crossed for Whiteside to tap in from close range. Then just five minutes later Kevin Sheedy volleyed home from a Pat Nevin corner and at that point our dreams of a famous victory were gone.

With 4–1 the aggregate score the tie was lost, but the O's kept battling away and we were rewarded with a second goal with just a minute left. Lee Harvey's through ball was met by Geoff Pike who fired past Southall from ten yards. A good goal, though not quite in the same class as Carter's effort.

So we ended up with an admirable 2–2 on the night after a wonderful performance. At the final whistle the Merseyside locals rightly applauded our boys off the pitch, as of course did those in the visitor's enclosure.

Like the team we too had given a fine account of ourselves that evening – said Frankie afterwards: 'Our supporters were superb. They certainly out-shouted the home fans.'

It certainly was a cracking display from the boys in red on the pitch against a side packed with internationals.

The papers were quick to praise the O's for the performance the next day – headlined the *Daily Express*: 'Carter gives mighty Everton the blues.'

For once I had to agree with them. (This was actually the newspaper that had told us just a couple of weeks before that Liverpool, having just lost John Aldridge to Real Sociedad for £1.2 million were tracking Mark Cooper as a possible replacement.

As bizarre Orient stories in the press go the only one I can ever remember coming close to matching that one was when some six years later the *Daily Mail* informed us that Rod Stewart was thinking of buying the club.

We had faltered somewhat in the league going into the second Everton match and it was hoped that the heroics at Goodison Park would help to kick start the season again for the O's.

But of course we are talking Leyton Orient here and in true Leyton Orient tradition we returned to Merseyside some three days later and lost 3–0 in the league to Tranmere, with a dismal showing.

Everton: Southall, Snodin, McDonald, Ratcliffe (Rehn 4), Watson, Whiteside, Nevin, McCall, Sharp (Cottee 71), Newell, Sheedy.
Goals: Whiteside (72), Sheedy (77).

Leyton Orient: Heald, Hoddle, Dickenson, Pike, Day (Baker 78), Sitton, Howard, Castle, Harvey, Cooper, Carter. Sub not used: Ward.
Goals: Carter (44), Pike (89).

Everton won 4–2 on aggregate.

Star Man: Danny Carter.
Attendance: 10,128.

And so a few months after the Everton game, the curtain came down on what was (just for a change) a generally disappointing decade for Orient/Leyton Orient Football Club.

Of course, the nineties would surely be a much better one for all at Brisbane Road, wouldn't it?

Game Thirty-five

The Elleray Experience

Leyton Orient 4 Brentford 2
Division 3. 28 December 1991

This was a Brisbane Road classic to be sure, yet the match will forever be remembered for the mass brawl four minutes from the end and a refereeing performance generally recognized as one of the worst ever seen at East London's theatre of dreams.

The O's went into the game on the back of a 2–1 victory against Bolton on Boxing Day and occupied ninth place in the Third, while Brentford were top of the league, though forwards Marcus Gayle and Gary Blissett were suspended having both been sent-off against Torquay the previous week. Top scorer Dean Holdsworth had a slight foot injury and was so named only as a sub, while ex-O Kevin Godfrey made a return to the East London club he had played for so many times.

The two teams had played out a classic on the opening day of the season, with the Bees victorious by the odd goal in seven, and indeed Orient were

looking to halt a run of nine consecutive defeats by our London rivals.

The first half turned into something of a shooting contest between Greg Berry and Brentford's Lee Luscombe with both netting twice before the break.

Berry scored first in the sixth minute with hesitancy in the opposition defence allowing our man a simple tap in, and after Luscombe's volley levelled the score, Bees 'keeper Benstead lost the ball at the feet of Mark Cooper who passed wide to an unmarked Berry who scored again.

Luscombe was then on target again at the end of a virtually unimpeded solo run, but even at 2–2 the home team looked the better team in the first forty-five.

After the break the O's made their dominance pay when Steve Castle, who had earlier hit the post, put the home side in front following a cross from substitute Wayne Burnett and then the other sub Andy Jones added a fourth when he turned away from a crowded midfield to drive past the Bees 'keeper.

It had been a bad tempered affair all game with five bookings and many a foul but everything that had gone on before paled into insignificance four minutes from the end when all hell broke out in the centre-circle when Elleray finally appeared to lose the plot.

Orient's Kenny Achampong had evaded two dreadful tackles but was finally sent tumbling to the turf on the third. Whether the referee was attempting to play an advantage or whether he had simply left his glasses in the dressing room was uncertain at the time, but Achampong reacted with a poor tackle of his own in retaliation.

Cue pandemonium in the middle of the park as sixteen players slugged it out in a scene not seen at Brizzy Road for many a year. Elleray appeared powerless to stop the mayhem, his two linesmen sheepishly keeping well out of it.

When things had finally calmed down the man in black went to talk to one of his assistants but it was clear that although they knew they had to take some kind of action, they didn't have a clue exactly who to send off.

So while five or six could have taken their bath four minutes early, to the astonishment of all present it was Kenny Achampong, who despite his initial involvement had pretty much taken a back seat at the height of the agro who was given his marching orders.

Despite being on course for a famous victory the home fans went berserk. The game ended minutes later though there were apparently heated exchanges in the player's tunnel as they came off, and the Orient faithful gave Mr Elleray a whole heap of abuse at the final whistle as he followed them.

I personally found events at the end all rather bizarre. For the first time in seven years we had defeated our foes from West London who happened to be top of the league, we had witnessed a cracker of a match yet ninety per cent of Leyton Orient supporters were going home as if we'd just been relegated to the Conference.

I must admit I've always had a bit of a Bee in my bonnet (if you'll excuse the pun) about sendings-off. How many times do you hear a commentator argue that the referee has ruined a game by producing a red card ? In my opinion it's often the very opposite. There nothing like a player being sent for an early bath to galvanize the remaining twenty-one left on the park, not to mention those on the terraces watching. Many a boring contest I've seen come to life at the production of red.

Some twenty years on Elleray's performance that day is still talked about by Orient veterans over pint or six, and it's fair to say good as the 4–2 victory was without our friend in black's performance, that afternoon would have been largely forgotten by now.

Even at the time O's boss Peter Eustace said the thing that would remain in people's memories were the last few minutes when there had been 'a free for all'. He continued, 'We all had a part to play in that, but I think that the referee has got to hold his hand up and realize he played a part in it as well'.

Unsurprisingly Orient appealed against Achampong's red card, and unsurprisingly the F.A. turned down the appeal. Said managing director Frank Clark, 'Kenny was cut off at the knees by an horrendous tackle and got punched in the face. He did hardly anything. He made an angry tackle, and he got sent off. Having watched it on video it was incredible.' Cheekily Frank said he was going to send a video of the match to Elleray.

On the day our biggest home crowd of the season had seen us climb up to seventh, while Brentford slipped down to second behind West Bromwich.

Whether it was coincidence or not it was many years before Elleray refereed another game at Brisbane Road. On that day however back in 1992 he certainly wrote himself into Orient folk-lore.

Leyton Orient: Turner, Howard, Hackett, Whitbread (Burnett), Day, Otto, Achampong, Castle, Cooper, Nugent (Jones), Berry
Goals: Berry (6n, 20n), Castle (47s), Jones (77s).

Brentford: Benstead, Bates, Rostron (Manuel), Millen, Evans, Ratcliffe, Sealy, Godfrey (Holdsworth), Luscombe, Smillie, Buckle.
Goals: Luscombe (12s, 31s).

Star Man: Greg Berry.
Attendance: 7,383.

Cup Glory

Leyton Orient 4 Oldham Athletic 2
F.A. Cup Fourth Round Replay. 15 January 1992

Orient's brawl of the nineties against Brentford was followed just a few weeks later by arguably the club's best cup performance of the decade against Oldham.

Strange as it may seem now the Lancashire club at the time were one of the top dozen teams in the country. They had been F.A.Cup semi-finalists a couple of years earlier and had recently spent serious money bringing the likes of Graeme Sharp, Mike Milligan and Neil McDonald to Boundary Park.

A magnificent performance had seen us hold the Latics to a 1–1 draw on 4 January – Man of the Match Keith Day had given us the lead after 20 minutes and it took a late Sharp equalizer to take the tie to a second game some eleven days later.

I remember as I left the ground at the conclusion of the first game, the Boundary Road scoreboard had flashed up a latest cup score as Wrexham 0 Arsenal 1. Boarding the supporter's club coach, however we heard that Wrexham had scored two late goals and had beaten the Gunners 2–1.

This actually gutted me at the time, because not for the first time a magnificent cup performance by the O's was going to be largely overlooked by the media because of a result elsewhere.

The build up to the second match saw a proper rant by our Frankie Clark regarding the T.V coverage on the day of the replay.

'It's absolutely disgraceful that the Leeds v. Manchester United game is live on the BBC. The average fan is fed up with the thought of seeing these two teams in action again.'

With the O's unable to change the date of the match to Tuesday as West Ham were at home to Farnborough that night, our Frankie for some reason thought that the Orient faithful were not going to turn up at Brizzy Road but stay at home to see the Roses game. As it was a crowd of 10,056 was pretty decent at Leyton Stadium and they saw a cracker.

When Adams scored for Oldham after twenty minutes there appeared no hint of an upset. Then just before half-time a wonderful save by Chris Turner from a Henry header probably kept the O's in the match.

It was fourteen minutes into the second period however, that for the first and not the last time that night we saw some woeful Oldham defending as Lee Harvey's pretty tame cross from the left evaded everybody and slipped into the corner for an equalizer.

Then on 77 minutes Greg Berry left Marshall for dead, and played in Kevin Nugent to give us the lead.

It took a freak equalizer for the visitors to send the game into extra-time as Marshall's cross was intercepted by Keith Day but his clearance rebounded off Roger Palmer's back and into the net.

You would not have liked to have picked a winner going into extra-time but the game was decided by two more awful bits of defending by the First Division outfit.

Firstly Richard Jobson needlessly dragged down Andy Jones inside the box. Initially Steve Castle's penalty was brilliantly saved by Jon Hallworth, but the referee ordered a retake for encroaching by Oldham defenders and Castle made no mistake second time round.

Then a woeful back pass from Jobson gifted Kevin Nugent with a fourth and his second of the evening.

There was mass celebration at the final whistle, though I must admit I nipped off quick so as I could get home in time to see the highlights of our game on Match of the Day later.

The idiots that had stayed at home to watch the live game on the telly were treated to a dull 1–0 victory by Manchester United at Elland Road, while we had witnessed a Brizzy Road Cup Classic.

Tony Gubba commentating on our game for the Beeb commented that it had been a wonderful match without a single booking and Frankie must have had more than a small grin on his face, when reflecting on the decision to show the game at Leeds rather than ours as the night's main event earlier on the terrestrial channel.

On the match itself, manager Peter Eustace said afterwards: 'There were a lot of 19 and 20 year old legs out there. It was the biggest day of their footballing lives and they came through it well. That's the greatest occasion since I've been at the club. We played well, the team were magnificent.'

For the record we played Portsmouth away in the next round and lost a disappointing game 2–0, but nothing could take away the memory of the Oldham game. It had been a wonderful evening and with no other cup shocks that night we got more than our fair share of publicity in the dailies the next morning.

Leyton Orient: Turner, Howard, Hackett, Burnett, Day, Whitbread, Harvey (R. Taylor), Castle, Jones, Nugent, Berry.
Goals: Harvey (58s), Nugent (77s, 108s, Castle (95 pen. n).

Oldham Athletic: Hallworth, Fleming, Bernard, Henry, Barrett, Jobson, Adams, Marshall, Sharp, Palmer, Holden.
Goals: Adams (19s), Palmer (80n).

Star Man: Kevin Nugent.
Attendance: 10,056.

Game Thirty-seven

Daggers dumped in nine-goal thriller

Dagenham and Redbridge 4 Leyton Orient 5
F.A. Cup First Round. 14 November 1992

As the score rightly suggests, this was quite possibly the cup game of the decade. Nowadays we seem to draw the Daggers in cup competitions about four or five times a season, yet this game back in '92 was the first competitive meeting of east London's two major teams.

With the O's flying high at fourth in Division Two at the time, and Dagenham lying fifth in the Conference there was much excitement in anticipation of the first ever 'Jellied Eels Derby'.

The tie was given extra spice by the fact that D and R manager John Still had made one appearance for the O's in the sixties, before injury had forced him to retire from the game.

The match certainly did not disappoint. The game was but minutes old when a poor Chris Turner clearance gifted the home side the lead through former Orient apprentice Jason Broom and not long afterwards Steve Conner doubled the Dagenham lead. As any veteran O will tell you, watching our boys at the time going a couple of goals down nearly always meant game, set and match to the opposition, yet that afternoon at Victoria Road it was clear from the start that the standard of defending from both sides was – to put it kindly – a little below average, and so a two goal deficit was always going to be retrievable.

It did not come as a major surprise then, when after thirty-seven minutes Robert Taylor's cross was met at the far post by Oooh Terry Howard

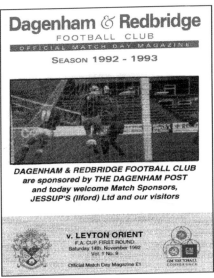

Dagenham & Redbridge
FOOTBALL CLUB
OFFICIAL MATCH DAY MAGAZINE

SEASON 1992 - 1993

DAGENHAM & REDBRIDGE FOOTBALL CLUB
are sponsored by THE DAGENHAM POST
and today welcome Match Sponsors,
JESSUP'S (Ilford) Ltd and our visitors

v. LEYTON ORIENT
F.A. CUP FIRST ROUND
Saturday 14th November 1992
Vol. 1 No. 9
Official Match Day Magazine £1

to give the visiting fans who had made the short journey more than a flicker of hope.

It took just three minutes for the two goal advantage to be restored however as Cavell set up Gary Butterworth for the Conference side.

Perhaps the games critical moment then came on the stroke of half-time. The linesman wrongly flagged for a corner kick to the Orient, when a goal-kick would have been the correct decision. Adrian Whitbread picked up the debris from the resulting Kevin Hales corner to crucially reduce the deficit to just one at the interval.

Taking my place in the long queue at the toilet (remember thinking at the time how lucky I was I did not have to put up with Vauxhall Conference loos every week) the general feeling amongst the O's contingent was that we would go on to win the match quite easily.

Indeed whilst not an earth shattering performance, we certainly turned on the heat in the early stages of the second period and it came as no surprise when a Simon Livett free-kick was met by Mark Cooper to give us an equalizer after 50 minutes. And twenty minutes later an almost identical goal gave us a 4–3 lead and eight minutes later yet another Livett free-kick was pushed on to the bar by 'keeper McKenna only for O's substitute Andy Jones to knock in our fifth.

Lots of credit had to be given to the Daggers on the day however, and within seconds of our last goal Paul Cavell – arguably the best forward on show on the day – burst through to set up a tense final ten.

Indeed if the non-league side had scored a fifth and taken it to a replay, it had been such a thrilling afternoon I don't think any O present would have complained too much.

The final score remained 5–4 however and as so often happened in those days we were given a scare by a non-league team yet survived. VS Rugby, Slough and Woodford had all taken us close in the greatest-cup-competition-in-the-world but some how or other we always seemed to come through.

After the game O's boss Peter Eustace said: 'I'm very relieved. But our goals showed our quality.'

An excited John Still said: 'That's the best performance I've ever seen in fourteen years as a manager. I've no complaints, I couldn't ask for any more of my players.'

We drew Reading away in the next round which gave us the novelty of a Saturday night game live on Sky. We lost a poor match 3–0, with Terry Howard commenting in his regular column in the local paper, saying that the most disappointing thing about the evening was that he was unable to spend his customary Saturday night at Walthamstow dogs.

Leyton Orient: Turner, Bellamy, Howard, Hales (Jones), Kitchen, Whitbread, Taylor, Achampong, Livett, Ryan, Cooper.
Goals: Howard (37), Whitbread (46), Cooper (50 and 70), Jones (78).

Dagenham and Redbridge: McKenna, Shirtliff (Kimble), Watts, Pamphlett, Conner, Broom, Owers (Georgiou), Butterworth, Cavell, Nuttell, Blackford.
Goals: Broom (3), Conner (26), Butterworth (41), Cavell (80).

Star Man: Simon Livett.
Attendance: 5,300

Game Thirty-eight

How's that?

Leyton Orient 5 Mansfield Town 1
League Division 2. 28 November 1992

Terry Howard was a really popular player at Brisbane Road and at our level a very good one, too. His record of 327 league games for the O's puts him fifth in the all time appearance list, and his tally of 35 goals when he played the majority of his matches in defence was to say the least admirable.

Yet for all this he will probably best be remembered in the football world as the player who got fired by his manager during a game at half-time. John Sitton was the boss, the game was Blackpool at home in the 1994–95 season, and the reason the world found out was because the cameras were in the dressing room at Brisbane Road, filming for the infamous 'Club for a Fiver' documentary.

He left us with some great memories as an O, however – Ooh Terry was on the pitch for every minute of all 61 games during the promotion season of 1988–89 and was a key member of the side that year. The fact that you could see him in an Orient shirt on a Saturday afternoon, then catch up with him

at Walthamstow dogs in the evening enhanced his popularity at Brizzy Road.

His greatest hour came with this match against Mansfield Town in the early nineties when he bagged a hat-trick.

Our start to the 92–93 season had been very good, entirely due to our home form. Going into this match against the Stags we had won eight and drawn one of our nine games in Leyton and were sitting fifth in the league.

Manager Peter Eustace had not been happy at all about events the week before however, when we had lost 3–1 at Wigan and had ordered four of the side including Howard, that played in that game to turn out for the reserves in mid-week.

It was only the second outing Howard had ever had for our second eleven, but it was clearly the kick up the backside that he needed. He was named in the eleven for the Mansfield game and Eustace recalled Paul Heald into the side after our 'keeper had been away training with Leeds.

The match started very open and the visitors had a couple of early chances when they could easily have found themselves in front. The O's first meaningful effort ironically came from Terry Howard, when our man powered a low free-kick through the Mansfield defensive wall after 17 minutes and Town 'keeper Jason Pearcey saved at the second attempt.

The O's had been playing a 'diamond formation' all season, which certainly at home had been very successful, with Kevin Hales playing as a sweeper and Howard pushed up into a mid-field role.

After 22 minutes the O's got the breakthrough that they had been starting to threaten. Simon Livett and Gary Bellamy combined to set up Robert Taylor to head home his ninth goal of the season.

Following this however Mansfield had their best spell of the entire game and twice almost equalized. First Steve Spooner burst through and rounded Paul Heald but the Mansfield midfield man was thwarted by a combination of Adrian Whitbread and Kevin Hales. Then Spooner had another opportunity, but this time Heald made a fine save.

After 38 minutes however Orient doubled their lead and Howard opened his account for the day. Kenny Achampong was causing all kinds of problems to the Town defence and it was his pace that created a shooting opportunity for Howard who volleyed past Pearcey.

Then just before half-time some more excellent work from Achampong resulted in a fine cross which Howard met with a magnificent diving header to make it 3–0. He said afterwards that it was only the second goal he had ever scored with his head, indeed I remember everybody was quite stunned on the Brizzy terraces when we saw what had happened.

After the break the O's continued to attack and made it four just six minutes after the restart when Mark Cooper seized the ball on the rebound and fired home, after Robert Taylor's initial header had come back off the post.

In fairness to Mansfield they kept trying to come forward and pulled a goal back after 68 minutes through Gary Ford, but they continued to be grateful to goalkeeper Jason Pearcey for keeping the score down, despite Orient's domination.

A fifth for us always looked on the cards however and it finally came after 86 minutes. Yet more good work from Kenny Achampong saw our midfielder brought down in the box, resulting in a penalty for the home side.

When the referee pointed to the spot, I remember the crowd, myself included, shouting for 'Ooh Terry' to take the kick so as he could go home with the match-ball, indeed I think regular taker Kevin Hales knew it was more than his life was worth to take the kick himself as we had the game won.

Howard duly converted and celebrated wildly, as indeed we all did on the terraces, delighted to witness a first Orient hat-trick of the season, and from an unlikely source at that.

He nearly snatched a fourth in injury time but his strike this time hit the underside of the bar.

Said assistant manager Chris Turner afterwards: 'It was important we won the game today and the crowd got right behind us. We are still trying to perfect the diamond formation and Kevin Hales played an important, but different role today. He is an experienced and skilful player, who can fit into the formation well. We have to be pleased with our performance.'

Said our Terry: 'Although the headed goal brought me the greatest joy from my hat-trick the penalty strike was a great feeling because it was my first goal from the spot in 12 years. I missed a penalty in an important cup final and vowed never to take one again.'

It had been a fine performance from the O's, Mansfield had created some chances but 5–1 did not flatter us in any way.

We moved up to second in the league and our home record was the best in the country. It was certainly good to be watching football at Brisbane Road at the time.

Leyton Orient: Heald, Bellamy, Howard, Hales, Kitchen (Carter 83), Whitbread, Taylor, Achampong, Warren, Livett, Cooper.
Goals: Taylor (22s), Howard (36s, 44s, 86s pen.) Cooper (51s).

Mansfield Town: Pearcey, Parkin (Gray 46), With, Holland, Walker, Spooner, Ford, Castledine (Noteman 62), Stant, Wilkinson, Fairclough.
Goal: Ford (68n).

Star Man: (Ooh) Terry Howard.
Attendance: 4,557.

Game Thirty-nine

Away The Lads! (Finally)

Northampton Town 1 Leyton Orient 2
Football League Division 3. 12 September 1995

When the O's defeated Hull City 1–0 away on 31 October 1993, no-one in their wildest nightmares would have imagined that it would be nearly two years before we were to register another success on the road in a league match.

In the middle of the barren run of course was the infamous 1994–95 season which produced an away record of played 23, won 0, drew 2, lost 21 with a monumental nine goals scored.

We all knew towards the latter stages of the run that when we did finally get that elusive victory it would be a moment to be remembered in our careers supporting the Orient, and that certainly proved correct, with this Tuesday evening win at the Cobblers Stadium breaking the seemingly never-ending sequence.

Over five-hundred O's had made the trip up to the semi-north, more than would normally be expected to for a not-too-local midweek match, but many were attracted by the prospect of a new ground – it was the first time we had played at Northampton's Sixfield Stadium – and the fact that we had not made a bad start to the season in our new, lower Division.

Even Mr Hearn, our new man in charge, had made the trip.

In fact the game saw a really good performance from the team with Ian Hendon and Colin West in particular outstanding for ninety minutes. We were indeed unlucky to go a goal down after thirty-eight when a Gareth Williams strike skimmed of O's defender Alan McCarthy's backside into the net.

1–0 down at the interval, the three words on everybody's lips in the queue for half-time burgers were 'same old story'.

Just three minutes into the second half however, the game changed from an unlikely source. A grass-cutting free-kick on the edge of the area from defender Ian Hendon found its way through the wall and into the bottom corner for 1–1.

It was Hendo's first goal for two years. Heaven only knows what he was doing taking the free-kick. He explained afterwards 'I've been messing around on the training ground with them and a couple had gone in. That goal's my quota for the season.'

In fact he did score one more time in 1995–96, at Torquay in January.

Although we continued to look the better side after the equalizer, particularly after Joe Baker had come on as substitute towards the end, it looked as though we were going to have to settle for a draw as the final whistle got ever nearer.

Then just before the end Hendon looped over a cross to Shaun Brooks who volleyed back into the area, where Alex Inglethorpe lunged in for the winner right in front of the win-starved travelling contingent. A bit untidy but did we care. Ecstasy ensued amongst the away support.

Only seconds remained and surely even Leyton Orient could not blow this one.

Sure enough the final whistle was blown and jubilation engulfed one stand behind the goal. There was a pitch invasion from the fans, and a mini lap of honour from the players.

What I remember most was the sheer bewilderment of the Northampton stewards. They could not understand how what looked to them like a routine 2–1 away win against not even local rivals could be greeted with such hysteria by the visiting hoards.

The game had certainly brought the best out of the players, the fans and of course Barry Hearn.

The great man was on top form after the first away win under his reign: 'That was marvellous. It was like a European Cup Final out there and great for the fans. Never mind taking drugs, just come and watch the Orient.'

It was for sure a wonderful evening. Certainly one of the nights of the nineties. The three home stands had long since been deserted while we were still there partying. And we all knew, of course that with the monkey finally off our back victories away from home would come two-a-penny from now on.

Well actually not. Our next away win remarkably enough was again at the home of the Cobblers on 10 September 1996, two days short of a year later.

Northampton Town: Woodman, Norton, Hughes, Grayson, Warburton, Sampson, Deer, Williams (Beckford), White, Burns, Colkin (Thompson),
Goal: Williams (37).

Leyton Orient: Caldwell, Stanislaus, Bellamy, McCarthy, Hendon, Brooks, Cockerill, Chapman, Kelly (Baker), Inglethorpe, West.
Goals: Hendon (48), Inglethorpe (90).

Star Man: Ian Hendon.
Attendance: 5,072.

Game Forty

O's Seaside Special

Brighton and Hove Albion 4 Leyton Orient 4
Football League Division 3. 8 March 1997

Now this really was a game and a half. It was an afternoon that had everything. Eight goals, umpteen chances, dodgy decisions, a sending off, cautions a plenty and a pitch invasion.

Bazza Hearn ranked the match alongside some of his all time sporting classics. 'It was the most amazing ninety minutes of football I've ever seen in my life', was the great man's verdict.

The league table before kick-off highlighted the importance of the match. Brighton were the 92nd club and in grave danger of going out of the league, while the O's were just seven places and nine points above them and by no means safe from relegation.

Ray Wilkins had joined Orient on a months contract a couple of weeks before, meaning that with Peter Shilton and Alvin Martin also in our squad we had more England caps than any other side in the country.

9,298, the divisions biggest crowd of the season, packed the Goldstone Ground delaying kick-off some five minutes and the atmosphere from the start was fierce to say the least.

With just five minutes on the clock a Danny Chapman mis-kick let in Craig Maskell to gift Brighton the advantage. The same player – who was to appear for the O's in the play-off final at Wembley a couple of years later – doubled the lead just two minutes later to put the east Londoners under considerable pressure.

Before half-time Brighton's Paul McDonald had what seemed a valid appeal for a penalty turned down, but at the break at 2–0 down things appeared grim for the O's.

As the game restarted, however, there followed twelve remarkable minutes during which time the two goal deficit was turned into a 3–2 score line. Carl Griffiths – who had re-signed permanently for us only the day before – ghosted in at the near post to pull one back just two minutes after the restart, Alex

Inglethorpe then glanced home a Justin Channing cross to level, and Griff again pounced to latch home a ball from Joe Baker and the O's amazingly had the lead.

It was never going to be the end of the goals, however and just a couple of minutes later Ian Baird headed home only for referee Frazer Stretton to disallow for a push.

The same player then had a carbon copy effort find its way into the back of the net and this time the goal was allowed to stand.

Amongst all this Tommy Taylor had wound up the home fans by refusing to throw the ball back at a Brighton throw, setting the scene for the mayhem that was to follow in the seventy-fifth minute.

With the game at 3–3 an Inglethorpe through ball set up Scott McGleish and the O's man slotted home to once again give us the lead.

All this proved too much for one Seagull who invaded the pitch and attacked Scotty. Two more home fans followed, one heading for the man in black before a wonderful tackle from Wilkins brought the intruder down. Police and the stewards eventually restored order dragging the 'fans' away. Four were arrested as the game was held up for four minutes.

The game restarted at 4–3 but when Danny Chapman slid in to bring down Maskell inside the box, a clearly flustered Stretton waved for a corner only to change his mind and point to the spot.

In the jostling on the edge of the box before the kick was taken Mark Warren clashed with Baird and the O's man got a second yellow resulting in an early shower.

McDonald scored the penalty with ten minutes to go during which time the Seagulls could easily have snatched a winner against the ten men O's – Danny Chapman clearing off the line and Maskell shooting into the side netting at the death.

At just before 5 o'clock the final whistle sounded at 4–4 and everyone paused to get their breath back.

Not surprisingly after such an afternoon a lot of people had a lot to say after the game.

Tommy Taylor – never one to sit on the fence – said of Brighton and the pitch invasion: 'If I was at the FA I would kick them out of the league'.

When pressed about the match he was unbelievably scathing about poor old Danny Chapman: 'Danny's had a hat-trick, they might as well give him the matchball as he has given three goals away. He has had a stinker.'

Last time Ray Wilkins had played against Brighton it was for Manchester United in the FA Cup Final replay and he had scored a cracker in the 4–0 win. This time things were a little different.

Said the man of the trouble ; 'One lad was about to banjo the referee so I stepped in front of him. After the match the referee thanked me. It's an unsavoury incident and it took the gloss off and exciting game of football.'

It had indeed been a day to remember. Brighton, who had already had two points taken away earlier in the season for a pitch invasion were lucky to escape a further deduction. This proved crucial looking at the final league table, with the Seagulls avoiding relegation to the Conference by goal difference as Hereford went down instead.

Wilkin's tackle on the fan proved to be the only real contribution the England international made in his one month at the club and at the end of his short contract he was not retained.

At least he can look back at his spell at the club (as I'm sure he often does) and reflect that he played a part in one of the all time great Orient matches.

Brighton and Hove Albion: Rust, Humphreys (Johnson), Tuck, Reinelt, Allan, Hobson, Storer, Peake, Baird, Maskell, McDonald.
Goals: Maskell (5 and 7), Baird (74), McDonald (85 pen.).

Leyton Orient: Weaver, Channing, Naylor, Chapman, Warren, Wilkins (Ling), Griffiths (Hanson), Inglethorpe, McGleish, Baker (McCarthy)
Goals: Griffiths (47 and 57), Inglethorpe (50), McGleish (75).

Star Man: Carl Griffiths.
Attendance: 9,298.

Game Forty-one

Eight-on Orient (take three)

Leyton Orient 8 Doncaster Rovers 0
Football League Division 3. 28 December 1997

Strange one this one. We equalled our best ever win, yet the mood amongst the Orient fans coming away from Brizzy that day was summed up by the headline in the local *Recorder* the following week: 'O's disappoint in eight goal anticlimax.'

The fact was that with just 64 minutes played the home team were eight up against a team nine points adrift at the bottom of the league, who had a seventeen-year-old goalkeeper making his debut, and it looked a certainty that Oriental all-time goalscoring feats were about to be superseded that winter's afternoon.

In the event Conference bound Rovers managed to keep a clean sheet for the remaining 26 minutes and we all went home a little frustrated.

All of our goals had been crammed into a forty-four minute spell in the middle of the game. It had been twenty minutes before an Alex Inglethorpe strike had been parried by rookie 'keeper Gary Hoggeth into the path of Carl Griffith to give us the lead.

Inglethorpe then scored the second when his shot was wickedly deflected over a helpless custodian and Dean Smith made it three from the spot after Martin Ling had been brought down.

When Tony Richards made it four just before the break there had been three goals in just five minutes.

Rovers made three substitutions at the interval, though even if they had let the replaced players remain on the turf it would have been debatable whether they would have been able to get back into the game.

Griffiths added two more in the ten minutes after the re-start only to be rewarded by being taken off, while Richards suffered the same fate after scoring his second. Sub Joe Baker scored the eighth, but our new three-man strike force of Harris, Baker and Simpson were actually pretty woeful and could not inflict further pain on the Yorkshire side.

The mood in the O's camp could be gauged by the post match interviews. A clearly underwhelmed Griff – he had been sub for the previous few games and was obviously not too impressed at having been taken off – said merely: 'It's nice to be back in the first team and get three points'.

Coach Paul Clark was actually highly critical of his player's performance: 'it was good enough to beat Doncaster, with all due respect to them, but probably not good enough to have beaten other teams.'

He said the team had been given a right rollicking at half-time, despite being four up.

Indeed the team that season were not really good enough and we finished a disappointing eleventh. Doncaster duly took their place in the Conference, though they resurrected themselves in the years that followed and seeing the League tables these days they can look back and laugh at that afternoon at Brizzy Road back in '97.

Leyton Orient: Hyde, Channing, Naylor, Smith, Hicks, Clark, Ling, Joseph, Griffiths (Harris), Richards (Baker), Inglethorpe (Simpson)
Goals: Griffiths (20n, 48s, 55s), Inglethorpe (40n), Smith (43 pen. n), Richards (45n, 59s), Baker (64s).

Doncaster Rovers: Hoggeth, Sanders (Pemberton), Smith, Hawthorne, Gore, Mike, Esdaille, Warren, Halliwell (Ramsay), Moncrieffe (Messer), Dobbin.

Star Man: Carl Griffiths.
Attendance: 4,437

Game Forty-two

Taylor made for Wembley

**Rotherham United 0 Leyton Orient 0 (after extra-time)
Leyton Orient win 4–2 on penalties. Division 3 Play-off Semi-final
Second Leg. 19 May 1999**

This was a game that was a million miles away from being a classic, yet with the prize at the end being a first ever trip to see the O's play at Wembley who cared.

The first leg of the play-off semi at Brisbane Road had been built up by Bazza as 'our biggest day in a decade' and that game too was dire, ending goalless. Our largest crowd of the season 9,419 had crammed into our Stadium for a Sunday lunchtime kick-off but in truth there would have been more fun to be had staying at home cooking the Sunday roast that day.

For the second meeting 2,000 O's made their way up north to be part of a crowd of 9,529 at Millmoor, so many that kick-off was delayed some fifteen minutes.

Some bright spark at Rotherham had the bright idea of putting Millers fans who could not be fitted into the home section in with the travelling contingent causing more than a little disruption before the game had started.

Once matters in the stands had been sorted out, those present were treated to a game in truth only slightly better than the first. Chances once more were rare as the tension clearly got to those on the park.

The nearest there came to a goal was in the 97th minute of normal time when a Rotherham free-kick on the edge of the area was veered past the Orient wall, only for Scott Barrett to tip away magnificently at full stretch, thus ensuring extra-time.

So late in the game was this that there was not even time for the home team to take what would have been their first corner of the evening.

Nothing at all happened in the half-hour of extra-time, so it was left to the penalty shoot-out to produce more action and talking points than the 210 minutes of football in the two games had done.

It was decided the shoot-out would take place in front of the home fans at the Tivoli End of the ground, though possibly crucially the O's were to take the first spot kick.

Manager Tommy Taylor confessed afterwards, perhaps surprisingly, that our players had not practiced penalties in the build up to the match.

'Five put their hands up to take them and they took them' he said, although in the end fifth choice Simon Clark was not required to take one. 'I was a bit surprised that one player did not want to take one, Amara Simba,' he added.

Dean Smith took our first and smashed it high into the net for 1–0. Thompson scored to level, then Martin Ling put his effort to the left of Pollitt for 2–1.

Then came the major point of controversy in the whole tie. With Andy Roscoe preparing to take the Miller's second kick referee Clive Wilkes was called away by the fourth official to marshall a dispute with Tommy Taylor.

Roscoe was forced to wait what at the time seemed an eternity while T.T. was ushered away from the playing area. Tommy said afterwards he had gone onto the pitch with his physio Tony Flynn to treat the injured Alex Inglthorpe. In truth this was a pretty lame excuse and our Tom was rightly ticked off by the FA in the days after the game.

Not surprisingly after the long delay Roscoe hit his spot kick too close to Barrett who was able to palm the ball away.

Substitute Dave Morrison made it 3–1, hitting his shot high to Pollitt's left. Paul Hurst then struck Rotherham's fourth effort only to see our Scott save superbly leaving Matt Lockwood with the chance to score and send us to Wembley.

Our Matt stepped up and left foot reliable as ever found the bottom corner and we had made it to the final.

Some of Rotherham's 'fans' invaded the turf and Locky got a nice kick from one of them as way of a congratulation, but even this was quickly forgotten by all on a night to remember.

It had certainly been a long one, but as we boarded our coaches to take us back to east London no one cared that it would be near dawn when we would arrive home.

We all looked forward to a memorable day out in front of the Twin Towers. Indeed it would be nice to have had the Play-off final as one of the 60 golden games, but it was not to be.

Sadly though as good as the build-up was to the Scunthorpe encounter it was just a shame the man in black had to spoil it all by blowing the whistle to start the match at 3 o'clock that afternoon. In truth we conceded after just six minutes and never really got going all game, losing 1–0. We were not helped, it has to be said by some strange selection choices by Mr Taylor on the big day.

Still nothing will ever take away the memory of the penalty shoot out and the aftermath on one of the O's glory nights at Rotherham that May evening in 1999.

Rotherham United: Pollitt, Vartry, Hurst, Thompson, Knill (Williams), Dillon, Fortune-West, Warne, Roscoe.

Leyton Orient: Barrett, Stimson (Hicks), Lockwood, Smith, Joseph, Clark, Ling, Richards (Morrison) Watts (Inglethorpe), Simba, Beal.

Star Man: Scott Barrett.
Attendance: 9,529.

A Corner Turned

Chester City 1 Leyton Orient 5
Football League Division 3. 28 December 1999

This was our final game of the nineties, and in fact there is a valid argument to call it the most important match of the decade.

Defeat would have left the O's entering the year 2000 the ninety-second team in the Football League, five points adrift of the rest and staring the Conference full on.

Travelling up to the North West that day the omens were not good.

We had not scored in five league matches, and had only netted twice in ten. An Orient striker had not found the back of the net in over two months. Two days previous to the match, we had been beaten at home 1–0 by Swansea.

We were at the bottom of the league, with Chester the nearest club to us at the time two points better off.

Remarkably though the afternoon turned out to be something of a thrashing for the O's.

From the eighth minute when Steve Watts gave us the lead, following a Lockwood/Griffiths sortie down the left there was only going to be one winner at the Deva Stadium that day.

We had to wait a little while for our second but it came seven minutes before the break when Watts was upended by Matthew Woods, giving Carl Griffiths the chance to double our lead from the spot. Griff had been resigned by the O's in the middle of December, just nine months after he had gone to Port Vale and he duly obliged with his first penalty success of the afternoon.

Indeed just six minutes after the restart he was given another chance to practice his spot-kick taking skills – this time Kwame Ampadu was upended by Darren Moss in the area.

The Welshman duly made it 3–0. In fact Carl could easily have had a hat-trick of penalties in just 23 minutes when Ahmet Brkovic was floored by

Brown in a one on one, but the ball broke to Griffiths who completed his hat-trick without the need for another effort from twelve yards.

At 4–0 the game was well and truly over as a contest and Griff was duly substituted.

Needless to say there was a great reception from those who had ventured up from east London that afternoon.

He had done his popularity with us O's no harm at all by appearing on the away terrace at Rotherham at the second leg of the Play-off semi-final some months previous, and a hat-trick in such a critical game here enhanced it even more.

Chester pulled back a consolation, but Orient's highly satisfactory afternoon was completed when substitute striker Iyseden Christie scored his first goal for the Club, heading home a Matt Lockwood cross to ensure a 5–1 score line.

The truth of the afternoon was that the result was probably more down to an inexperienced Chester sides incompetence rather than a Barcelona like performance from the O's but no matter we had secured a much needed win, and in the process had scored five away from home for the first time in a league match for thirty-five years.

The game certainly proved a turning point. It was the start of a run where we collected twenty points from eight games to see us to safety, and we ended the season thirteen clear of Chester who unsurprisingly went down to the Conference.

Upon entering the year 2000, although no-one knew how the next decade would pan out, there was a general feeling around Brisbane Road that it surely could not be any worse than the nineties, and as events turned out it certainly wasn't.

Chester City: Brown, Moss, Doughty, Eve, Spooner, Woods, Nash, Richardson (Reid), Beckett, Laird (Wright), Fisher.
Goal: Wright (66).

Leyton Orient: Barrett, Smith, Clark, Downer, M. Joseph, Walschaerts, Brkovic, Ampudu, Lockwood, Griffiths (Christie), Watts (Rowbottom).
Goals: Watts (8), Griffiths (38 pen, 50 pen, 61), Christie (69).

Star Man: Carl Griffiths.
Attendance: 3,160.

Magpie's millionaires matched at the Matchroom

Leyton Orient 1 Newcastle United 1
Worthington Cup Second Round. Second Leg. 26 September 2000
(Newcastle won 3–1 on aggregate)

As I've mentioned before, one of the great mysteries about supporting Leyton Orient for as long as many of us have, is why their record in the League Cup, (in what ever disguise the competition has taken over the years), has always been so poor.

Given that the FA Cup has given us so many memorable moments over the years – from Fairbrother in '72 through to Tehoue in '11 – it's rather strange that the country's second most important Cup competition simply has not.

Ok so it's an event that we are never going to win, but amazingly the 2011–2012 season saw the first time in twenty years that we were still in it come the Third Round. Unlike the FA Cup, giant-killings and upsets and indeed merely stirring performances in the League Cup, have been few and far between for the O's since its inception. The two matches against Newcastle in 2000, especially the second one however, were an exception to the rule.

In the first game 37,284 had packed St. James' Park, such was the pulling power of the Orient, a team some 69 places lower than the Toon in the League, and our boys gave a highly commendable account of themselves. Until Gary Speed's goal thirteen minutes from time which made it 2–0, we were still very much in the game and could easily have sneaked a draw.

Bobby Robson had played a full strength team for Newcastle in the first leg, and gave the O's a nice tribute afterwards by saying: 'I was hoping to rest five or six players for the second leg. I don't think I can do that now.'

Some 800 of us had made the trip up the A1, but my overriding memory from the evening was the shattering climb up seven levels to get to the away supporters seats behind a corner flag.

Somebody told me that from the furthest seat in our stand to the far corner flag it was actually a quarter of a mile. You simply could not pick out which player was which at the opposite goal and it did not help that the Geordies shirts were striped, making it almost impossible to read the numbers on their backs.

It was my fourth visit to St. James' park to cheer on the O's and we've now lost every game, but at least on the previous three occasions I'd actually been able to see all the action, without at times having to guess what was happening down the other end of the ground.

The O's beat Lincoln 1–0 at Brizzy Road on the Saturday after the away leg, and 9,522 welcomed the north-easterners to London the following Tuesday for the tie's conclusion.

Somewhat surprisingly Orient boss Tommy Taylor, who was celebrating his 49th birthday, left out Carl Griffiths, Ahmet Brkovic and John Martin, bringing in Jason Brissett, Steve Watts and Iyesden Christie as replacements, though the new players it has to be said all performed admirably on the night.

Initially the O's were somewhat overawed in the second game – Robert Lee, who had learned his footy up the road in east London's Echo League, hit a thunderous drive in the first minute which Ashley Bayes tipped against the inside of the post, then Alan Shearer's 15th minute free-kick again saw the Brisbane Road woodwork tested.

The O's gradually got themselves into the contest however, so that it came as a big disappointment when United's Andy Griffin got to the byline on the right after 32 minutes and crossed for Kevin Gallacher to score at the far post.

The east Londoners did not let their heads drop however, and it came as no surprise when with the last kick of the first half Steve Watts flicked in his first goal of the season from Richard Garcia's low cross.

The second half was proving quite even and boldly T.T. brought on young forwards Jay Murray and Jabo Ibehre towards the end to try to snatch the two goals that could have taken the tie into extra-time.

Indeed Jabo could easily have won a penalty as he rounded Shay Given and was brought down, while Murray brought a fine save out of the 'keeper after a storming run from his own half.

Victory on the night was a whisker away when David McGee's last minute header from Matt Lockwood's corner clipped the cross-bar, but even so a 1–1 draw against a team costing £42 million was for sure a moral victory on the night for our boys.

Much credit had to be given to Dean Smith who kept Alan Shearer goalless for 180 minutes over the two ties, and he was rewarded with the England centre-forward's shirt after the second encounter.

Said Bobby Robson after the tie: 'Over the two matches they (Orient) did very well and gave us a game. One goal was a poor reward for our endeavour but you've got to give them credit for a workmanlike performance. They were never afraid of us and never stopped working.'

Robson, of course was an amazing football man. I remember just before the end of the second game after we had hit the cross-bar he was running up and down the touchline screaming and gesticulating wildly at his players, furious they had nearly conceded, even though it would have made little difference to the tie's final result.

The ultimate professional, I would imagine a few of the Toon defenders got a bit of a roasting when they got back to the dressing room after the game.

In true Orient tradition we came back down to earth with a bang the following Saturday, losing 2–0 to Brighton at the Withdean with a performance a million miles away from the two encounters of the Geordie kind.

Leyton Orient: Bayes, Joseph, Smith, McGee, Harris, Christie (Murray 74), Garcia, Walschaerts, Watts (Downer 81), Brissett (Ibhere 64). Goal: Watts(45s).

Newcastle United: Given, Griffin, Domi, Charvet, Hughes, Lee, Dyer, Cort (Cordone), Shearer, Gallagher (Solano), Speed. Goal: Gallagher (32n).

Star Man: Dean Smith. Attendance: 9,522.

Tigers tamed by Matt's magic

Leyton Orient 2 Hull City 0
Division 3 Play-off Semi-final. Second Leg. 16 May 2001
(Leyton Orient won 2–1 on aggregate)

If our general record in the League Cup over the years can best be described as pants, then the same can certainly not be levelled at our participation in play-off semi-finals. Played 3 Won 3 is a nice one to have on your club's C.V. even if a 33% success rate when it comes to the final could maybe be improved upon.

I love the play-offs. You really do wonder these days how we ever lived without them. Your club can be languishing in the bottom four in any league well into the season, yet with a decent run you can still get your team up there vying for promotion come May, thanks to the wonderful thing that is the play-offs.

Grumpy old man that I am, still consider footy was far better and more enjoyable to watch when I first started going many years ago than it is now, however the two changes for the better, in my opinion, have been the arrival of the play-offs and the introduction – thanks to Jimmy Hill let us not forget – of three points for a win.

When you only got two most teams used to go away and park nine or ten behind the ball knowing that a point for a 0–0 would be a fantastic result. Nowadays it's just not done.

Yes looking back, before the above two rule changes you wonder some seasons when you were mid-table come Christmas, why you ever bothered going to any games in the second half of the season , when there was absolutely sod all to play for.

Anyway back to this Brisbane Road classic from 2001, our last sortie into the play-offs and a never to be forgotten night in Leyton.

Unlike our previous two semi-finals play-off wise, on this occasion we were at home in the second leg and it was up to us to press forward to wipe out the one goal deficit we had succumbed to in the first leg.

The previous Sunday had seen a close match at Boothferry Park, the O's going down to a John Eyre goal in the second half.

It's fair to say we did not get the rub of the refereeing decisions that afternoon – Eyre admitted afterwards that he had used his arm in the build up to the goal, and we appeared to be denied a penalty when Scott Houghton's shot hit Mark Greaves on the arm, but we were still well and truly in the tie for the second encounter.

There was great anticipation pre-match for all O's, in my opinion the atmosphere generated before the game that night was one of the best ever at east London's premier football venue.

Nothing at Brisbane Road of course, will ever beat the atmosphere before the Aston Villa home game in May 1974 when a win would have taken us into the top Division. Thirty thousand were packed into the stadium that night, and with three sides standing the ground was full and rocking well over an hour before kick-off in '74, but the evening twenty seven years on certainly did it's best to rival that infamous occasion.

My first recollection of the Hull night was doing my usual and getting a big bag of chips from the wonderful chippy that used to be on the High Road, coming out of the shop to find I was surrounded by City fans who were being herded by the police from the tube station to the away end at the Winsor Road end of the ground.

Friendly enough they were however, even more so when they were offered a chip or two. In fact I actually had more trouble from the local boys in blue who seemed reluctant to let me leave the group of 100 or so they had surrounded, to let me take my place in the East Stand for the game.

I eventually made it though and settled down to watch what became a wonderful night's entertainment.

Predictably enough unlike the first-leg the O's were on the front foot from the start attempting to claw back the narrow deficit. It was a cagey affair from the off, with very few chances.

The breakthrough came just before the break. Their big man Kevin Francis, who had a bit of a history of doing well against us, wonderfully lost control of the ball in his own half for it to fall into Scott Houghton's path.

The Orient man's cross was magnificently met by Steve Watts for a stooping header past Paul Musselwhite to level the tie at 1–1.

Needless to say the goal totally changed the atmosphere at half-time amongst supporters and one would imagine in the dressing rooms too.

The O's continued to push forward after the break and we gradually got more and more on top. Wim Walschaerts and Steve Castle both came close and Matt Lockwood saw a thirty yarder saved by Musselwhite. That Locky effort however turned out to be just a 'sighter'. Soon afterwards, with seventy gone on the clock, the magical full-back picked up the ball just inside the Hull half, advanced a little before unleashing an unstoppable thirty-yarder into the top corner at the Coronation Gardens end of the ground. Three sides of the Stadium erupted. It was looking back, **the** moment of the noughties at Brisbane Road, indeed for me it took nearly ten years for a better one at the home of football to arrive with Tehoue's stunner against the Goons in 2011.

The result was that we were now 2–1 up and well and truly in the driving seat for a place in the Play-off Final at the Millennium.

Hull came forward, but never really seriously threatened Ashley Bayes in our goal. However the night just had one, what turned out to be serious downside In the 85th minute Steve Watts was given his marching orders for a second yellow card.

It was a stupid one too. He had raced fifty yards to lunge in totally unnecessarily to a Hull player, leaving the ref no option but to give him an early bath.

With our top scorer Carl Griffiths having also ridiculously got himself sent off at Mansfield for striking an opponent, it meant that our main two strikers were both suspended for the Play-off Final, which not surprisingly told in the end as we crashed out to Blackpool.

After the red card Hull tried to throw the kitchen sink at us but even with 'keeper Musselwhite up in our penalty area at the end of the game we held out and despite the Watts incident had still witnessed one of the glory nights at Leyton Stadium.

The players hung around the pitch at the end taking the cheers of the fans as we anticipated a first visit to the Millennium for the O's.

It was a truly wonderful evening – Brisbane Road announcer Andrew Buonocore said afterwards it was the best night of football he had known, though no-one knew if it was because of our victory or if it was because it was also the night Liverpool won the UEFA Cup beating Alkmar 5-4 (Buonocore having confessed to being a follower of the scousers for many years before taking the mike at Brizzy Road).

As it was the suspensions of Griffiths and Watts did prove crucial in the final so that while we went 2-1 up at one stage, as the players tired in the second period there was little to offer from the bench and we ended up losing 4-2 to Blackpool.

Nothing could ever take away however, the excitement of that May evening in Leyton.

Leyton Orient: Bayes, Joseph, Smith, Downer, Lockwood, McGee, Castle (Harris 67), Walschaerts, Houghton (Brkovic 88), Ibere (Tate 85), Watts.
Goals: Watts (44n), Lockwood (70s).

Hull City: Musselwhite, Edwoods, Whittle, Greaves, Holt (Philpott 38), Whitley, Atkins, Brabin, Matthews (Brown 70), Francis (Rowe 64), Eyre.

Star Man: Matt Lockwood.
Attendance: 9,419.

Game Forty-six

Pompey Chimed Out

Portsmouth 1 Leyton Orient 4
FA Cup Third Round. 5 January 2002

Now this really was a game and a half. Purely looking at League positions it could be argued that our victory over Premier League Fulham at Craven Cottage in the Third Round in 2006 was our best FA Cup performance of the decade, yet for various reasons this for me was the most enjoyable.

For starters I've always had a theory (probably dating back to the Chelsea game in '72) that the most pleasing matches are always those where you come from behind to win.

Also unlike the Fulham encounter, the Pompey result was totally unexpected as we had been playing very poorly in the league at the time.

And another difference from the Cottage afternoon was that most of the action – all five goals – took place down our end, in front of the O's masses gathered behind the goal.

It was, for sure Paul Brushes finest hour – or to be more precise 45 minutes, as we were one down at the interval – in his time as Orient manager, (although there was, to be honest very little in the way of competition for this accolade.)

Looking back now it was indeed a pretty strange match. At the start of the game we were awful. After seven minutes Nigel Quashie latched on to a Steve Lovell knock down to hit a twenty-five yard shot which cannoned off the bar.

Then just five minutes later we went a goal down. Courtney Pitt swung over a speculative cross from the left which appeared to be going straight to Scott Barrett in the O's goal. As he came out however, Dean Smith appeared from seemingly nowhere to nod the ball past his 'keeper and into the net.

It was for sure a pretty stupid goal to give away by Deano, inexcusable really for a player of his experience. Occurring right in front of me I remember there was absolutely no show of any emotion at all from our captain. He just turned expressionless and went back to take his place for the restart without a word to anyone.

Clearly he had the idea of just putting the mistake behind him, moving on and winning the game for the O's. And boy did his cunning plan work.

Not initially it has to be said. Nigel Quashie and Croat Robert Prosinecki continued to dominate midfield and Courtney Pitt was giving young full-back Chris Dorrian a torrid time down the wing. It needed a couple of good saves from Barrett and a bad miss from a header by Peter Crouch to keep us in the game, and at half-time we were desperately lucky to be just one down.

I recall trudging off to the loo which it has to be said was tiny for the amount of supporters in the away end. Topic of conversation amongst O's was divided between how badly we had played in the first half and just how bad the facilities were at a big club in the second tier of English Football.

There was certainly nothing to suggest at what we were about to witness in the next daft forty-five minutes of football.

At half-time Paul Brush had made one tactical change replacing the out-of-his-depth full back Dorrian with the more experienced Donny Barnard and this proved a good move as the threat of Pitt was virtually removed for the reminder of the afternoon.

As the players emerged for the second half the 1,000 or so O's gathered behind the goal welcomed the Japanese goalkeeper - and indeed captain – Yoshikatsu Kawaguchi to our end of the ground, though the way the first half had gone I think many of us considered he'd be mainly redundant in the second period. How wrong we were.

Within three minutes we manufactured a free-kick on the edge of the area. I recall watching the man from Japan standing right in front of me near the post, waving his hands frantically like a madman trying to line up a wall to cover any goal bound attempts.

Meanwhile Dean Smith quite unexpectedly suddenly unleashed to low shot into the opposite corner to where the stationary 'keeper was standing to make it 1–1, and the villain of the first period became the hero of the second.

Said Deano afterwards 'I saw the 'keeper at his post and the wall was still lining up, so I thought I'd take a chance'

Brush said 'I don't know why Smith took the free-kick but it changed the game.'

Indeed it did. Kawaguchi continued to look all at sea and was lucky to get away with dropping a Jeff Minton cross before helping to gift the O's a second after 66 minutes.

A long through ball from Andy Harris should not have presented the 'keeper with any problems but the man from Asia hesitated badly allowing Steve Watts to knock it past him and tap the ball into an empty net, to put us 2–1 up.

It was another very strange goal and once again shocking defending from the team 49 places above us in the League.

And things just got better and better.

After 77 minutes a long kick by Scott Barrett caused confusion and the ball broke to Wayne Gray who left footed magnificently into the bottom corner to give us a two goal advantage. In the context of the game with all of it's – shall we say – rather unorthodox goals it was weird to see what one would term a normal one.

By now the feeling on in our stand was one of stunned disbelief. Even the ritual of the half-time struggle for the toilet had just about been forgotten.

At 3–1 down many of the home fans started to disappear.

Paul Brush replaced Watts and Gray with Jabo Ibhere and Iyseden Christie just before the end with the game won, and the day was rounded off magnificently in injury time with an O's fourth.

Pompey appeared to have totally given up when a fine ball from Mikele Leigertwood found its way to an unmarked Jeff Minton on the left who crossed the ball past Kawaguchi to Christie.

The O's sub was making his first appearance after a 14 month lay-off through injury, and within minutes of coming on remarkably found himself with the ball at his feet looking at an empty net.

Such had been the nature of the game with so much strange stuff going on, it would have fitted into its ethos for Christie to miss.

In fact he did his best to do so, his effort just going in via the underside of the crossbar, but go in it did and we ended up 4–1 winners.

At the final whistle the players came over to us and there were the expected wild celebrations. Credit to the Pompey faithful who had stayed to the end and gave our boys a very generous round of applause as they finally left the pitch, and credit to the Pompey man behind the P.A. system who hilariously played 'We're on the road to nowhere' as their boys went back to the dressing room.

Talking to few of their supporters while on the way back to our coach they were actually quite happy that we had beaten them as they said it would mean the end for their manager Graham Rix and it would give them the opportunity to bring in Harry Rednapp who was at the club, as manager. This, in fact was exactly what did eventually happen.

I had no complaints about this. I'd never liked Rix since his goal against us for Arsenal in the Cup Semi in '78.

With no Premier teams falling to sides from the lower divisions this was the major cup shock of Third Round Saturday and so our game got heaps of coverage in the Sunday papers the next day.

Probably unsurprisingly a lot of the space was taken up by quotes from the irrepressible Bazza Hearn, who was on top form.

'This is an expensive hobby but it's days like today that makes you realize why you do it. The buzz is up there with anything I've done. To hear the home fans chanting our name at the end was special. You don't see boxing fans applauding the guy who's just knocked out their man.'

At the end of the day you could excuse the great man for feeling a little elated - his man Phil Taylor defeated Peter Manley 7–0 in the World Darts Championship final that evening to secure his eighth successive title in the event, so an 11–1 aggregate score marked a decent return that day for our Chairman.

It was certainly an amazing afternoon and we were rewarded with a lovely tie at Everton in the next round, where we far from disgraced ourselves going down 4–1. The Pompey game certainly gave everyone at the club a much needed lift at a time when we were really struggling on the park and it was hoped the result would see a change of fortunes in the league at the time.

We are though Leyton Orient.

The following Saturday we went to Carlisle and lost 6–1.

Portsmouth: Kawaguchi, Primus, Hiley (Crowe 80), Tiler, Harper, Quashie, O'Neil (Derry 70), Pitt, Prosinecki, Crouch, Lovell.
Goal: Smith (O.G. 12).

Leyton Orient: Barrett, Dorrien (Barnard 46), Smith, Leigertwood, Harris, McGee, Martin, Jones, Minton, Gray, (Ibhere 90), Watts (Christie 88).
Goals: Smith 48, Watts 66, Gray 77, Christie 90.

Star Man: Steve Watts.
Attendance: 12,936.

Game Forty-seven

Lee licks Lincoln

Lincoln City 3 Leyton Orient 4
League 2. 23 October 2004

Brushes torrid time as O's boss had come to an end in October 2002 and he had been replaced by Martin Ling, in true Orient tradition the Assistant Manager being made up to be the new man in charge.

Our fortunes had certainly improved under the new manager so that coming into this encounter in 2004 we were up to third in the bottom division and playing some entertaining football.

The 543 who had made their way up from Brizzy this afternoon were treated to a classic game with the O's three times going behind only to score the winner some thirty seconds from the end.

Striker Gary Alexander had been injured in the week ruling him out until the new year with ankle problems, but Lee Steele more than made up for Gazza's absence netting a memorable hat-trick in this Sincil Bank encounter.

Although much of the afternoon's defending from both teams left much to

be desired, it made for a highly entertaining affair.

A sign of things to come came after just two minutes when it needed a superb save from Lee Harrison to deny the Imp's Francis Green from scoring, but the let off was short lived with Gareth McAuley heading home unchallenged from a corner seconds later.

The response from our boys was excellent however and just eight minutes later Stuart Wardley headed against the bar, only for Steele to knock home the rebound from eight yards.

It took just three more minutes for Lincoln to regain the lead when our centre half Gabby Zakuani misjudged the bounce of the ball allowing Simon Yeo to slot past Harrison.

It was very nearly 3–1 soon after when a Francis Green cross took a deflection off Justin Miller, Harrison having to re-adjust to save low down.

The game had made a breathtaking start, though it calmed down for a short period before some fine work in midfield by Michael Simpson saw him play in Alexander's replacement Jabo Ibehere and the unmarked striker volleyed home from ten yards.

At 2–2 the first half drama still wasn't finished when just before the interval the O's 'keeper came rushing out of his area to collide with Martin Carruthers – many a ref may have sent our man off – but the man in black Anthony Leake decided a yellow was sufficient punishment much to the relief of all O's present.

It had been a frantic first period to say the least and the drama continued a plenty after the re-start.

Within three minutes Gareth McAuley for the second time in the match found himself unmarked and able to head home this time from a Kevin Sandwith free-kick.

At 3–2 down the game looked like it could be slipping away, so Ling replaced Carlisle and Wardley with Newey and Hunt with twenty minutes to go, and the changes had the desired effect as we dramatically turned thing round with two goals in the last twelve minutes.

With 78 on the clock a superb Matt Lockwood delivery from a free-kick saw probably the smallest man on the park Lee Steele rise superbly to glance a header into the net for the equalizer.

Credit to the O's who weren't content to sit back on their point and their continued pressure found it's reward in the last minute when Matt Lockwood managed some fine work in midfield before threading an inch perfect through ball to Steele who calmly chipped past Marriot to snatch all three points.

Needless to say Pandemonium broke out on the away bench and in the Orient stand as we had secured an unlikely and dramatic victory.

In fact the most dramatic reaction was surprisingly on 'Orient World' with the normally cool Matt Porter, now of course chief executive, going completely bananas at the winner's arrival.

The win took us up to second in the table and Lee Steele went top of the goalscorers list in League Two, a feat very few Orient strikers ever seem to have achieved over the years.

With things going really well under Martin Ling most O's were confident of the club gaining automatic promotion in 2004–05, or at the very least making the play-offs. Being Leyton Orient however, after the Lincoln game we won just one out of the next nine and ended the season in eleventh place.

**Lincoln City: Marriott, Sandwith, Morgan, Butcher, Yeo (Peat 69), Carruthers (McNamara 69), McAuley Bloomer, McCombe, Green.
Goals: McAuley (2, 47), Yeo (14).**

**Leyton Orient: Harrison, Miller, White, Zakuani, Lockwood, Carslile (Newey 70), Simpson, Wardley (Hunt 70), Scott, Steele, Ibehere.
Goals: Steele (11, 78, 89), Ibehre (37).**

**Star Man: Lee Steele.
Attendance: 4,246.**

Game Forty-eight

Messin' around by the river

Fulham 1 Leyton Orient 2
FA Cup Third Round. 8 January 2006

Truly memorable Sunday afternoon this one. Over six thousand O's had ventured across to the other side of London, our best following away from Brisbane Road since the play-off final in 2001. We packed the covered stand behind the goal and made up almost half of the crowd, while making about four times more noise all afternoon than the home contingent.

There's no doubt that the FA Cup certainly brings out the best in O's supporters. Two hundred had ventured to the game by boat on the Thames and win lose or draw there was always going to be a party atmosphere amongst the away fans at the Cottage.

As I've already said, in my opinion for various reasons the Portsmouth game in 2002 was the most enjoyable cup game of the noughties but it has to be said that this match provided the best display by an Orient team in the competition in the decade.

At the end of the day we had become the first side from the fourth tier to defeat a Premiership club since Shrewsbury had beaten Everton some three years earlier.

And it has to be said that the result was thoroughly deserved. Whilst at Fratton Park we could easily have been three down at the interval, here we took charge virtually from the kick-off and for long periods were by far the better team.

In 2005–06, manager Martin Ling had finally assembled an Orient squad that actually looked capable of getting us out of the bottom division for the first time in eleven attempts. When they were put to the test here against top flight opposition they showed the nation just how good they were.

Come January we were handily placed in the League for a real push for promotion and we were playing some highly entertaining stuff. Lingy clearly saw making it up to the third tier as by far the club's number one priority, so much so that he had banned the players mentioning the word 'Fulham' at the club until the Thursday before the game, with a ten pound fine the penalty for any offenders.

When the game started at 2.00pm the O's took the game to the home team from the kick-off, and it came as something against the run of play when Thomas Radzinski raced onto a through ball from Luis Boa-Morte after ten minutes to fire the ball past Glyn Gardner and into the net, right in front of the 6,000 away fans.

There was a sight from heaven for all O's however, as the linesman stood arm aloft flagging for offside.

It was a minor blip for the away team as we continued to press forward and it came as little surprise when just five minutes later Joe Keith found Craig Easton on the edge of the area and our Scottish midfielder sent a shot into the net, via the foot of Fulham debutant Simon Elliott.

I think most of us thought the goal would be a wake up call for the home team, but in fact they were forced further back into their shell as the O's confidence rose even more.

We started spreading the ball around and passing with all the panache we'd got used to seeing in the League all season. I remember the O's having the ball after only about twenty minutes played, and after about the fifth pass of a move, cries of 'Ole !' incredibly started breaking out in our stand.

Our midfield continued to dominate through Easton and Michael Simpson, the later having been a former FA Cup semi-finalist with Wycombe, and with Shane Tudor and Keith providing the width we looked comfortable at 1–0.

The only first half effort from the home side after our goal was a Stern John header which went over the bar, and it came as no great surprise when the O's doubled their lead two minutes before the break.

Gary Alexander held up the ball and laid it back to Easton on the edge of the area. Our midfielder slipped it through to Joe Keith coming in from the left and our man picked his spot to fire past Warner, again with the help of a deflection as Liam Rosenior threw himself in the way of the shot.

The away stand went balmy, as we went into the break with a not undeserved 2–0 lead.

We knew that well as we had played however Fulham would throw everything at us in the second period and they surely could not be as bad as they had been in the first .

Credit must be given to Martin Ling here. Many a lower league manager in a similar position would I'm sure have made defensive substitutions and try to defend the two goal advantage, but Ling continued to press forward with Jabo and Gazza Alexander upfront and the first defensive substitution did not arrive until the last minute when he took off Alexander and replaced him with defender Donny Barnard.

Fulham did improve after the restart and their best move of the match resulted in them pulling a goal back after 50 minutes when Rosenior picked out Radzinski just inside the O's half and he slipped a neat ball through to the edge of the area where Stern John drilled home a right footer past Garner.

We knew the rest of the game was going to be tough, but our defence continued to look strong until twenty-two minutes from the end when it appeared it had finally cracked with Gabby Zakuani giving away a penalty.

From where we were it looked a little harsh but we knew all was not lost with Glyn Garner having a good record in saving penalties – he had saved five the previous season.

Regular penalty taker Heidar Helguson was injured so Stern John stepped up to try to equalize. Garner reacted magnificently however, diving to his left to push the effort out.

Much credit too must be given to Craig Easton who was the first to react to the rebound and clear the danger.

Yet again the 6,027 O's went wild.

Indeed the penalty miss seemed to knock the stuffing out of the home side some what. Zak Knight headed a corner over and Sylvain Legwinski saw his twenty-five yard volley knocked over by Garner, but the O's regained their composure and even enjoyed the better of the dying stages as they closed in on a famous win.

Needless to say when the final whistle sounded we all went potty. Three sides of the ground quickly emptied but we stayed to party. The team went in and came back out again and celebrated in front of us. There was a mass dive from all the players and even Bazza Hearn came to mingle with the masses.

It had been a wonderful performance. True Fulham had a few injuries and were pretty woeful, but they were still a Premiership side and as Matty Lockwood pointed out in his column in the local paper, Lois Boa-Morte earned more in a month than the entire Orient team did.

Martin Ling said it was the best moment he had had in his nine and a half years at the club as player and manager though predictably he said that the next league match against Northampton was more important.

It was the biggest shock of the Round and rightly got lots of coverage in the papers the next day.

When Leyton Orient have a decent result of course, the press love it. We are, lets be honest the headline makers dream team.

On the Monday we had: 'O's what a lovely score !' from the *Daily Mirror*, 'O Yes – Hero Easton's Scot a lot to smile about' from the *Sun*, while the *Metro* chipped in with 'Cottagers sickened by taste of the Orient.'

The press and T.V. flocked to Brisbane Road to see the players and management reaction to the Fourth Round draw as it happened at lunch-time on the Monday – there were indeed about twice as many pressmen there at 1.30 that afternoon as we normally saw at any time for a routine league fixture.

We got a good draw too. Charlton away meant another Premiership Club and a few more bob for Barry while the short distance saw that another 6,000 would be able to travel to the match.

Unfortunately the build up to the game was somewhat overshadowed by the ticketing at the Orient, as season ticket holders were not given initial priority and some missed out as we quickly sold our allocation.

The game itself however, saw another fine performance as we lost only in the final minute to a Jay Boothroyd free-kick and we all had another good day out in London. The highlight of the 2005–06 Cup campaign remained that day out by the river though, when we defeated a club miles above us league position wise, and we showed everybody what a good team Lingy had turned us into.

Fulham: Warner, Legwinski, Knight, Boa Morte, Radzinski, John, Rosenior, Elrich (Timlin 62), Elliott, Jensen, Pearce (Goma 84).
Goal: John (50).

Leyton Orient: Garner, Lockwood, Simpson, Mackie, Easton, Alexander (Barnard 90), Keith (Carlisle 84), Zakuani, Miller, Tudor (McMahon 71), Ibehre.
Goals: Easton (16), Keith (43).

Star Man: Craig Easton.
Attendance: 13,394.

O's Steele promotion at the death

Oxford United 2 Leyton Orient 3
League 2. 6 May 2006

This was the undisputed game of the decade. Indeed for many an O the undisputed best game ever. Personally it stands as runner-up in my all time list, beaten only by the Chelsea cup classic from '72.

I had said for many a year that nothing would ever come close to coming from two goals down to defeat the European Cup Winners Cup holders some forty years ago, well this afternoon at the Kassam had a mighty good try.

I remember telling everybody in those final few months of the 2005–06 season that if we were to get promoted I wanted to do it as Champions or else via a Play-off Final. If we were to go up by coming second or third it would probably be quite boring.

Not one of my better quotes.

The game at Oxford has been called many things over the years but one word that could never be used to describe it was boring.

The scene for the final day showdown had been set the weekend before. The O's had beaten Peterborough 2–1 at Brisbane Road, a fine performance against a useful Boro team, who themselves were on the fringes of the promotion race. We had made heavy weather of it with Paul Conner getting himself sent off after just twenty minutes after misuse of his elbow, but a Matty Lockwood penalty and a Wayne Corden effort had secured the win.

Just as important however had been Grimsby's failure to win at Macclesfield. A 1–1 draw in that game meant that automatic promotion on the last day was in Orient's own hands. We were a point clear of the Mariners, so a win would take us up.

Oxford, meanwhile had drawn 1–1 at Wrexham to leave them on 49 points and in a relegation place, one but bottom of the league. Five clubs were just above them on 51 points but with two of them, Bury and Notts. County playing each other on the last day and both having a worse goal difference than Oxford, it meant that a win for the U's against us would keep them up.

In fact any two of seven teams could have gone down to the Conference that afternoon, setting it up for a dramatic finale to the season at both ends of the table.

In the run up to the Oxford game the home team sprung a real surprise by announcing that they would be giving the whole of their side stand to the O's. To me at the time it seemed like an amazing own goal by them. It was probably the biggest game in their side's history and being a well supported club would have had no problems selling around ten thousand tickets for the game. Yet they gave us over four and a half thousand and an entire stand leaving them with only two, the Kassam being a three-sided ground. It was great, of course for all of us from east London but must admit if I had been an Oxford fan I would not have been happy with my Club.

It went without saying that the atmosphere in our stand pre-match was magnificent.

Everyone was nervous, but at least we knew worst case scenario we would be in the play-offs and it would not be the end of the world. For two sides to the ground, however they knew they could end the afternoon in the Conference and that certainly **would** feel like it was the end of the world for them.

It was rather strange as well to know that come 5 o'clock both sets of supporters could be happy, only one set may have been over the moon, or everyone could have gone home fed up.

When the match began the O's raced out of the blocks and could have gone a goal up with just ninety seconds played, when Adam Tann's cross was met on the volley by Joe Keith. One time Orient 'keeper Billy Turley – not for the last time that afternoon – made a fine close-range save however to keep it at 0–0. Just five minutes later a Michael Simpson through ball put in

Lee Steele, but the ex-Oxford man saw his effort tipped onto the post by Turley.

The O's paid the price for the early misses as the hosts went ahead on 14 with their first attack of the game. John Mackie conceded a free-kick on the right and John Dempster whipped the ball in. With Tann playing the U's forwards onside, Eric Sabin bundled the ball home.

The lead lasted just three minutes, however. Wayne Corden sent in a cross which Craig Easton headed home, an effort Turley should really have dealt with a lot better. From where I was sitting down the other end it looked like he had carried the ball over his own line before trying to clear it.

It was certainly a deserved equalizer, but a mixture of nerves and good keeping meant that we were unable to press home our undoubted superiority in the first half.

Indeed a rare Lockwood slip let in Sabin just before the break, but Gaby Zakuani's excellent challenge put the striker off as he fired wide.

1–1 it was at the break. In truth, we had been all over a very poor team. We all knew we should go on and win the game but we all knew were Leyton Orient. In the queue for refreshment at the interval, I heard someone mention the Villa game in '74, which to be honest was the last thing I wanted to be reminded of at the time, but I knew what he was getting at and he had a point.

We heard that it was still goalless at Grimsby, but four thousand six hundred O's knew that it was only a matter of time before Grimsby would go ahead at Blundell Park.

When the game restarted we continued to dominate but still could not break the U's down. Oxford even managed to force their first corner after 56 minutes, though nothing came of it. Then after 64 came the moment we had all been praying for. Joe Keith picked out Gary Alexander on the left, the O's man – without a goal since January – advanced forward and coolly lobbed over Turley and into the net.

The way the home side had played you just could not see them getting back into the game at 2–1 down. They were though playing the O's. It therefore took them all of three minutes to be back on level terms.

It was another free-kick that proved our undoing this time conceded by Matty. Glyn Gardner initially made a fine save from Sabin's close range header but Chris Willmott followed up to score.

The goal certainly lifted the home fans and their team. Half way through the second half and they finally started to cause us some serious problems. They started to push forward knowing one more could well preserve their League status. Garner had to make a wonderful save from substitute Steve Basham and we were a little bit on the ropes.

I remember when someone sitting near to me said not to worry we were ok, Grimsby were still drawing, you just knew what was coming next.

Yep, Grimsby Town 1 Northampton Town 0. Jean-Paul Kamudimba had scored for the Mariners with just fifteen left to play.

With our game moving towards its final stages both sides at the Kassam now knew they had to win. We looked the more likely as the end neared but when a goal bound effort from Wayne Corden hit Lee Steele just two yards out, you thought it was just not going to happen. Lingy sent on Shane Tudor and Jabo Ibehre in an attempt to get the winner but we all feared the worst.

With 85 gone Oxford got a free-kick and there ensued a fracas in the O's box. Johnnie Mack went down and Chris Willmott, the earlier goal scoring hero for the U's was sent for an early bath for apparently using an elbow. Still though we could not make the breakthrough.

With ninety minutes played the score remained 2–2. No good to anybody. We all looked to the board to see how many minutes injury time there would be and five was the answer.

Now I remember thinking at the time this was – shall we say – a tiny bit generous. True an Oxford nutter had ran onto the pitch in the second half causing a brief delay, but you could not help wondering if the referee Andy Woolmer maybe knew a draw was no good to anyone and therefore gave both teams the best possible chance of finding glory.

You knew it was going to be a farcical five minutes with Oxford basically playing 1–2–6 and the O's 2–2–6 as it was do or die for both sides, and so it was.

The first injury time chance fell to the home side. A long through ball saw a suspiciously offside looking United forward chasing down a high ball dropping in our area. From where I was down the other end Glyn Garner seemed to take an eternity to come off his line to punch the ball clear from the oncoming forwards head, but clear the danger he did.

Then a minute later the one Oxford defender the U's were still employing slipped to let in Ibehre on the left. He reigned in on Turley, this surely was the moment. It was three against one with Jabo having two fellow forwards to his right who would have had an open goal. But Jabo inexplicably shot and Turley saved.

At that moment I think everyone of us in the away stand just collapsed in despair. Poor old Jabo. He had been with the O's for years. In fairness he had had some wonderful moments, loved the Orient and was a really nice bloke.

Yet my two lasting memories of him in an O's shirt will always be when he hit the post in the Blackpool play-off final at 2–2 which proved crucial, and this miss against Oxford which could have been fatal.

Still the game continued and both teams pressed. Just ninety seconds remained when Alexander got the ball on the left and crossed only for Steele to head over a not-too-easy chance.

That surely was it. The ball was launched into the O's half. To the left of me a massive cheer went up. What was going on? I think I was sitting in the only part of the O's stand where nobody within about thirty yards had a radio. You hoped the Cobblers had equalized but the previous week I had got caught out by wrong information that had come from Grimsby's match at Wrexham, so I wasn't going to celebrate.

Northampton had nothing to play for, they were already promoted, no way were they going to equalize, were they?

Meanwhile the balls been played back high into the Oxford half, Gazza has it down the left and he's crossed it into the box. Now I'm sitting dead level to where it comes and there's three O's forwards (some might say two plus Jabo) all a mile offside, with every Oxford player camped down the other end.

Steelo was the one who gets the ball and knocks it into the net, though I'm just sitting there waiting for the linesman's flag to go up and still not believing Grimsby weren't winning. But go up the linesman's flag did not do. Blimey the ref's given it.

All hell breaks loose, even finally where I'm sitting. And yes Northampton have equalized. I've watched the wonderful DVD of the game so many times since, and in fairness to making the wrong decision, the poor old lino was yards behind the play when Steelo put the ball away – it was the 95th minute and the ball had just been going up one end then down the other for the last ten and he was probably just too knackered to keep up with the play and make the right decision at the time.

The final whistle sounded ten seconds after the restart and low and behold we were up. Cue wild mass celebrations in one stand, sheer despair in the other two along with at Grimsby.

In a nutshell, we were up and Oxford were out of the League. Ironically they were to be replaced by Accrington Stanley, whose place they had taken some forty-four years previously in 1962.

There was needless to say mass hysteria amongst the 4,603. Wisely none of us invaded the pitch – everybody knew it would not be a good idea as the locals were not too happy - but all the team came over to us to share the wonderful moment. A first automatic promotion for thirty-six years. Amidst all the elation there was a wonderful picture of John Mackie in the 'Mail on Sunday' the next day consoling United's Steve Basham a la Freddie Flintoff on Brett Lee in 2005. A real nice touch from our captain on the day. Of course in many ways the promotion was probably made all the sweeter by the dramatic way things had turned in those unbelievable twenty seconds at five to five on the last day of the season.

Goalkeeper Jimmy Glasses winning goal for Carlisle in '99 may go down as the most dramatic finish to a season ever, but our effort at the Kassam in 2006 can't be too far behind it for sheer drama.

Orient may not have had too many promotions in our 130 year history, but when we do go up we like to do it with a touch of class as '62, '89 and '06 will testify. Roll on the next one.

You had to have a little sympathy for Oxford, although they had been badly managed for many years since the Maxwell days, but the team to really feel for that day were surely Grimsby. Until Northampton's Ryan Gilligan had equalized in the ninetieth minute of their game, they probably thought they were up. There boss was a bright young manager who was tipped for great things called Russell Slade. He said afterwards: 'Sometimes the game kicks you in the teeth. We're very disappointed.' Whatever became of Slade I know not, though rumour has it that the shock of that day back in 2006 made him lose his hair.

You actually knew that who ever did not go up automatically that day out of us and Grimsby would not go up in the play-offs as it would have had such a demoralizing effect to have missed out having gone so close. As it was the Mariners did indeed miss out and stayed in the bottom division.

You also had to feel a bit sorry for them as the papers, rather than giving them much sympathy seemed more preoccupied by the story that their player Curtis Woodhouse was giving up the game to become a professional boxer.

Possibly unsurprisingly they went downhill rapidly afterwards and now find themselves in the Conference.

One wonders what would have become of the O's as a club had we not gone up that day in 2006.

The celebrations rightly were huge for everyone connected with Brisbane Road after the Oxford triumph. It was actually quite amusing that in the post match photos in the dressing room, captain Johnny Mack is nowhere to be seen. It transpired that he was called back after finally leaving the pitch to give a drugs test. He really struggled to pass urine however, so much so that he was held up for ages and in the end was so delayed he had to board the team coach still in his playing gear.

Some things, needless to say were entirely predictable after the triumph. Bazza Hearn was on tip top form: 'With apologies to Steve Davis, Eubank, Benn and Lennox Lewis, it's the greatest day of my life in a sporting sense.' (I must admit if I was Phil Taylor, I'd have been pretty upset upon hearing this, that I didn't get a mention from the great man.)

The Club laid on a wonderful day of celebration the following Saturday with a parade by the promotion winning squad. This followed the Orient Play-off final squad of 1999 playing a team of 2006 youth team and staff in a thirty minute each-way challenge match.

We all then made our way to the Supporter's Club for a pint or six to enjoy watching West Sham getting beat by Liverpool in the FA Cup Final. Happy days, indeed.

And the final League table showed we finished a clear three points ahead of Grimsby – very comfortable indeed in the end – so that my statement that finishing third would in fact be boring was in the end proved to be correct.

Oxford United: Turley, Robinson, Dempster, Willmott, Mansell (Brooks 76), Burgess, Hargreaves, Smith (Beechers 89), Quinn, N'Toya, Sabin (Basham 69).
Goals: Sabin (14), Willmott (66).

Leyton Orient: Garner, Lockwood, Mackie, Zakuani, Tann, Keith (Tudor 79), Easton, Simpson (McMahon 87), Corden (Ibehere 82), Alexander, Steele.
Goals: Easton (17), Alexander (64), Steele (90 +5).

Star Man: Lee Steele.
Attendance: 12,243.

Game Fifty

Matt's perfect finish

Leyton Orient 3 Gillingham 3
League 1. 26 September 2006

Matt Lockwood's finest personal moments as an O were probably the winning penalty shoot-out goal he scored at Rotherham in '99, and the 25 yard screamer against Hull to take us to the Millenium in '01. This Gillingham match however, probably represented his most memorable game – or to put it more precisely his most memorable thirteen minutes in an Orient shirt.

After all the euphoria of Oxford in May, the O's had predictably found life in the higher division very much harder.

We had defeated Millwall and Bournemouth at home early in the season, but as we prepared to face the Gills on this Tuesday night we had lost seven out of the previous eight and with just seven points from ten games stood third from bottom of the league.

Just three days earlier a woeful performance had seen us go down 3–2 at home to Rotherham.

Lingy clearly knew we had problems and that he had to change something, so his answer this evening was to ditch the 4–4–2 which had served him so well in the bottom division and go with three up top, basically doing away with the two wide men.

As a result Paul Conner was brought into the side to replace Wayne Corden.

Initially this didn't look a bad change – Gazza Alex saw a fine header flash just wide after two minutes, and after sixteen Lee Steele came within inches of connecting to Alexander's knock down, following a fine diagonal ball from Matt Lockwood.

As the game progressed however, the visitors started to get more and more into the match and they created their first real chance after half an hour when Matt Jarvis – by far the Gill's best player on the night – got to the by-line and crossed low towards Michael Finn, whose low drive was parried away by Glyn Garner.

Our 'keeper was then nearly caught out four minutes later when Guylain Ndumbu-Nsungu's shot at the near post almost beat him, but the Welshman just got down in time to save.

The O's had a chance to open the scoring after thirty-nine minutes when John Mackie headed a Locky corner over the bar, but by now Gillingham had the upper hand and it came as no great surprise when they took the lead with forty-three played.

The opening goal summed up just how our season had gone up till then. The entire defence went to sleep when a short corner was played to Danny Jackman and the Gillingham man was allowed to cruise into the box and cross to Mark Bentley who planted a header past Garner.

And there was still time for more damage to be done before half-time when a poor clearance from Garner went to Michael Flynn who fed Jarvis on the left who crossed low for Ndumbu-Nsungu to pass the ball home.

The five minutes before the break had certainly been a disaster for the O's, the lucky ones being the punters who had nipped off early to get in the queue for half-time refreshments.

Despite its bright opening, the cunning plan by Ling to play with three strikers had by and large been a failure in the opening period, as it basically meant we were playing without anything like a proper midfield.

Unsurprisingly Wayne Corden was introduced for the second period with Conner the man to make way.

The Gills however continued to dominate. Jarvis threatened to make it three after fifty minutes when he turned inside Johnny Mack, but the O's skipper recovered sufficiently to get in a block and divert the ball for a corner.

The Gillingham man finally got the goal he thoughougly deserved however some twelve minutes after the break. He held off Brian Saah on the edge of the area to fire home from twelve yards.

0–3. The O's were dead and buried. Still over half an hour to go, and we were looking at a proper mauling. Folk in the two home stands – we had a three sided ground at the time – started to leave even with over a quarter of the game to go. I actually even saw a few from the East Stand, which was housing the away fans going home – well it was quite a journey back to Kent, it was a Tuesday night and after all the game was over as a contest.

Seventy-five gone, nothing much happening on the pitch and many more had disappeared in the stands. The next fifteen minutes however, summed up just why us punters pay a fortune to go and watch 11 idiots run around every Saturday and sometimes Tuesday, attempting to get the better of 11 other idiots more often than not with not very good results at the end of it.

Because on the odd occasion that they do get it right the feeling is just unbeatable.

Seventy-seven gone the balls played down the right into the corner. Shouldn't be too much hassle for the Gill's defence, but Adam Chambers sees it differently. He chases down a seemingly hopeless cause, just manages to get the round thing and takes it into the box where he's brought down by 'keeper Scott Flinders. A penalty is given and there's not too much argument from the Gillingham players. Well even if they score it's only a consolation, after all.

Up steps Matty-the-pen and it's 1–3 as Flinders goes in the opposite direction. (Incidentally, piece of useless info here, the Orient legend that is Matt Lockwood took 22 penalties including this one, at the 'Tommy Johnston Stand' end of the ground and scored every one of them.)

Then eight minutes later Jabo, who had come on for Steelo after an hour makes a strong run down the right to win a corner.

At the kick Daryl McMahon picks out Matty on the edge of the box and the legend takes one touch, looks up to size up his options and fires goalwards. To be fair it was not the best of efforts by the great man. The box was packed however, and a Gillingham boot got in the way and deflected a not too powerful effort into the centre of the goal, totally wrong footing the custodian. Blimey it's 2–3 and there's still five minutes to play.

Those that were still in the ground came alive as we sensed an amazing equalizer, and sure enough it came. There was more excellent work from McMahon on the edge of the area and he spotted our lively full-back haring on the overlap into the box to his left, so he picked him out with an exquisite through ball. Matty collected, and lets be honest any half-decent left-back would have centered to one of the forwards who were approaching the six yard box.

Matt though chose to thunder an attempt on goal and Flinders was beaten all ends up at the near post. Incredible, unbelievable. Matt goes berserk, the other players go berserk and we all go mad. In eleven minutes we've discovered just why we go to football matches.

In injury time Daryl McMahon had a shot from the edge of the area that could actually have given us a 4–3 win, but it was not to be. But anyway who were we to be greedy. The final whistle went, it was only a point but Christ it felt like fifty.

When you're down the bottom and you get only a draw against a fellow team from the bottom ten then that's normally a couple of points dropped, but not this time.

Matty carried off the match ball and we all celebrated wildly at the end. It was the first time he had scored more than one in a game, and his three made him our top scorer for the season at the time with five, which included three penalties. Not bad for a bloke wearing the number three shirt.

Talk amongst O's in the Supporters Club and on the message board post-match should have been about Matty's performance or failing that our shoddy effort over the first 77 minutes, where Lingy's tactics had got it all wrong and we had been hopeless.

Actually the main talking point was pointing the finger at all those 'part-time supporters' who had left well before the end and so missed one of the most glorious comebacks ever at Brisbane Road.

In the weeks after the game a few admitted to going early, but many an O kept very quiet. I'm still trying to find an Orient fan who did the 'double' of leaving this game early, and also leaving the Droylesden match before the end in 2010, when we were 2–0 down with five to go and ended up winning 8–2 after extra-time.

I can think of only one thing that must have been worse that night than being an Orient supporter who left at 0–3 to get home and find the score finished 3–3, and that would have been being a Gillingham fan who left at 3–0 only to discover the final score on getting back to Kent.

Leyton Orient: Garner, Lockwood, Simpson, Mackie, Alexander, Steele (Ibehre 60), Miller, McMahon, Conner (Corden 45), Saah, Chambers.
Goals: Lockwood (pen 77s, 85s, 88s).

Gillingham: Flinders, Jupp, Jackman, Flynn, Cox, Crofts, Bentley, Easton, Johnson, Jarvis, Ndumbu-Nsungu.
Goals: Bentley (43), Ndumbu-Nsungu (45+1), Jarvis (57).

Star Man: Matt Lockwood.
Attendance: 3,978.

Table toppers toppled by the Trent

Nottingham Forest 1 Leyton Orient 3
League 1. 16 December 2006

If there were a poll for the most unexpected Leyton Orient victory of the noughties, then this game at the City Ground would surely win hands down.

Ok so we defeated Pompey and Fulham away in the Cup during the decade when they were in leagues above us, but just looking at the bare facts going into this contest, we were complete no hopers before the game. Indeed the bookmakers agreed at the time and had made us 7–1 to win before a ball had been kicked.

Forest went into the match five points clear at the top the league. Orient meanwhile were sitting twenty-third only off the bottom spot on goal difference, a massive twenty-six points behind their opponents that day.

We had failed to gain momentum from the moral boosting salvaging of a late point against the Gills and were still finding life in our new division a real struggle. On the Tuesday before the Forest clash we had crashed out of the FA Cup by losing 2–1 at home to Torquay who were one off the foot of the division below us. It had been a truly awful performance by everyone that night.

It turned out however, to be an unforgettable afternoon at the City Ground this afternoon for all O's present. 1,030 of us had ventured to the midlands, a good 350 more than we had taken to any other away game that season enticed partly by the prospect of a new ground – we hadn't played Forest away since the seventies.

It was a terrific showing especially considering we had not won an away game all season, the day's performance creating a wonderful atmosphere in the stand we had behind the goal.

Backs to the wall it might have been for periods of the game for the boys in their away-day blue, but in the end thanks to good finishing and a resilient defensive showing we just about deserved the three points.

After a quiet opening to the game Gary Alexander was presented with the first opportunity after ten minutes when James Walker's flick header appeared to be going through to home 'keeper Paul Smith, but Danny Cullip decided to attempt a clearance. The ball found its way to Gazza who volleyed just wide.

Forest went into the game with a strong three man strike force of Grant Holt, Nathan Tyson and Kris Commons and the previous Saturday they had hit four at Crewe with Tyson scoring a hat-trick. Here though the three were being wonderfully shackled at the start by the O's defence, so much so that Glyn Garner had not been seriously tested with half an hour played.

The O's in fact looked the more likely to score, with Walker sending in a dipping effort after twenty-three minutes that Smith did well to hold, and it came as no great surprise two minutes later when we got a deserved lead.

Wayne Corden collected a Justin Miller cross and laid the ball back to the edge of the area where Luke Gutteridge smashed the ball home left footed, in front of the home fans at the Trent End. Needless to say not for the last time that afternoon there were wild celebrations down the other end of the ground amongst the 1,030.

The goal appeared to wake up the home team however and Nicky Southall had a couple of chances to equalize as Forest at last began to give some indication why they were top of the league.

As the interval approached we were all just praying for the half-time whistle to come so that we could regroup for the second period, but then came possibly the games pivotal moment.

On the stroke of forty-five minutes Gutteridge released Walker down the left and our on-loan forward took the ball round a leaden-footed Gary Holt before squaring to Adam Chambers. Chambers took a touch and then somewhat scuffed his shot, but somehow or other – from the other end of the ground I don't know how – it ended up in the back of the onion bag.

We were all going loopy of course but there was still time for the home side to mount an attack straight from the kick-off. It needed a fine save from Garner to deny Grant Holt from finding the back of the net in first half injury time.

The whistle then sounded however and quite amazingly we were 2–0 up at the break.

There was certainly an air of stunned disbelief in the away supporters stand though we knew the game was far from over, of course.

From the restart Forest not unexpectedly upped their game and Garner again had to react brilliantly to a Grant Holt effort after just a minute of the second period to keep our two goal advantage.

As had been the case all season we started to give away silly free-kicks and from one of them in the fifty-eighth minute Ian Breckin rose well at the near post to glance in Southall's delivery to make it 2–1.

At this point I would imagine many an O would have taken a point. Forest were beginning to look far superior and we continued to give away far too many free-kicks in threatening positions. It was becoming increasingly rare for those gathered in our away stand to see the ball down our end of play.

After sixty-nine minutes however, quite unexpectedly we were to see one of the moments of the season happen right in front of us.

Chambers advanced into the Forest half and passed to Walker. Our man spotted Wayne Corden to the left of him whom he played in. Corden skipped round Wes Morgan on the edge of the area and our wide man unleashed an unstoppable twenty yarder into the top corner.

Cue the inevitable pandemonium in the Orient end and the stunned silence in the other three parts of the ground.

Corden's corker seemed to knock the stuffing out of the Forest side and the final twenty minutes amazingly enough were quite comfortable for our boys. Indeed Gary Alex could easily have made it four in stoppage time when he broke away only for Smith to make a fine save.

It mattered little however as the final whistle blew and we had secured our first away win to lift us up to twenty-first in the table.

The players came to us and there was a mass celebration of a stunning victory by all O's present, both players and supporters.

It's pretty fair to say the result had a massive impact on both Clubs for the remainder of the 2006–07 season.

The momentum we gained at the City Ground we took up to Northampton the following Tuesday where a Paul Conner goal gave us a second away victory in four days. We all knew it was still going to be a struggle all season, but the two wins certainly gave us hope.

As for Forest the home loss to a struggling side appeared to have a rather devastating effect. After the 1–3 reverse they only won two out of the next eight, and after looking nailed on for automatic promotion ended up only finishing fourth.

They played a play-off semi-final against Yeovil and incredibly went out after losing 5–2 at home, having won the away leg 2–0.

Terrell Forbes, who went on to play for the O's, played for Yeovil in those games and I remember watching the then Yeovil manager in a bright green cap going bonkers at the end of the tie. Guys name was Russell Slade. The fact that he wore the cap all evening made me think that it was highly likely he had no hair, but it appeared their fans didn't seem to care.

Nottingham Forest: Smith, Curtis (Agogo 46), Cullip, Breckin, Morgan, Southall, Clingan, Gary Holt (Perch 78), Grant Holt, Tyson (Dobie 85), Commons.

Goal: Breckin (58).

Leyton Orient: Garner, Miller, Mackie, Saah, Lockwood, Chambers, Easton, Gutteridge (Barnard 85), Corden (Tudor 89), Alexander, Walker.

Goals: Gutteridge (25), Chambers (45), Corden (69).

Star Man: Wayne Corden.
Attendance: 23,109.

Game Fifty-two

Lion's mauled

Millwall 2 Leyton Orient 5
League 1. 20 February 2007

When you see your team score five away from home it's always going to be a special occasion. When you see them do it do it against one of your fiercest rivals who you haven't played away for thirteen years it just about becomes unbeatable. This really was a wonderful evening in south London.

Trips to play Millwall away had always been unique before we went our separate ways in the early eighties.

The old Den was always a pretty intimidating place to go to for all away supporters. The visitors section was right in a corner with a very poor view, not helped by having a whacking great big floodlight pylon in the middle of it. There was an unpleasant walk down an alley to get to it, (which of course became a lot more unpleasant after the match if your team had won).

Like many an O when we played there in the seventies and eighties I used to stand in amongst the Lion faithful in the home end (scarf-less of course) just

trying to blend in with the locals. We considered it the safest option, though if the O's scored it was always hard work not celebrating.

Remember the game there on Boxing Day 1982 – Keith Houchen got the winner for us and when you looked round after he scored there were pockets of supporters scattered round the ground starting to jump up and then stopping, doubtless thinking of their own safety.

It's fair to say Cold Blow Lane was a real dump of a place and the New Den really was a ground that badly needed building. With the Lions going in one direction, however – even up to the top flight briefly – and the O's going the other way we had to wait till this memorable day in 2007 until we first visited the new venue.

And blimey was it worth the wait. Like the Forest game earlier in the season expectations pre-match were not high. We were in a relegation place and had lost our last away game 5–0 at Bournemouth. On the previous Tuesday night we had got hammered 4–1 at home by Brighton.

Millwall meanwhile after a poor start to the season had picked themselves up and were in the top half of the table.

What we witnessed that night were ninety highly entertaining minutes. Aside from the seven goals the crossbar was rattled five times and we had a perfectly good goal ruled out because the ref did not think the ball had crossed the line. It's no exaggeration to say the final score could have been seven-all.

The fun and games started in the fifth minute. Gary Alexander rose to meet Matt Lockwood's excellent corner to head home from six yards.

Then just two minutes later, Shane Tudor played in Ryan Jarvis down the right and the O's forward, who was on loan from Norwich, raced towards the goal. He squared to Alexander but Gazza scuffed his shot somewhat allowing Richard Shaw to clear off the line. The ball bounced up to the oncoming Jarvis however, and our man bundled the ball home.

Neil Harris immediately went down the other end and tested the crossbar, but incredibly we came back at them just a few minutes later with a third.

This one came about from some shocking Millwall defending. Mark Phillips attempted a pass back to 'keeper Lenny Pidgeley but his effort was woefully short and Jarvis intercepted half way inside the Lion's half.

Pidgeley stood up well to block the striker's first effort, but Ryan raced onto the rebound and fired home from a tight angle.

3–0 up after just eleven minutes. No-one in the away end, the opposite one to where the goals had been scored, could quite believe what we were watching. Orient just never went 3–0 up after eleven minutes home or away.

Having squandered two goal advantages against Oldham and Rotherham that season and with still bags of time to play none of us were counting on three points though. Some of us still remembered Hull at home in '84 –4–1 up with twenty to play and we lost 5–4.

And Millwall continued to look dangerous. After eighteen minutes Tom Brighton headed against the bar for them, but we countered that by hitting the bar ourselves Justin Miller this time testing the woodwork.

Alexander wasted a glorious chance to make it 4–0 just before the break when he blazed over from Locky's long through ball, but going in three up at the interval was to say the least highly acceptable.

The atmosphere in the queue for refreshment at half-time was one of stunned disbelief.

Had we really just seen what we thought we had ?

Millwall came out for the second period knowing that actually they had not played too badly in the first forty-five, creating plenty of chances and that if they continued to press they surely had to get some reward eventually.

After fifty minutes they hit the crossbar for a third time through a Danny Senda free-kick and they finally got on the scoresheet after sixty-six when Dave Brammer's free-kick struck Alexander and ended in the back of the O's goal.

Then just three minutes later Poul Hubertz cut the deficit to just one, when he flicked the ball over John Mackie in our area and lashed the ball home.

2–3 and still twenty minutes to play. I think we all feared the worst in the Orient end.

Our defence at the time – as the recent matches against Bournemouth and Brighton had shown – was not the best around.

We continued to be pushed back, but then after seventy-six came the games defining moment. Pidgeley took a goal-kick, but it was a shocker. Not even reaching the halfway line it found Gazza Alex, who offloaded immediately to the forward running Jarvis. The Wall 'keeper came rushing out like a mad man, but Jarvis easily beat him to the ball and poked it past him and into the net.

Queue mass wild celebrations from the travelling O's. Our fourth goal of the evening but this was the first we'd scored at the away end and it crucially gave us a two goal cushion.

Millwall heads finally went down after the latest set back and we even had time to add a fifth in injury time.

Again poor defending was to blame as Shaw headed straight to Alexander, and Gazza unselfishly squared to our unmarked substitute James Walker, who rounded Pidgeley to stroke home.

Indeed the final score should have been 6–2 with Adam Tann firing a 15 yarder against the bar and over the line soon afterwards, but referee Alan Wiley obviously felt a little sorry for Pidgeley and the home defence and ruled that the ball had not crossed the line.

None of us really cared of course. We'd just witnessed a stunning Orient win.

Our new striker Ryan Jarvis had hit a hat-trick in only his second match, though a lot of credit also had to be given to Gary Alexander. Gazza – a life long Millwall fan – had had a fine game, despite scoring an own-goal.

Jarvis had a strange career at Leyton Orient. He followed up his wonderful evening at the New Den by scoring two against Tranmere the following Saturday. We ended up signing him on a permanent basis. He then went on to do pretty much nothing in an Orient shirt for the next four years, until he scored a ninety-fourth minute winner against Peterborough at the end of the 2010–11 campaign. We then let him go on a free. He will always have a place in all O's hearts however, thanks to his hat-trick against our rivals that night.

And as for the New Den, well it was certainly a lot different to the old one. Some things hadn't changed, however. I've worked with many Lions fans over the years and they've all been really good blokes. Millwall still seem to have a small following however that are real idiots.

At the new stadium they seemed to like to congregate in the parts of their stands as near to the O's end as possible, even though that gave them a shocking view near the corner flag. The whole point of the evening appeared for them to be to hurl abuse at us for ninety minutes.

Normally they would have looked fairly stupid, but with their side three down after eleven and going on to concede five its fair to say they looked extra silly that evening.

Millwall: Pidgeley, Craig (Zebroski 78), Elliott, Harris (Hubertz 38), Byfield, Brammer, Brighton (Hackett 45), Senda, Shaw, Phillips, Williams.
Goals: Alexander (og 66), Hubertz (69).

Leyton Orient: Garner, Barnard (Corden 20), Lockwood, Mackie, Tudor (Tann 75), Easton, Alexander, Jarvis (Walker 90), Miller, Saah, Chambers.
Goals: Alexander (5), Jarvis (7, 11, 76), Walker (90+1).

Star Man: Ryan Jarvis.
Attendance: 10,356.

Game Fifty-three

Bantam's battered

Bradford City 0 Leyton Orient 2
League 1. 21 April 2007

This was a very poor game, played by two very poor teams, near the bottom of the table but one look at the league table before and after the match shows why it has to have a place in the '60 memorable games' book.

		P	PTS.	G/D
19	Cheltenham	43	50	-13
20	Leyton Orient	43	48	-14
21	Bradford City	43	46	-13
22	Chesterfield	43	44	-9
23	Rotherham Utd	43	38	-12
24	Brentford	43	34	-35

…was the state of play before the Valley Parade encounter.

18	Leyton Orient	44	51	-12
19	Bournemouth	44	51	-13
20	Cheltenham	44	50	-14
21	Bradford City	44	46	-15
22	Chesterfield	44	44	-10
23	Rotherham	44	38	-13
24	Brentford	44	34	-38

…was how the bottom of League one looked after it.

While defeat that day in Yorkshire would have taken us into the bottom four, with our own fate taken out of our own hands, victory in effect meant that we needed only one point from the final two matches to virtually guarantee safety.

In terms of our league status, the match drew comparisons to the away game at Chester in 1999, when defeat would have seen the O's the ninety-second team in the league at staring the Conference full on, but a 5–1 victory then proved a turning point.

Who knows now what would have happened had we lost that April day at Bradford, but I'd wager there would have been a fair chance the O's could have found themselves playing in the bottom division in 2007–08, where we might still be playing today.

And it was a game we could easily have lost. The home team could quite easily have found themselves a couple up at half-time, instead of 0–0, had they taken their chances.

After only seven minutes Glyn Garner made a brilliant save with his legs to deny City's on loan striker Billy Paynter. Our 'keeper then did well after fifteen to gather a low drive from Omar Daley.

Bradford really should then have taken the lead after twenty-four when Daley broke clear and found himself in the box. He had two teammates unmarked waiting for a pass and an easy tap-in, but the Jamaican undid all his good work by attempting to score himself from a tight angle and Garner again saved.

You could sense the despair amongst the home crowd, and there was more to come.

Spencer Weir-Daley ran on to a through ball and found himself one-on-one with Orient's custodian. He had options a plenty, but chose to lob and got it horribly wrong, the ball finishing yards wide.

At 0–0 the O's must have felt they had got out of jail in the first half. The forwards had created nothing, our most threatening player had been Matty through his in swinging corners and a couple of long range efforts.

The second half started pretty even but chances were few, but then came the crucial moment with just over an hour gone. Our Substitute Jabo Ibehre showed great strength to hold off Mark Bower and our man played in Gary Alexander who smashed home past Donovan Ricketts to give us the lead.

This was a body blow to the home side and as heads started to drop we added a second just three minutes later.

A long free-kick from Matt Lockwood was headed across goal by John Mackie and Adam Tann took advantage of confusion in the Bradford defence to nip in and double our lead.

At 2–0 the game was effectively over and we survived the last twenty-five minutes fairly comfortably.

With other results going our way it was, as the table above shows a massive win.

Martin Ling said afterwards: 'We went in with a game plan – a little more defensive than normal – and it worked perfectly. David Wetherall (the Bradford manager) will be disappointed with their finishing in the first half, but personally, I put that down to good goalkeeping from Glyn Garner.'

Not unsurprisingly we lost both of our last two games – at home to Nottingham Forest and away to Huddersfield – but thanks in the main to the win at Bradford just about managed to stay up.

When followers of many a club recall memorable matches from decades past Cup Final victories, Championship winning matches, European glory nights will come to the fore.

When you support Leyton Orient it's 2–0 wins on bleak afternoons in Yorkshire that you remember. And I would not want it any other way.

Bradford City: Ricketts, Edghill, Parker, Wetherall, Bower, Schumacher, Johnson, Daley, Paynter, Youga (Colbeck 63).

Leyton Orient: Garner, Barnard, Lockwood (Miller 72), Mackie, Tudor, Alexander, Jarvis (Ibehre 48), Tann, Gutteridge, Chambers, Thelwell. Goals: Alexander (62), Tann (65).

Star Man: Glyn Garner.
Attendance: 10,665.

Game Fifty-four

Canaries kop it again

Leyton Orient 2 Norwich City 1
League 1. 13 April 2010

The end of the noughties had been somewhat of a struggle for the O's, and the new decade started no better. A disastrous 3–1 home defeat by Hartlepool on 3 April 2010 saw us fall to nineteenth in League 1, with a fall to the bottom division at the end of the season a distinct possibility. We had lost five out of the previous six.

After the game unsurprisingly Barry Hearn took the step of saying goodbye to manager Geraint Williams, ending fourteen months in charge for the Welshman.

He replaced him with former Scarborough, Grimsby, Yeovil and Brighton manager 49-year-old Russell Slade. A first game in charge saw us draw 0–0 at Exeter and a second pitched us against high flying Norwich City.

The Canaries were eight points clear at the top of the league which they appeared to be strolling. They had hammered us 4–0 earlier in the season. The general feeling amongst most O's going into this Tuesday night encounter was that we could write it off as a chance to pick up any points in the relegation struggle and that it would be down to the last four matches against teams on paper not so strong as Norwich, to save us.

How wrong we all were, however. A magnificent – totally unexpected – performance saw us rise just one place, but crucially increase the gap between Orient and the bottom four from one to four points. It may seem a bit over the top to say that this one match saved our season, but there is certainly an argument to say that it probably did. We had home games against the bottom two Stockport and Wycombe to follow, but the breathing space the Norwich victory gave us was key to survival.

Norwich were boosted before the game by the return of their first-choice goalkeeper Fraser Forster after suspension, but the match also saw the return to the starting eleven of Sean Thornton for the O's. Our man had missed the previous two games and turned out to be the key figure in the crucial game.

It took just three minutes for our midfield man to make an impact. A long free-kick bounced awkwardly in the area. Scott McGleish managed to knock the ball down to Thornton who chested it before knocking it past Forster to give us the lead. Three sides of Brisbane Road erupted with joy, though the goal was greeted with silence by the whole of the East Stand which was home to over three thousand travelling Canaries that night.

The new manager certainly appeared to have galvanized the team, the difference between the previous home encounter with Hartlepool and this one was clear from the start, with every ball being fought for by all those in a red shirt.

Norwich still looked a class side however, and they equalized with a fine goal after nineteen minutes. City midfielder Korey Smith swapped passes on the edge of the area with Stephen Elliot, before side footing into the bottom corner past Jamie Jones.

Well as we had started I think most of us present, with one eye on the league table, would have expected the away side to then go on and take control but amazingly this did not happen at all.

Though just three minutes later Norwich striker Chris Martin sent in a volley from twenty-five yards which beat Jones but cannoned off a post, for the rest of the half Orient more than held their own, and deservedly scored a second.

Again it came from a free-kick this time taken by Charlie Daniels. Thornton found himself unmarked in the six yard box after a fine delivery, and he headed home for 2–1.

Before half-time Daniels was close to making it three when his free-kick from an acute angle warmed Forster's hands at the near post, but at the interval a narrow lead for the under-dogs was an excellent reward for a battling display from the boys in red.

Norwich actually had not played too badly but the O's were really up for it and though we knew they would come at us hard in the second half we had shown more than enough to suggest that an upset was possible.

The Canaries indeed did push forward after the break, but although Smith and Darel Russell produced some good work in the middle of the park, our defensive pairing of Ben Chorley and Tamika Mkandawire stood up to everything they threw at us.

Indeed the O's were starting to look very dangerous on the counter attack and another rasping shot from the excellent Daniels produced a fine save from Forster.

With just eleven minutes left Norwich boss Paul Lambert sent on Stephen Hughes and Cody McDonald and the two new players seemed to give the away side a much needed late boost. Hughes hit a fierce shot from twelve yards, which Jones blocked brilliantly, and it's fair to say that in the last few minutes we were hanging on grimly.

As the game moved into injury time another Norwich substitute Anthony McNamee, put in a cross-cum-shot which beat Jones all ends up, but much to the great relief of all O's the ball rebounded to safety off the post.

The final whistle sounded soon after and a famous and extremely important victory had been achieved. At 7.45 I'd have taken a point from the game so that to get three was just incredible.

There was ecstasy in three sides of Brisbane Road and in front of us we saw Russell Slade punching the air wildly in front of us, for the first time. It was a sight that we were to see quite a bit more of at our ground in the following years.

Slade had only been given a contract until the end of the season, but after the start he had given us that evening there seemed a fair chance that if we survived he would still be with us come August.

Said our new man afterwards: 'It turned out to be a real cup tie in many ways, particularly in the second half. We opened them up and had one or two opportunities to perhaps get that third goal. I'm really pleased and we couldn't have done any more on the night.'

Lambert countered: ' We never got going and defended poorly at set-pieces. We were well beaten.'

It was indeed a brilliant performance from the O's, totally out of character with what we'd seen all season up till then.

2–0 victories against Stockport and Wycombe ensured third tier football at Brisbane Road for 2010–11, with our Russell initially looking an excellent choice of manager from Bazza and Managing Director Matt Porter.

For the first time in ages, our players all appeared to be fully behind the man in charge who was given a new contract at the end of the campaign.

Little things from certain matches for some reason remain in your mind, and from this evening I can remember going ballistic in the West Stand over our ball-boys. With the game entering the final minutes, they kept quickly giving the ball back to a white-Norwich shirt as soon as the ball went out of play.

In similar circumstances at every other ground in the country the home ball-boys would not have acted in this way at all, I felt. Looking back now abusing the young lads only doing their job was not one of my finest hours as an O's fan, but then I suppose, that's just how much being a supporter of Leyton Orient supporter can corrupt your senses.

Leyton Orient: Jones, Chorley, Mkandawire, Chambers, McGleish, Thornton, Daniels, Jarvis (Pires 86), Spicer, Smith, Lichaj.
Goals: Thornton (3s, 29s).

Norwich City: Forster, Drury, Nelson, Martin R., Elliot (McDonald 79), Doherty, Martin C., Lappin (McNamee 68), Russell, Smith, Johnson (Hughes 79).
Goal: Smith (19n).

Star Man: Sean Thornton.
Attendance: 7,520 (3,028 away).

Game Fifty-five

Eight-on Orient (take four)

Leyton Orient 8 Droylsden 2
FA Cup Second Round Replay. 7 December 2010

Over the years the O's have had some pretty fierce battles in the FA Cup against non-league sides. There has generally been a pattern to the way the encounters have gone. We always seem to struggle, often looking like we are on the point of being on the receiving end of a giant-killing, but somehow or other, more often than not we just about manage to scramble through.

My first experience of seeing us on a non-league ground was against Altrincham in 1980 when we were near to elimination until a late Billy Jennings goal saved us.

Somehow or other since then we have always managed to get through the banana skin of away ties against the minnows, the only defeat I can remember at the home of a non-league club was at Dover's ground against Margate in 2002.

Our two games against Droylsden back in 2010 in many ways epitomized

BATTLING BACK
Comeback kings show fighting qualities

our battles against the small teams over the years. Drawn away, we escaped with a 1–1 in the first game, thanks to a late own goal when Scott McGleish's header hit the post then the back of the 'keepers head and rebounded into the net.

That set up this replay, which turned out to be one of the most astonishing games ever seen at Brisbane Road.

Ten goals – six in extra-time, thirty-four shots on target, four sending's off, the O's two minutes away from elimination summed up an extraordinary evening.

Orient started the game well, a cheeky back-heel by Alex Revell almost resulted in a goal, before Scott McGleish powered a thirty-yarder against the bar. It was the visitors who took the lead however, when Jody Banim crossed from the left and though Ciaran Kilheeney saw his first effort blocked by Ben Chorley, he smashed the rebound into the net.

The O's continued to press forward and an equalizer looked on the cards but the complexion of the match changed on thirty-seven minutes when Terrell Forbes became the first Orient player of the season to be shown a red card. He lunged in on Banim on the half way line when there was no danger, giving referee Graham Scott no real option but to send him off.

1–0 down and with only ten men, at half-time we had still done enough to warrant hope for the second period, especially as the Droylsden defence did not look full of world beaters.

After the break Russell introduced Jonathan Tehoue for Jimmy Smith, who felt unwell, and we went to playing just three at the back.

Both sides continued to attack and the second goal of the evening came after 55 minutes, again though it went to the visitors. The ever dangerous Banim saw a shot parried, but Alex Brown followed up to scramble the ball past O's 'keeper Jason Brown.

Though two down we had seen enough to make us believe we were still in the game, our young winger Paul-Jose M'Poku, was continually causing them all kinds of problems at the back and indeed it was our loanee from Spurs who brought us back into the tie with just thirteen minutes remaining.

A run into the box saw our man go down under a challenge from Liam Brownhill and Ben Chorley stepped up to score the resulting penalty.

It became clear that the non-leaguers were tiring badly as we started to put them under intense pressure and their cause was not helped seven minutes from time when Nat Kerr was sent off for a bad foul on M'Poko.

An equalizer looked inevitable and sure enough it arrived with just two minutes left. A M'Poku cross from the left found its way to Tehoue who swept home from close range.

2–2 and there was another twist in the dying moments when Chorley picked up his second yellow and the O's were down to nine.

And so it went to extra-time. It started 9 v. 10, yet the momentum was with us and the non-leaguers seemed absolutely knackered.

Sure enough after just three minutes M'Poku – who by now was becoming almost unplayable – went on a superb solo run down the left and fired home at the near post to give us the lead for the first time in the whole tie.

Our man on loan from Spurs was clearly becoming too much for the northerners to handle and the next time he picked up the ball he was the victim of an x-rated challenge that earned Lee Roche a deserved red. As if the evening hadn't been lively enough already, this sparked a heated confrontation between the two benches and ended up with the Droylsden manager Dave Pace being sent to the stand. Over the two games there had been some pretty bad challenges, especially from the non-leaguers, but this one on M'Poku, most certainly won the prize for the worst of the lot.

It was now nine-a-side and with Droylsden looking down and out, it came as no surprise when Scott McGleish opened his account for the evening minutes later with a shot from the edge of the area.

Then after 99 minutes there was more excellent work from M'Poku, as he set up Tehoue for his second of the night.

As the teams turned round at 5–2 it was clearly a question of how many the O's could get in the last fifteen minutes playing against nine men who could barely stand up. The answer was three.

First Tehoue completed his hat-trick with a fine strike from the edge of the area, then McGleish struck twice more to complete the rout.

A truly amazing game saw the non-league side coming mighty close to recording an upset, yet had ended up on the wrong end of a drubbing. Orient's tally of six goals in extra time set a new record for the FA Cup and it must have seemed like a very long journey back to Lancashire for the minnows.

Despite all of the goals the highlight of the night for me was when our seventh goal went in and the 69 away supporters who had made the trip, started to do the conga in the East Stand. Some of the challenges from the players and the actions of their manager had not endured the non-leaguers to us, but you simply could not fault their fans all of whom were still there and singing, at the end.

I'm sure there must have been more than a few O's supporters who actually left when we were 2–0 down – you would love to know their reaction on finding out the final result.

Said our Russ afterwards ; 'M'Poku was key as was Jonathan Tehoue. We stayed positive and it paid off. Eight probably flattered us in many ways, but the character was there for all to see.'

A gutted Dave Pace said: ' At 2–0 all we had to be was disciplined. But they were hanging on for grim death. They did not know what they were doing.'

We had been drawn away to Norwich in the Third Round, who were high flying in the division above us at the time. I expected us to get well beaten at Carrow Road, but I remember coming away from the Droylsden match thinking that at least the FA Cup had provided us with one highlight that season in the shape of the 8–2 match.

Little did we know at the time of course, that it would provide a few more before we were to get eventually knocked out that year.

Leyton Orient: J. Brown, Omozusi, Chorley, Forbes, Dawson, McGleish, Revell (A. Brown 90+2), Daniels, Spring, Smith (Tehoue 46), M'Poku (Walker 101).
Goals: Chorley (77s pen.), Tehoue (89s, 99n, 107s) M'Poku (93n), Mcleish (97n, 108s, 119s).
Sent off: Forbes, Chorley.

Droylsden: Phillips, Roche, Brownhill, Kerr, Hardiker, Brown (Byron 61), Killen (Cryan 87), Gardener, Kiheeney, Banim, McNiven (Rouse 72).
Goals: Kilheeney (6s), Brown (54n).
Sent off: Kerr, Roche.

Star Man: Paul-Jose M'Poku.
Attendance: 1,345.

Game Fifty-six

Delia dumped out

Norwich City 0 Leyton Orient 1
FA Cup Third Round. 8 January 2011

After defeating Droylsden in the 2nd Round, the O's reward was a trip to face Norwich City in the Third. City were going great guns in the Championship at the time, sitting third, and had had just one defeat in their last eleven. They stood 40 places above us in terms of league placings and the O's came into the game on the back of a 5–0 hammering at Brighton on New Years Day.

Nevertheless a Third Round FA Cup game at Carrow Road brought back many a memory of 1978 when we went up there in the same round and in a replay unexpectedly won 1–0.

Some thirty-three years earlier we had had Peter Kitchen in the ranks to score the winner. In 2011 as it transpired we had Jimmy Smith.

two thousand made their way up the A11 for the game creating a wonderful atmosphere in the away end before the action started. Most of us would have taken a draw but then you never know, of course, when it comes to the Orient and the FA Cup.

Norwich came at us from the start and could have taken an early lead, but the O's started to work their way into the match with Smith giving an early warning as to the danger he posed, when a smart shot on the turn tested Declan Rudd.

Then came the big moment of the afternoon with twenty minutes played. Dean Cox, who was having a wonderful season, put in a teasing cross from the left and there to meet it was Jimmy Smith with a powerful header which sailed past the Norwich custodian. The goal came just in front of where we were seated along the side and was obviously met with total ecstasy by the travelling 2,000.

Norwich continued to create chances, David Fox had their best opportunity of the first half, but he dragged his shot wide after 34 minutes and we went in still holding our one goal lead at half-time.

The second half saw more pressure from the Canaries in the early stages, and after an hour they brought on leading scorer Grant Holt to bolster their attack.

The introduction of their Club captain made an immediate difference and Holt almost grabbed an equalizer when he just failed to make contact from a curling cross from Anthony McNamee with 67 played.

Attacks for the O's were rare and it was not until 75 minutes that we created our first real attempt at goal in the half, when Paul Jose-M'Poku shot over.

For all their pressure however, Norwich did not make too many clear cut chances with our defence playing magnificently and indeed it was not until the last minute that Jamie Jones was really tested when he was called upon to turn a curling effort from McNamee past the post.

We held on and so recorded another famous FA Cup victory. The stars of the show for the O's had been in the defence, Terrell Forbes having arguably his best game in an Orient shirt, with Ben Chorley too a colossus at the back.

It had been a few years since we had caused one of our famous cup upsets at the Orient, so there was of course much jubilation amongst Russell's travelling army at the end.

Said the man with no hair afterwards: 'There was an unbelievable spirit about us, from the first minute of the game. To get that goal was crucial because I thought it settled us down and gave us something to hang on to. And boy did we hang on to it. We defended well at centre-half, and not only that but the likes of Alex Revell and the midfielders too. They all put their bodies on the line.'

Norwich boss Paul Lambert said, 'We didn't deserve anything from the game. We have set ourselves high standards this season and we didn't match them. We seemed to be trying to score the perfect goal. They played really well and deserved to go through.'

The irrepressible Barry Hearn needless to say had a magnificent day, though hearing him speak afterwards he gave the impression that the pre-match catering provided courtesy of Delia Smith was just as important to him as the final score.

Slade said of Hearn: ' It's the happiest I've seen him. He was jumping for joy. He loves the FA Cup.' Our Barry also likes a nice bit of hospitality, he might have added.

It was indeed a very good performance – apart from the Brighton set back we were actually playing very well at the time and coming back down the A11 after the match we looked forward to a possible tie against a major Premiership club in the following round.

As it was we only got Swansea away in the Fourth, another team looking for promotion out of the Championship at the time, but they were not Premiership and as such it was a bit of a disappointment to everyone. The Swans were not Premiership and did not even have Delia Smith, so were not known for their pre-match grub which must have been a great annoyance to our Barry.

Norwich City: Rudd, Martin R., Drury (Lapin 63), Whitbread, Hoolahan, Fox, Martin C. (Simeon 72), Smith, Barnett, Wilbraham (Holt 63), McNamee.

Leyton Orient: Jones, Omozusi (Whing 26), Chorley, Forbes, Cox (M'Poku 58), Dawson, Revell, Daniels, Spring, Tehoue (McGleish 71), Smith.
Goal: Smith (20).

Star Man: Terrell Forbes.
Attendance: 18,087 (2,125 away).

Game Fifty-seven

Wednesday walloped

Leyton Orient 4 Sheffield Wednesday 0
League 1. 22 January 2011

Whilst the FA Cup run to the Fifth Round in 2010–11 was a magnificent achievement by the O's, it should not be forgotten that the season also saw us finish in our highest league position for some eighteen years.

To finish in seventh position just one place away from a play-off place represented a fine performance from Sladey and the team, especially considering that after defeat at Sheffield Wednesday on 9 October we were one but bottom of the league, and appeared destined for a winter of discontent, fighting relegation.

After Brighton hammered us 5–0 on New Years Day we went on a wonderful record-equaling run of fourteen league matches without defeat, which was made all the more remarkable by the fact that it coincided with the potentially distracting cup run.

There were some very good performances in it too, none more so than this four goal thrashing of Sheffield Wednesday, played a week before we went to Swansea in the cup.

When the Yorkies visited us on 22 January our rise up the table had well and truly begun and we stood eighteenth with twenty-eight points from twenty-two played.

We had taken Harry Kane and Paul-Jose M'Poku on loan from Spurs who both looked decent young players and a third was to follow shortly afterwards in Tom Carroll.

Both sides came out attacking, though the nearest either side came in the first quarter of an hour was when Orient defender Charlie Daniels headed a high hanging Wednesday cross over our 'keeper Jamie Jones, and it needed a recovery from our defender to clear the resulting Chris Sedgwick effort off the line.

Nine minutes later visiting winger Gary Teale had a fine shot from twenty-five yards, but Jamie Jones dived to his right to save. Then just two minutes later the O's had the ball in the visitors net, but Alex Revell was flagged offside after converting Charlie Daniel's driven low cross.

Teale had another attempt well saved by Jones just after the half-hour mark, but though it had been an open game the two sides went in 0–0 at the break.

It had been a pretty even first period, but Orient came out all guns blazing after the interval and produced a stunning forty-five minutes football, during which time they scored four goals.

Ben Chorley started it all off after 51 minutes when he converted a penalty after Teale had been penalized for a hand ball in the box. Kane then started to become a real handful for Wednesday, five minutes after our first he collected a Jimmy Smith pass and forced a smart one-handed save from Nicky Weaver. It came as no surprise when the man from Spurs doubled our lead just a minute later when he nodded home Dean Cox's free-kick from close range.

A flying header from Kane then produced another decent save from Weaver, by now Wednesday heads appeared to have gone down and it was one-way traffic.

A third goal came for the O's with eleven minutes left when the visitors once more failed to deal with a free-kick and this time Alex Revell stole in to nod home. The scoring was completed after 84 when yet another free-kick this time by M'Poku saw the faintest of touches by substitute Scott McGleish leave Weaver once again stranded.

4–0 certainly did not flatter us after the second half display which was certainly one of the best halves of football the O's had produced in the league for some years.

Said assistant manager Kevin Nugent afterwards: 'It was a good second half performance, and equally it was a good first half performance. We came in at 0–0, which is no mean feat against a team like Sheffield Wednesday, and we upped it again after half-time and it was a very pleasing result. There are goals in this team, so we always say to stay in the game, and then it gives us the chance to push on and get something out of it.'

We were indeed starting to get together a very decent squad of players at Brisbane Road. Top scorer Scott McGleish, soon to be cup hero Jonathan Tehoue and M'Poku all started on the bench against Wednesday, highlighting the strength in depth we had at the time.

2011 had started very well for us, and the best was yet to come.

Leyton Orient: Jones, Whing, Chorley, Forbes, Cox (M'Poku 80), Dawson, Revell (Tehoue 80), Daniels, Spring, Smith, Kane (McGleish 70). Goals: Chorley (51s pen), Kane (57s), Revell (79s), McGleish (84s).

Sheffield Wednesday: Weaver, Buxton (Beavers 46), Morrison, Miller (Johnson J. 59), Jones, O'Conner, Teale, Johnson R., Sedgwick, Morrison, Madine (Mellor 46).

Star Man: Harry Kane.
Attendance: 6,449 (2,350 away).

Game Fifty-eight

Swans silenced

Swansea City 1 Leyton Orient 2
FA Cup Fourth Round. 29 January 2011

And so, with the O's starting to climb up the league the 2010–11 FA Cup band-wagon rolled onto Wales, with a game against Swansea in the Fourth Round.

Being drawn against the welsh side had been a bit of a let down. Not a game against a Premiership team and not even at home. There was also the burden of a 12.50pm kick-off as the match was to be broadcast live on Welsh-language channel SC4, which meant the pain of a very early start for those travelling from east London.

Just like Norwich had been in the previous round, Swansea went onto our encounter riding high in the division above us. They sat fourth, only out of an automatic promotion place on goal difference. The Swans had not conceded a goal at home for four matches, winning them all, and had only let in five at the Liberty Stadium all season.

We were not on a bad run ourselves, but still went into the game as outsiders, as we looked to reach the Fifth Round for the first time in twenty-nine years.

Swansea started on the front foot and could have been two up inside the opening ten minutes with a Scott Sinclair effort producing a fine save from Jamie Jones, and then a 25-yarder from Kerry Agustien glancing off Ben Chorley to go for a corner.

Sinclair continued to cause our right-back Andrew Whing all kinds of problems down the Swansea left, he continuously cut inside our defender and tried his luck, but luckily for the O's he did not appear to have put his shooting boots on that day.

In truth we were struggling to get any kind of foothold in the game but the score remained 0–0. Then out of the blue, and totally against the run of play we scored. The ball found its way up the end Swansea were defending and a clearance from a home defender saw a push in the back on our skipper Steve Dawson.

From the resulting free-kick Charlie Daniels put in a really tasty delivery from the right, deep into the Swan's box. Jimmy Smith rose superbly between 'keeper Yves Ma-Kalambay and defender Alan Tate to head the ball into the net.

It was into the goal right in front of the away end and needless to say the 678 of us in the stand went delirious with joy. As in the Norwich game we had taken a first half lead through a Jimmy Smith header, though it has to be said that our performance leading up to the goal had been much better up in East Anglia some three weeks earlier than it had been in late January in South Wales.

Swansea came back at us straight away and continued to look threatening. It came as no surprise when they equalized with forty-five minutes on the clock. A Darren Pratley dipped cross was met by the head of Cedric van der Gun with the O's central defence for once no where to be seen, and the ball sailed past Jamie Jones for 1–1.

The Swans had scored at a crucial time just before the break and there was still time for more incident before half-time, with a critical moment just before the ref blew up. Sinclair once more cut in from the left and let fly for once with a terrific shot, which sailed past Jones. It was heading into the corner but there on the goal-line was Pratley to help the ball home.

The ref rightly blew for offside against the Swansea player and the 'goal' was wiped out. It was dreadful play by Pratley – if he had let the ball go he would not have been deemed interfering with play and the goal would have stood.

If we had gone in 2–1 down I do not think we would have recovered, but at 1–1, although the momentum was certainly with the Jacks, we were far from out of it.

I remember the mood in the away end at the break was one of relief that although it had not been one of our better performances in the first half, this was the FA Cup and being Orient we still had a very good chance in the match.

As it transpired the second half proved to be Jamie Jones time. Our 'keeper had what can only be described as a truly blinding forty-five minutes. It started just two minutes after the restart when van der Gun was put through one-on-one against our man, who saved brilliantly. Two more blinding saves followed from Sinclair and substitute Dobbie, and Jones was starting to look unbeatable.

We were defending for long periods and seeing very little of the ball. There was just one break when Alex Revell charged forward and had a great chance to put substitute Jonathan Tehoue in on the left, but his cross was far to near the 'keeper who gathered easily.

As the game entered the last two minutes, I remember thinking that a draw – thanks mainly to Jamie – was going to be a magnificent result for us, especially as we had not been at our best, but then came one of those magical moments that make you realize just why you turn up to watch an often rubbish football team every week.

Jonathan Tehoue got the ball on the edge of the Swansea area, and although he had two defenders around him, he somehow managed to slip the ball to fellow substitute Paul-Jose M'Poku on the right. Our Spurs loanee from the Congo put in a low – to be honest not very good – cross into the six yard box, where City captain Alan Tate swung a boot. The Swansea man somehow however, managed to slice his attempted clearance past a helpless Ma-Kalambay and into the net.

Looking back now, for me it all then became a little bit bizarre. We were up the other end and I saw everyone trooping back to the centre for the restart, yet no Orient player was being congratulated – initially I wasn't even certain we had scored. It was in truth a very poor own-goal to give away, but we of course cared little.

The O's actually quite comfortably saw out the remaining minutes. The goal – and probably the nature of it – seemed to have really knocked the stuffing out of the Welshmen and we thus recorded another famous cup win at the sound of the final whistle.

There were wild celebrations among the near seven hundred travelling supporters, as we were joined just in front of us by the team, as well as the man without any hair at the end of the match.

Afterwards our Russell summed up the game perfectly; 'It's unbelievable really. I don't know how we did it I have to say. Swansea are a very, very good side, but we managed somehow to stay in the game. Scoring the first goal clearly helped us. We hung in there and managed to get a fortunate goal towards the end so we're in the last sixteen and I'm absolutely delighted.'

Said Swansea manager Brendan Rodgers: 'I never thought with this group a result like that would happen because the key to our success in the Championship has been our ability to work hard. But we just weren't quite at our best.'

Indeed it really had been a heroic backs to the wall performance. Swansea like Norwich ended up getting promoted to the Premiership at the end of the season. We had actually played a lot better at Carrow Road a few weeks earlier where Jamie Jones did not have a great deal to do. This time round however, he had been outstanding and was easily the man-of-the-match.

As I boarded the supporter's coach outside the ground to take me back to Leyton it all seemed a bit surreal.

It was not even three o'clock, yet we had already booked our place in the last sixteen of the old tin pot for the first time in nearly thirty years.

It was strange on the way home to hear scores come in from the other ties that were still being played. Supporting what you might call one of the smaller clubs in Leyton Orient, I usually root for the underdogs in the Cup, but on this occasion I was cheering for all the big boys to succeed with the hope that we might draw one of them in the next round.

I even found myself wanting Manchester United to win at Southampton when they kicked off at 5.15 that evening, even though I truly hate the Red Devils after the carnage they caused at Brisbane Road back in 1974. (Not that I'm one to bear a grudge for long).

I got home around half past seven. It had been a wonderful day and there was more to come, as I immediately relived the whole of the game again thanks to the coverage on SC4 and my Sky + box.

There was even a magnificent commentary in Welsh to further enhance the enjoyment (well it was certainly no worse than what one usually has to put up with on ITV.) John Hartson was their guest pundit and I'm sure he was very complementary to us, although I could not be sure.

Part of the magic of the cup I always think, is anticipating after you have won, just who you are going to get in the draw for the next round. Saddo that I am, I always look at the teams left in it and analyse what are the best and worst draws we could possibly get.

The draws for the Third and Fourth Round in 2011 had not looked very inspiring initially, although they both resulted in two memorable days out.

Surely though one thought that we were due a real humdinger of a tie as reward for our performance at the Liberty, in the Fifth. One of the big London boys or one of the Manchester giants was what I was after.

When the balls came out Sunday afternoon, Arsenal at home suited me just nicely.

Swansea City: Ma-Kalambay, Williams, Tate, Pratley, Orlandi (Angel Rangel 63), van der Gun (Dyer 87), Moore, Sinclair, Allen, Agustien (Dobbie 69), Alfei.
Goal: van der Gun (45).

Leyton Orient: Jones, Whing, Chorley, Forbes, Cox, Dawson (Chambers 64), McGleish (Tehoue 46), Revell (M'Poku 79), Daniels, Spring, Smith.
Goals: Smith (35), Tate (og 88).

Star Man: Jamie Jones.
Attendance: 6,281 (678 away).

Game Fifty-nine

The O's are better than Barcelona

Leyton Orient 1 Arsenal 1
FA Cup Fifth Round. 20 February 2011

So it was Arsenal at home. No question about it an absolutely brilliant draw for us. We were due a nice one and boy did we finally get it.

It was a game where we were going to get heaps of publicity raising the profile of our club at least for a short while, and of course make lots of money which as always with the O's, we certainly needed.

Our boys would in all likelihood get well and truly hammered but it would still be an occasion, the kind of experience that as an Orient fan you get to savour only once in a blue moon. And if we could somehow get to nick some kind of result it would for sure put it up there with the all-time great games.

It was certainly one of the ties of the round and was inevitably going to be live on the box. As it was ESPN ended up the lucky station getting it, with a 4.30 kick off on the Sunday of the cup weekend.

When we do get a game like this one every now and again, I just love the build up to the match. Supporting a small club it's so nice to actually be able to pick up a daily newspaper and read about your team for a change.

There was a lot the nationals could focus on as well. Our centre-half Ben Chorley had skippered Arsenal's youth team to success in the 2001 FA Youth Cup before they had let him go, and our veteran striker Scott McGleish was a lifelong fan of the Gunners. His two young sons were also followers of the team from the Emirates and questioned their Dad as to who they should support for the big day. One of them ended up being O's mascot for the encounter.

It also did not go unnoticed that with Tottenham already having got knocked out of the cup 4–0 by Fulham, the three players we had on loan from Arsenal's north London rivals – Tommy Carroll, Harry Kane and Paul-Jose M'Puko were left to fly the flag for Spurs in the competition.

Needless to say every paper you picked up had some kind of quote from Bazza Hearn and every time you turned on Sky Sports News in the week before the game, you had Barry in front of you.

It was great. A 9,000 capacity crowd was guaranteed – Brisbane Road could probably have sold out three times – and for once at our Club there weren't even many quibbles about how the tickets were sold. We seemed to have learnt from our mistakes of the past, notably from the Charlton game in 2006.

The O's went into the match on the back of a really good run of form. We had lost just once in twenty matches – the 5–0 hammering on New Years Day at Brighton – and we were playing with plenty of confidence.

And what of Arsenal's form at the time ? Well in their game on the previous Wednesday they had had the small boost of defeating Barcelona 2–1 in the Champions League last sixteen, first leg.

Sure they would rest a lot for the game against us, but it was still set up nicely for an historic encounter.

If there was one team in the country that many O's wanted us to do well against it was the Gunners. Many of us still had bad memories about the semi-final in '78, with MacDonald's two deflections and then there was the game in '72 when everyone agreed we were unlucky to lose in the Cup quarter-final against them.

We had been trying for nearly one hundred years to defeat them and had never succeeded. I never for one minute expected us to beat them, but even a narrow defeat I felt at the time would be a moral victory for Leyton Orient.

It was strange taking my normal seat high in the West Stand late on a Sunday afternoon, but it was lovely to see our magnificent stadium chock-a-block full. Even the four blocks of flats in the corners of the ground had balconies crammed with people, just for a change.

Interestingly the draw for the quarter-finals took place just before the two teams came out, so that when the game began we both knew what the prize for the winners would be. And some prize it was too – Manchester United away.

I remember there was an amazing reaction all round the ground when the news quickly came through. For the O's of course this was another brilliant draw. If just somehow we could get the better of the Goons then there was the prospect of much more publicity and much, much more cash with a trip to Old Trafford.

At the same time however, you could hear the groans from the East Stand where the away support were gathered. It was of course, the worst tie imaginable for any Club that harboured thoughts of actually winning the old tin pot, which Arsenal always did. Even if they as expected defeated us their chances of progressing too much further had just received a mighty blow.

I felt the O's had actually received a big physiological boost by this news pre-kick off.

After for once having had the pleasure of hearing *Tijuana Taxi* being played in front of a full arena, and after all the (wonderful) hype leading up to match, the game at long last began.

And the mighty reds started off on the front foot. With just a minute gone Orient captain Steven Dawson fired the first shot of the game which 'keeper Manuel Almunia saved somewhat unconvincingly at the second attempt.

It did not take Arsenal long to get into their stride however, as they started to impose their passing game on proceedings. A slick build-up culminated in Andrey Arshavin's pinpoint cross being met by Marouane Chamakh, but the visiting striker's header flew straight at Jamie Jones.

Then after thirteen minutes Chamakh found space on the edge of the box, but his effort was again weak with Jones once more saving easily.

Just a minute later Orient won a first corner and the ball found its way to Charlie Daniels wide on the left who tried his luck from twenty-five yards, his effort whistling over the bar.

This was merely a blip in Arsenal's dominance however, and the ball seemed forever with the visitors as they looked to open the scoring. An Andrey Arshavin effort from eighteen yards again called Jones into action and then with thirty-four minutes played came their best opening to date. Good work from Gunners full-back Kieran Gibbs resulted in a low cross that went straight to an unmarked Chamakh just six yards out. The Moroccan however contrived to mis-kick woefully, the ball going painfully wide for the Arsenal front man.

Maybe, just maybe it was going to be our day after all. Half time came and it was still 0–0. In truth we had been totally outplayed and had hardly had the ball at all. Feeling amongst most of us was that surely our defence would eventually cave in to the relentless onslaught in the second half. On the other hand however we were talking about Leyton Orient and the FA Cup so you just never knew.

It actually took eight minutes after the restart for our admirable defence to finally be broken. Nicklas Bentner crossed from the right and Thomas Rosicky flicked a header past Jamie Jones and into the bottom corner.

At this point I fancy even the most optimistic of O's would have thought that our chances of getting anything out of the game were looking very slim. On sixty-three minutes however came what proved to be a masterstroke from Russell Slade. He decided to replace thirty-seven-year-old Scott McGleish who had run himself to the ground, with our super-sub Paris born Jonathan Tehoue.

The Frenchman had scored nine goals that season after coming on as a substitute with eight of these coming after at least eighty-five minutes had been played. This in fact was no coincidence. Tehoue was big and strong and quick. He was just the kind of player as a tiring defender at the end of a game you just did not want to see haring towards you.

In the week preceding the Arsenal encounter he had come off the bench at MK Dons to notch the winner in a 3–2 victory. Unfortunately though good as he was for us as an impact player, he was just unable to keep it up for ninety minutes and so very rarely started a game in an Orient shirt.

On this February evening however, this was a fact that at the end of it mattered little to anyone of an Orient disposition.

Minutes after he entered the field of play, Arsenal had a very good chance to double their lead. Arashavin, who was looking the away side's most threatening player crossed from the right to Rosicky and the scorer of their goal forced a fine double save from Jones to keep us in the game.

From here on in though, Tehoue started to make an impact. A fine run on the right ended with a cross from him finding its way to Alex Revell who swept a shot wide. He then cut back to Revell again in the area and this time our forward's fiercely hit drive was blocked heroically by Sebastien Squillaci. There were the inevitable shouts from the O's faithful behind the goal in the Tommy Johnston Stand for a penalty, but it never was.

We had come much more into the game following the Frenchman's introduction but as the game approached its closing stages we were pushing further forward, and so leaving ourselves rather more open at the back.

With 87 played the ball found its way to Arshavin just inside our half, and with our defence pushed up the Arsenal player ran forward and let fly a shot which sailed past Jones. Luckily for the O's however, the ball brushed the outside of the far post and went out for a goal kick.

A minute later with both teams starting to become sloppy, Tehoue found the ball at his feet just outside the Gunners penalty area. Defenders Igasi Miquel and Gibbs were between our man and the goal, but the Frenchman charged between them and with only Alminia to beat unleashed a stunning low shot that flew past the 'keeper and into the net for the equalizer.

What a moment. Bar one corner of the East Stand the ground just erupted. 8,000 O's going mad. Russell Slade running down the touchline delirious. The players and Theo celebrating wildly in front of the South Stand. It truly was one of the all time great Orient moments.

All of a sudden you realized why you put up with those home loses to Hartlepool, that 6–0 defeat at Huddersfield on a Tuesday night, defeat by Margate in the FA Cup. It was for moments like these.

Two minutes remained of course, they naturally appeared like two hours but we held out for a famous draw and resulting ecstasy around Brisbane Road.

Looking back now – and I know I'm being greedy here – we could actually have gone on and won the game. Arsenal heads had clearly gone down and Jonathan Tehoue was scaring the life out of them.

But at the end of the day of course, no one had the slightest complaint about a draw and a trip to the Emirates. The players stayed on the pitch and we stayed in the stands celebrating unreservedly. As an Orient fan you knew it was an occasion the likes of which that may not come around again for a very long time and you just wanted to make the most of it.

The team eventually left the field of play and we started to very, very slowly leave the ground. In a far corner Steve McManaman and Robbie Savage sat around a desk the ESPN team had erected and started to analyse the goings on with presenter Ray Stubbs.

Unsurprisingly they were joined minutes later by Russell Slade and Barry Hearn. Needless to say our unflappable chairman just would not shut up.

I eventually left and got outside the ground but just stood there for about three quarters of an hour. I quite simply just did not want to go away. Many others had the same feeling and were just milling around with big smiles on their faces.

There were of course wild scenes that we saw on the telly later, in the Orient dressing room after the game. Bazza had promised the team a trip to Las Vegas if they managed to get a draw and the great man was greeted with a chorus of 'Viva Las Vegas' as he entered the dressing room.

I eventually got home about nine o'clock, drank a bottle of wine and watched the highlights still on cloud nine.

The one thing I remember watching the game again, was realizing what a good strike it was by Tehoue for the equalizer. My initial reaction at the game was that maybe Almunia might have stopped it, but watching it again I saw what a really powerful shot it was, and that any 'keeper would have been hard pushed to keep it out.

So Sunday was very pleasant and I have to add that Monday was too. As has become traditional for me after a classic Leyton Orient victory, the next day I buy every one of the national newspapers to take in the full reaction.

As I've said before, it's a headline makers dream when our boys achieve a corking result, and the Arsenal game was no different.

'Our Her-O's' said the *Daily Mail*, as well as 'Jewel of the Orient' on their inside.'

'O yes !' was the *Sun's* take on proceedings, with 'Tehoue are you ?' to back this up.

The latter was a reference to Arsene Wenger's admission that before the match he had never heard of our goal scoring hero. Wenger was well known for his encyclopedic knowledge of foreign players especially French ones, so that this really was quite a quote from the Arsenal top man.

In fairness to him, Wenger was highly gracious in his assessment of the game, afterwards:

'That's what football is all about. I believe we played the game with the right attitude and I cannot fault our fighting spirit. You have to give credit to Leyton Orient. They never gave up and, as long as you don't score the second goal, these kind of things can happen.'

The *Daily Mirror* said 'Messi to messy', highlighting the fact that the Gunners could defeat Barcelona mid-week but were unable to beat us four days later. The *Sun* did a cheeky comparison between Orient and the Spanish giants, highlighting our 9,271 capacity compared with their 99,354 and the fact that while our team cost nothing, theirs was assembled for £88 million. Marvellous stuff.

Our Russell was quoted in the papers as saying: 'It's a fantastic night for the football club, and it was a great performance in terms of our resilience and never-say-die attitude. We're just over the moon. When we went 1–0 down the fans were fantastic and helped us so much. We've come from behind before, we never give up, and to keep this unbeaten run going after a game against Arsenal is great.'

It was also highlighted in the papers that Arsenal had officially managed a massive 801 passes during the game, compared to our 298. As an Orient fan, who cared.

A week after our game with them, Arsenal went to Wembley to play Birmingham City in the Carling Cup Final. They were overwhelming favourites to lift the trophy, yet lost 2–1. This reminded me so much of 1972, when we had beaten Chelsea 3–2 in the FA Cup and they too got beat seven days later by massive underdogs Stoke City in the League Cup Final.

Three days after their Birmingham encounter, 9,000 of us made our first trip to the Emirates to watch the O's. I think deep down we all knew that it would be near impossible to hold them on their own patch and so it proved with a 5–0 defeat in the replay.

Never mind, the travelling Gooners had taunted us with the chant of 'We'll never play you again.' when they were winning at Brisbane Road, and they had been proved wrong thanks to Tehoue. And we made lots of money in the second game, with officially 60,000 present that night.

And of course not even a 15–0 drubbing would ever have taken away the magnificence of that late February afternoon in Leyton in 2011.

A true Oriental classic.

Leyton Orient: Jones, Whing, Chorley, Forbes, Cox, Dawson, McGleish (Tehoue 63), Revell (M'Puko 84), Daniels, Crowe (Carroll 46), Smith.
Goal: Tehoue (89s).

Arsenal: Almunia, Sagna, Rosicky, Denilson, Song, Squillaci, Arshavin, Gibbs, Chamakh, Miquel, Bentner.
Goal: Rosicky (53n).

Star Man: Jonathan Tehoue.
Attendance: 9,136 (away 1,604).

Game Sixty

Over the Mooney in Derbyshire

Alfreton Town 2 Leyton Orient 4
FA Cup Second Round. 2 December 2012

The sixtieth and last unforgettable game for the O's over the last forty-five years was fittingly in the FA Cup. A very large percentage of my happy memories supporting the team from Leyton in that time have come in the competition so it's probably appropriate to sign off with a game from the old tin pot. I love these, what I like to call 'novelty' matches, away to non-league opposition in the early rounds of the FA Cup. The locals are thrilled to be playing what they consider a 'big team', giving players, officials and generally fans of the visitors a nice welcome, and the bonus for Orient is that we usually mange to find a way through to the next round in the end.

And its always nice to see our boys playing on a new ground as opposed to the same old Tranmere, Oldham, Colchester etc where we've all been to God knows how many times before.

This game came in the middle of the fine 2012–13 season, and was a

thoughoughly entertaining encounter shown live on ESPN, with a nice highlights package in the evening on ITV.

It was our first Sunday afternoon match since the legendary Arsenal game nearly two years before and like the Gooner fixture whilst awaiting kick-off we heard our draw for the next round.

Alas Hull City away was not the tie any O would have wanted in the Third, but it did not distract from a riveting encounter, made all the more watchable thanks to two dreadfully poor defences on the day, which meant that you always felt that a goal for either side was never far away.

Alfreton began the day fourteenth in the Conference, while the O's were in the middle of a cracking run. We were looking for our sixth consecutive victory to give us our best winning run since 1961.

As the game started however you would never have known that Orient were in such a purple patch. For the first twenty minutes we just never got going at all.

It took the non-league outfit just four minutes to go 1–0 up when Paul Clayton ran onto Ben Tomlinson's flick inside the box and the home striker shot early to beat Ryan Allsop, firing low to the 'keeper's right.

Alfreton continued to set the pace and very nearly doubled their lead just before the quarter of an hour mark when Tomlinson got the better of Ben Chorley and hammered a low shot against the base of the near post.

We started to give away silly free-kicks and from one of these Josh Law – who was the son of the Alfreton manager – saw his shot deflect off of an Orient body and onto the cross bar. So with a quarter of the match played we were really on the ropes, lucky to be just 1–0 down.

As we've seen many a time over the years however, gallant as the small teams are, the better fitness of the league players usually becomes a telling factor as the games progresses and there had also been signs that the home sides defence was not the best around, so that we always looked as if we would claw things back in the end.

Indeed after twenty-five minutes we did get back on level terms thanks to some wonderful play from Dean Cox on the right. David Mooney fed our wide-man who cut inside Conner Franklin and from just inside the box Deano fired a wonderful curing shot beyond 'keeper Jon Stewart and into the net.

The game had suddenly turned and within five minutes we had established a 2–1 lead. A Lee Cook corner was flicked on by Alfreton front man Tomlinson who was back defending, and the ball dropped nicely for an unmarked Mooney at the far post to rifle home.

Lloyd James had an excellent chance for us, but saw his effort kept out by Stewart, but with thirty-six gone we did indeed score a third. A Cook cross, this time from the left was met by the head of Mooney to establish a two goal cushion.

Just before the break some more excellent work from Moons saw our striker very near complete a fifteen minute hat-trick but his shot was saved by the 'keeper and we had to settle for 3–1 at half-time.

It was a score that flattered us enormously. Most O's must have felt that the way our defence had played for the first forty-five there was no reason why the home side could not get back into the game, and so it proved.

More sloppy play from the back four saw the deficit reduced to just one after fifty-one minutes when Tomlinson was allowed to turn and shoot home from six yards following a corner.

Just like the start of the first half the O's appeared to still have their heads in the dressing room and two minutes later Alfreton again rattled the woodwork with Tomlinson scooping the ball onto the bar from close range.

It continued to be a really open game and you knew that with the defending that had been on show from both sides the scoring was not going to end at five goals, though we just hoped that our league pedigree would see us through in the end.

After 67 minutes a fine Orient move resulted in Kevin Lisbie, who was making his fourhundredth senior appearance, heading goalward, and a resulting scramble brought about a goalline clearance from the non-leaguers.

Alfreton, although tiring still kept battling away, and after eighty-three minutes hit the woodwork for the fourth time. This time a Josh Law free-kick beat Allsop all end up, but the frame of the goal once more came to the O's rescue.

Then with 86 played Orient finally once more gave themselves some breathing space when Cox played a one-two with Mooney just inside the Alfreton box, and our tiny wide man slotted under Stewart for 4–2.

That concluded the scoring for the day, and the O's took their place along side the big boys in Round Three.

It had been a very entertaining afternoon, even if the crowd figure of 1,104 was disappointing.

Said Russell: 'It was a great Cup Tie. We didn't start well and that didn't please me. Their early goal set us back, but I felt that once we got our first goal, we then played some fantastic football and got three goals to put us in the driving seat. When we got hold of the ball and started moving it we caused them problems.'

Not surprisingly Alfreton manager Nicky Law saw the game in a different light: 'I thought that we dominated the game from the start. Then we had a fifteen minute spell where it cost us, and after that I think we dominated again. I think we came out second half and dominated. We got caught at the end, but we were having to go for it then.'

Though he had a point it was certainly not as one sided as Law had made out. That said though, after being hit four times there was a good case to make the frame of the goal behind Ryan Allsop, our man-of-the-match.

Alfreton Town: Stewart, Law, Franklin, Kempson, Killock, Streete, Meadows (Emerton 90+2), Bradley, Arnold, Clayton (Worsfold 90+2), Tomlinson (Denton 82).
Goals: Clayton (4), Tomlinson (51).

Leyton Orient: Allsop, Smith A. (Cuthbert 87), Odubajo, Baudry, Chorley, Cox, James, Rowlands, Cook (Smith J. 79), Lisbie (Brunt 90+5), Mooney.
Goals: Cox (25,86), Mooney (30, 36).

Star Man: David Mooney.
Attendance: 1,104 (away 281).

So that's it. I hope you've enjoyed my recollections of sixty of the best O's games from the past six decades and that they've maybe brought back a happy memory or two of watching our beloved team over the years. Recalling magical matches for supporters of some sides may mean reminiscing upon Premiership winning encounters, FA Cup triumphs at Wembley or glory nights in Europe. With the O's I've given you a 3–7 home defeat, a 4–5 loss when 4–1 up with 20 minutes to play, a game that took us off the bottom of the league, along with one that gave us our first away league victory for two years.

That's what it is to be a supporter at our wonderful little club, and personally I wouldn't want it any other way.

Here's to the next sixty crackers.

Up the O's and Herb Alpert.

16308341R00145

Printed in Poland
by Amazon Fulfillment
Poland Sp. z o.o., Wrocław